Y0-CAS-354

Social security and retirement :
368.4 CON   11418

Medway High School

SOCIAL SECURITY

AND

RETIREMENT

PRIVATE GOALS, PUBLIC POLICY

DATE DUE

CONGRESSIC
1414 2
WASHI

30 505 JOSTEN'S

368.4
C

Congressional Quarterly Inc.

Congressional Quarterly Inc., an editorial research service and publishing company, serves clients in the fields of news, education, business and government. It combines specific coverage of Congress, government and politics by Congressional Quarterly with the more general subject range of an affiliated service, Editorial Research Reports.

Congressional Quarterly publishes the *Congressional Quarterly Weekly Report* and a variety of books, including college political science textbooks under the CQ Press imprint and public affairs paperbacks designed as timely reports to keep journalists, scholars and the public abreast of developing issues and events. CQ also publishes information directories and reference books on the federal government, national elections and politics, including the *Guide to Congress*, the *Guide to the U.S. Supreme Court*, the *Guide to U.S. Elections* and *Politics in America*. The *CQ Almanac*, a compendium of legislation for one session of Congress, is published each year. *Congress and the Nation*, a record of government for a presidential term, is published every four years.

CQ publishes *The Congressional Monitor*, a daily report on current and future activities of congressional committees, and several newsletters including *Congressional Insight*, a weekly analysis of congressional action, and *Campaign Practices Reports*, a semimonthly update on campaign laws.

CQ conducts seminars and conferences on Congress, the legislative process, the federal budget, national elections and politics, and other current issues. CQ Direct Research is a consulting service that performs contract research and maintains a reference library and query desk for clients.

Copyright © 1983 Congressional Quarterly Inc.

All rights reserved. No part of this publication may be reproduced or transmitted in any form or by any means, electronic or mechanical, including photocopy, recording, or any information storage and retrieval system, without permission in writing from the publisher.

Printed in the United States of America

Library of Congress Cataloging in Publication Data

Main entry under title:

Social Security and Retirement.

    Bibliography: p.
    Includes index.
    1. Old age pensions — United States. 2. Social Security — United States. 3. Retirement Income — United States. I. Congressional Quarterly, inc.
HD7105.35.U6S62   1983   368.4′3′00973   83-14349
ISBN 0-87187-274-9

Editor: Robert S. Mudge
Supervisory Editor: Michael D. Wormser
Major Contributors: Janet E. Hoffman, Robert W. Merry, John L. Moore, Margaret C. Thompson
Contributors: Harrison Donnelly, Pamela Fessler, Kathy Goodwin, Diane Granat, Diane C. Hill, Sandra Stencel, William Sweet, Elizabeth Wehr
Designer: Mary L. McNeil
Cover Design: Richard A. Pottern
Cover Illustration/Graphics: Robert O. Redding
Photo Credits: p. 44—Brad Markel; p. 158—Wide World Photos; p. 198—Robert L. Knudsen
Indexer: Jodean Marks

Congressional Quarterly Inc.

Eugene Patterson *Editor and President*
Wayne P. Kelley *Publisher*
Peter A. Harkness *Deputy Publisher and Executive Editor*
Robert E. Cuthriell *Director, Research and Development*
Robert C. Hur *General Manager*
I. D. Fuller *Production Manager*
Maceo Mayo *Assistant Production Manager*
Sydney E. Garriss *Computer Services Manager*

Book Department

David R. Tarr *Director*
Joanne D. Daniels *Director, CQ Press*
John L. Moore *Assistant Director*
Michael D. Wormser *Associate Editor*
Martha V. Gottron *Associate Editor*
Barbara R. de Boinville *Senior Editor, CQ Press*
Nancy Lammers *Senior Editor*
Susan D. Sullivan *Developmental Editor, CQ Press*
Margaret C. Thompson *Senior Writer*
Carolyn Goldinger *Project Editor*
Janet E. Hoffman *Project Editor*
Mary L. McNeil *Project Editor/Design Coordinator*
Robert S. Mudge *Project Editor*
Patricia M. Russotto *Editorial Assistant*
Mary Ames Booker *Editorial Assistant*
Judith Aldock *Editorial Assistant*
Elizabeth H. Summers *Editorial Assistant*
Nancy A. Blanpied *Indexer*
Barbara March *Secretary*
Patricia Ann O'Connor *Contributing Editor*
Elder Witt *Contributing Editor*

Table of Contents

Tables, Figures and Graphs

PREFACE

This book appears in the wake of major legislation to rescue Social Security — the largest single pension in the United States and the biggest entitlement program in the federal government. Had the program gone bankrupt it would have deprived 36 million retirees of a significant, for some essential, portion of their income. Because a failure of Social Security's largest and most troubled trust fund, Old Age and Survivors' Insurance (OASI) would have dragged down the other two, Disability Insurance and Hospital Insurance, federal payments for medical costs beyond the reach of most elderly Americans would have ceased. The fate of the program also held consequences for the federal budget deficit in that the Social Security trust funds, while kept separate from general Treasury revenues, were counted as part of the unified federal budget.

It is fitting, however, that two thirds of the book deals with pension programs other than Social Security. Although none of them have undergone so complete an overhaul so recently, the fate of Social Security affects them all. Where Social Security fails, other plans — private, state and local government and federal — must take up the slack. On the other hand, the massive growth of Social Security far beyond its founders' expectations probably has inhibited the development of private and individual retirement funding and demonstrably makes some public sector plans redundant. Indeed, coordination of the various programs that make up the U.S. pension system is, after financing, the main concern for many policy makers and pension managers.

For ease of identification, the pension programs in this book are discussed according to who runs them. Public and private pensions, and the pension organizations that make up those categories, are discussed each in turn. The reader will note, however, that there are factors, other than administrative differences, by which these programs could be categorized.

A 1981 report for the House Select Committee on Aging observed that pension systems may be broken down according to the particular needs they are intended to meet — retirement, health and survivors' benefits are the three main concerns of retirees — to what degree those needs will be met and for what part of the population. Or the plans may be grouped according to the funding principles to which they subscribe and the contributions required of participants: are they welfare or "insurance" oriented? These questions, upon which many public-policy decisions turn, are highlighted to some degree in the context of each pension plan discussed in *Social Security and Retirement*.

Chapter 1 provides a basic history of Social Security and an explanation of the funding crisis addressed by Congress in March 1983; Chapter 2 surveys recently proposed methods of salvaging Social Security and the major issues debated by Congress in 1983. Chapter 3 explains the health-care components of Social Security: Medicare and Medicaid. Private pensions, the laws that regulate them and their costs to recipients and providers are the main subjects of Chapter 4. Public-sector plans on the federal, state and local level are discussed in Chapter 5. Finally, Chapter 6 goes into the opportunities presented to the independent investor by Individual Retirement Accounts (IRAs) and Keogh plans.

A chronology of pension development and a selected bibliography follow in an appendix section.

CQ Book Department editor/writers Janet Hoffman, Robert Mudge and Margaret C. Thompson compiled and wrote most of the book on the basis of coverage by reporters for the *Congressional Quarterly Weekly Report* and CQ's Editorial Research Reports service. Robert W. Merry, a Congress and economic affairs reporter for *The Wall Street Journal*, wrote the chapter on IRAs and Keoghs.

INTRODUCTION

Since World War II pension systems in the United States have grown massively in scope and have come to exert an unprecedented influence upon the lives of American retirees. In 1950 about one-third of the elderly population was covered by some sort of pension; by 1983 more than 90 percent enjoyed such coverage. The assets and reserves held by private and public pension funds have been estimated to constitute nearly 17 percent of all financial assets in the nation and more than 8 percent of its gross national product.

However, if an overall pension system can be said to exist in the United States, it has evolved piecemeal since the first military, government employee and private programs were set up in the 18th and 19th centuries. Throughout American history, hundreds of private corporations, labor unions, state and local governments, federal agencies and Congress have independently established pension plans for workers in a wide range of occupations.

The plans have evolved to meet the various needs of their participants and of society as a whole: Military pensions to clear the ranks of older men for rising young officers and enlisted men; government pensions to reward workers for public service; Social Security to provide for the many left destitute by the Depression without unemployment or retirement insurance; corporate and union pensions to meet the demands of employees in the post-World War II prosperity; Keogh plans for the self-employed and Individual Retirement Accounts (IRAs) to allow for individual retirement planning; and health insurance to cover the medical costs that fall most heavily upon the elderly.

Thus a central feature of the nation's pension system in the 1980s — and one of its most significant problems — is the great diversity of pension programs within it and the lack of coordination among them. Early in the decade, some pension experts believed that the lack of a comprehensive national policy left pensions financially vulnerable as they faced economic stress and a growing population of beneficiaries, and acted as an administrative stumbling block to the equitable provision of income to the elderly. On the other hand, President Ronald Reagan and members of his administration claimed that pension systems left to the laws of supply and demand would provide genuinely needed benefits while keeping their costs under control.

The differences among today's major pension systems — Social Security, federal employee, private and state and local government pensions — are marked. An important distinction can be made first of all between Social Security, which favors retirees with modest earnings records, and most other plans, which reward long years of service and tailor benefits more closely to pre-retirement earning power.

Benefits also vary by the degree to which a given pension plan attempts to replace pre-retirement income. While Social Security is meant to provide minimum benefits to be supplemented by other pensions or private savings, other public sector pensions frequently are intended to provide complete retirement coverage. Thus, the average monthly benefit for civil service retirees in 1983 ($1,047) was more than double that for Social Security recipients. Private pensions, often supplementary rather than comprehensive, are smaller on average than civil service payments. State and local government pensions, sometimes providing full retirement income *on top* of Social Security, can provide benefits twice the size of those in the private sector.

While Social Security, many state and local plans and the large Civil Service Retirement system index their benefits to inflation, most private pensions do not. The age at which a participant is eligible to receive full benefits usually comes earlier in the federal employee programs than in private plans or Social Security.

Employees participating in pension plans contribute to the various systems in amounts ranging from none at all in most private plans to payroll taxes of 6.7 percent for Social Security participants and 7 percent for federal workers.

Standards for funding and financial accountability also vary among the plans. Since its founding in 1935 — with the idea that it would imitate commercial insurance policies to some degree (accumulating reserves for future obligatons) — Social Security has become a pay-as-you-go system that funds its benefit payments with revenues from taxes almost as soon as they are collected. The federal civilian employee plans operate similarly, with the additional security of being able to draw on general Treasury revenues to make up for any shortfall. Military pensions are funded entirely through congressional appropriations. By contrast, private pensions are often "advance funded" with an accumulation of reserves to cover some portion of future obligations. State and local plans are financed through a combination of advance and pay-as-you-go funding in the absence of any overarching system of federal regulations.

In the 1970s, the major pension programs showed the strain of operating in an unforgiving economy. Partly due to their vulnerability to high inflation (including soaring medical costs) and lagging wages, the Social Security trust funds experienced severe cash-flow problems after 1972. Default on benefit payments in 1983 was averted by a last-minute Social Security rescue bill (PL 98-21) in March of that year.

Private pension plans had experienced financial difficulties long before the Social Security crisis. Funds accumulated by private pensions before 1974, in the absence of statutory provisions for oversight or auditing, were highly vulnerable to fluctuations in the economy and poor investment practices on the part of their managers. As a consequence they suffered from real and potential funding shortfalls. To ensure against abuses or defaults on the part of private plans, the Employee Retirement Income Security Act of 1974 (ERISA) established funding and financial disclosure requirements as well as federal insurance for private pensions through the Pension Benefit Guaranty Corporation (PBGC). However, ERISA left some issues — such as coordination of private plan benefits with Social Security — unresolved, and many plans, struggling under the dual burdens of hard economic times and the new financial standards, were forced to terminate. The PBGC itself encountered financial trouble because the insurance premiums employers paid for PBGC coverage increasingly were inadequate to meet obligations to cover the benefits of terminated plans.

Like Social Security, state and local government pensions faced unfunded future obligations. Critics pointed to the disparity between dwindling tax revenues and generous benefits, which in combination (but not coordination) with Social Security could yield for some recipients retirement income greater than their pre-retirement salaries.

As the large benefits offered by the Civil Service Retirement system (CSRS) and certain among the other federal pension plans began to outstrip the contributions of participants and their employer agencies in the late 1960s, the federal government had to chip in, to the tune of $11.2 billion by 1980. The comfortable position of federal retirees was contributing to the deficit in general Treasury revenues and thus to the federal budget deficit (Social Security contributed to the federal deficit in that its separate trust funds were accounted for under the unified federal budget).

All of these funding crises were precipitated by inflation and the general sluggishness of the U.S. economy, as the value of accumulated contributions declined and the cost of benefits went up. The problems promised to become worse in the next century as a number of demographic factors — increasing longevity, a declining birth rate, and the sudden retirement of the baby-boom generation between 2010 and 2030 — would reduce drastically the ratio of active workers contributing to pension plans to retirees receiving benefits.

Coping with these economic and demographic changes would be even more difficult, according to a number of pension experts — including Robert M. Ball, social security commissioner from 1962 to 1973, and Wilbur J. Cohen, head of the lobbying group Save Our Security (SOS) and a founder of Social Security — because there was no overall coordination among pension systems.

In an analysis for the House Select Aging Committee in 1981, pension expert Michael S. March elaborated this theme. He argued that where pensions plans were regulated at all, they answered to many masters. This applied particularly to private pensions, which, under ERISA, were regulated by the PBGC as well as the Labor and Treasury departments. As a result of this disorganization, March continued, there was a dearth of uniform guidelines for pensions, particularly regarding their obligations to beneficiaries and their own financial solvency. Under these circumstances, coordination of policy among various plans was difficult, if not impossible.

The President's Commission on Pension Policy pointed out in 1981 that the major pension systems — public, private and Social Security — were meant to act as a "three-legged stool," providing adequate retirement income for an individual in various combinations. However, because of the great disparities among the systems, some pensioners — particularly those in the civil service, military and state and local government programs — got relatively high (and sometimes duplicated) benefits, while many workers in the private sector remained uncovered or received disproportionately low benefits. Some plans had no provisions for the survivors and dependents of beneficiaries.

Workers not provided for under government or private sector plans were forced to look to Social Security and any savings they might have.

In the early 1980s about 75 percent of all pension benefits were paid by Social Security. One consequence of this was that a significant number of retirees depended on Social Security — originally conceived as only a partial replacement of pre-retirement income — as their sole means of support.

By contrast to those who would remedy these ills by more comprehensive federal regulation, the Reagan administration sought to stimulate private sector initiatives. The administration proposed additional tax breaks for private pension plans (they had been encouraged this way since World War II) and greater accessibility to IRAs. The latter was provided in the Economic Recovery Tax Act of 1981.

Perhaps the most dramatic strides toward a "free market" pension system were made in the area of health insurance. Between 1981 and 1983, the administration succeeded in giving the states greater flexibility to develop cost-effective health-insurance procedures. The federal Medicare program eventually adopted a cost-cutting billing scheme — pioneered by the states — as part of the 1983 Social Security rescue bill.

Other pension reforms in the early 1980s reflected concern for a better-integrated national pension system. The President's Commission on Pension Policy in 1981 proposed a minimum universal pension system that would establish national standards for private pension plans. Members of Congress in 1976 and again in 1982 introduced so-called "PERISA" bills to regulate state and local pensions along the lines of ERISA regulations for private plans. While neither proposal had made headway in Congress by 1983, the PERISA concept enjoyed bipartisan support and was likely to be proposed again.

The Social Security rescue bill of 1983 responded primarily to the immediate funding crisis. Its provisions to include federal employees under Social Security and to prohibit the exodus of state and local governments from the system were more to enhance the trust funds' tax base than to provide a structure for integrated policy making. However, the urgency of the funding crisis — as evidenced by the formation of a National Commission on Social Security Reform to grapple with the issue and the dispatch with which Congress approved most of the commission's recommendations — underscored the need for a more orderly and deliberate national pension policy.

Robert S. Mudge
July 1983

Enacted in 1935, today's Social Security system provides retirement income to 36 million Americans. But the system has faced severe cash-flow problems in recent years.

Chapter 1

SOCIAL SECURITY: THE FUNDING CRISIS

The massive U.S. Social Security pension system — a program that directly affects more than 60 percent of the U.S. population — underwent statutory changes in 1983 that reaffirmed its role as the key source of income for the vast majority of U.S. retirees, regardless of their economic status.

Despite serious funding shortfalls in the 1970s, and projections of more intractable problems in the next century, Congress and a joint executive-congressional commission set up to study these problems endorsed the fundamental concept of Social Security. The commission argued that "Congress . . . should not alter the fundamental structure of the Social Security program or undermine its fundamental principles." Its 1983 recommendations formed the basis for the comprehensive changes approved by Congress that year.

This confidence in the Social Security concept was buttressed by the program's spectacular record in improving the economic status of America's elderly. By 1983, the program encompassed more than 90 percent of the retired population and had reduced the proportion of this group living in poverty by 50 percent over the preceding two decades.

However, in the mid-1970s Social Security became a victim of its own success and of uncontrollable economic factors. Over the years the system had built a large constituency of beneficiaries who came to expect more and more in benefits. At the same time, Social Security was buffeted by economic developments that reduced the program's funds while increasing the cost of delivering benefits.

Social Security's severe financial position was augmented by political obstacles that plagued efforts to forge a consensus on solutions or even to reach an agreement between Congress and the executive branch on the extent of the system's troubles. Congress had rebuffed suggestions by President Carter that the system be financed in new ways or that benefits be cut. In 1981, the Reagan administration made dire predictions about Social Security's future and called for cutbacks in benefits. Democrats said the administration was overstating the problem and charged that the president was trying to balance the budget at the expense of America's elderly. A legislative standoff ensued and the president established the National Commission on Social Security Reform to assemble a bipartisan package of changes in the system.

Meanwhile, Reagan was stung by the public outcry and the sharp drop in public confidence in the future viability of the system. Democrats made Social Security a major issue in the November 1982 congressional elections and were able to increase their strength in the House. But partisan victories did not ease the problems of Social Security or comfort the large segment of the public — 63 percent according to a January 1983 CBS/*New York Times* poll — that doubted they would ever receive benefits from the troubled system.

The public's reaction to Social Security's problems reflected the extent to which millions of Americans had come to rely upon it at retirement. Any fundamental changes in the system would affect 36 million beneficiaries — one-seventh of the population — by 1983. Social Security paid out $206 billion in benefits and administrative costs in fiscal 1982. This amount constituted more than 25 percent of the federal budget for that fiscal year, equal to about 7 percent of the gross national product, as compared to 6 percent in the early years of the system. During the same period, about half the population — 116 million — contributed $183 billion to the system's trust funds through payroll taxes and health premiums. A large proportion of U.S. taxpayers — particularly those with low incomes — were paying more in Social Security taxes than in income taxes. Wage earners in 1982 paid an average of $971 in Social Security taxes; the maximum tax was $2,170.

The health of the system also had consequences for the national economy and the federal deficit. The Congressional Budget Office (CBO) projected that Social Security would comprise more than 30 percent of the federal budget by 1985.

The National Commission's recommendations — many of which ultimately were enacted into law — were acceptable to just over half the public, according to a poll made by *Newsweek* in the spring of 1983. The 1983 legislation, while preserving the essentials of the system, signaled a period of retrenchment relative to the beneficence of preceding decades. The payroll tax rate was increased sooner than previously scheduled. A new tax on certain benefits was established and the retirement age would be gradually increased in the next century. A more overt benefit cut came in the form of a one-time delay in the annual cost-of-living allowance. On the other hand, additional revenues would be gained by the inclusion of new federal employees under the system.

While the 1983 changes would mean some hardship for many Social Security participants, some observers considered the funding crisis of the 1970s and 1980s a fortuitous exercise in preparing for more serious challenges to the system expected in the next century.

A Social Revolution

Passage of the Social Security Act of 1935 (PL 74-271) — one of the most comprehensive welfare bills ever cleared by Congress — was a major political event. Enacted at the urgent request of President Franklin D. Roosevelt in the midst of the worst depression in the nation's history, the act changed both the concept of personal economic security in the United States and the nature of federal-state relations in the welfare field.

Redressing a Faulty Economy

The heart of the Social Security Act consisted of several "income replacement" programs. They were designed to assure that individuals had some income for essential expenses when their regular source of income was cut off by retirement, loss of job, disability or death of a working spouse. Of these, the main program was Old Age Insurance, a federal retirement insurance plan financed by a payroll tax, for persons presumed to be too old to work.

This was accompanied by a federal-state unemployment insurance system for persons temporarily unable to find work and a system of federal grants to the states to reimburse them for part of the costs of charity aid to the indigent — the aged, the blind and children deprived of the support of a parent — who were unable to seek work or support themselves. Using a variety of approaches, the income replacement programs were to provide individuals with weekly or monthly cash payments from government sources to cover living expenses.

A Radical Concept. The income replacement programs represented, in many ways, a revolution in American life. Before the Roosevelt New Deal, security against old age, unemployment and other economic hardships was considered the responsibility primarily of the individual himself, his family and local private charitable institutions.

9

For isolated groups in the country — federal employees under the civil service system, some state and local government employees, and small numbers of workers covered by private pension plans at their place of employment — relatively dependable retirement pension systems did exist. But for the bulk of the population there was no systematic program — public or private — to guarantee income after retirement and no organized program at all except charity (where available) to counter economic hazards. Even the minimal level of economic security afforded the individual by these traditional and uncoordinated sources of aid often was non-existent for much of the working population.

The Depression of the 1930s, which left millions destitute, generated both public pressure for some sort of economic security program and greater public willingness to accept remedial action by the federal government. Other factors leading to passage of the Social Security Act were the personal prestige of President Roosevelt and the large Democratic majorities in both houses of Congress that were ready to follow his lead.

A Moderate Federal Role. The Roosevelt administration's specific proposals for social insurance were viewed by conservatives as relatively moderate compared with other income security schemes that were being considered during the Depression. One such proposal drew from a plan devised by Dr. Francis Townsend, a physician and social reformer, that would have provided a monthly $200 federal pension for everyone aged 60 or older, to be financed by a new sales tax. The Townsend plan was a politically potent issue at the time, with widespread support among the nation's elderly. However, the plan was too radical for many members of Congress, including Democrats, who thought it would be too costly and would impose too large a federal role in personal economic security. The Roosevelt proposals, on the other hand, minimized both the breach with the tradition of individual self-sufficiency and eased the new tax burden that would be imposed on business.

By establishing a mandatory, nationwide program of income security, the U.S. government for the first time assumed permanent responsibility for functions traditionally reserved for the family and local governments. The income replacement programs, particularly unemployment insurance, also had the secondary function of stabilizing the national economy by keeping steady the purchasing power of different groups in good and bad economic times.

The programs furnishing income to the aged had another function that was important in the context of the Depression: They were intended to help clear the labor market of the surplus of older workers competing with younger persons for scarce jobs. The expansion of benefits in ensuing years was successful in drawing eligible retirees from the work force. In other ways, however, Congress backed away from this strategy as early as 1939 when it allowed workers over 65 to earn up to a specified amount while continuing to receive benefits.

Insurance and Assistance

From the inception of the Social Security system, there was considerable disagreement about how the program would be financed and benefits distributed. A major issue was whether the government should use a welfare approach, an insurance approach, or both, to safeguard the individual against economic misfortunes. In drafting the Social Security legislation in 1935, Congress devised a program that drew partly on insurance principles and partly on traditions of social welfare.

Old Age Insurance. The centerpiece of the Social Security Act, Old Age Insurance, would be a large national pension system based on social insurance principles, bearing a loose resemblance to those prevailing in the private insurance industry. As with a commercial insurance company, a prospective beneficiary would pay a "premium" in the form of a payroll tax and could expect to be compensated under specified circumstances, in this case, retirement.

Congress was attracted to the insurance approach to retirement income for several reasons. It was generally believed that a self-financing insurance-type mechanism would isolate Social Security from the kind of political and economic stresses involved in deciding annual appropriations for most government programs. In addition, many experts felt the insurance method would permit benefits at a higher level than the subsistence level, providing better security for the retired individual. By making retirement benefits automatic without consideration of need or the humiliation of a means test, it was hoped that Old Age Insurance would provide surer and truer income security than a charity approach.

However, the insurance protection envisioned under Social Security departed increasingly from private-sector insurance plans. Social Security was made compulsory at the outset, and in recent years, benefits have been paid out at a faster rate than revenue has come in through the payroll tax, depleting the funds reserved for future obligations.

An Income Supplement. Congress intended Social Security payments to be one source of supplemental income to an individual after retirement.

An individual's monthly benefits were calculated through a formula based on a statistically determined average life expectancy. Initially, the formula was applied to a worker's complete earnings record to yield the proper amount of his monthly payment. A retiree's Social Security payment was intended to provide a "replacement rate" — that portion of a worker's paycheck at retirement that Social Security was intended to replace — of about 40 percent. Private pensions and savings were expected to make up the remainder of the retiree's income.

For any one year of work, a ceiling was placed on the amount that could be counted in determining a worker's lifetime earnings. This ceiling — which defined a worker's "benefit base" — began at $3,000 for the years 1937-1939.

The Payroll Tax. The Old Age Insurance system was financed through a federal payroll tax, imposed on most industrial and white-collar employees and their employers. As in the calculation of benefits, the amount of a worker's annual earnings that could be taxed was initially set at $3,000. There was no tax on earnings above that amount. Assessments on taxable earnings began in 1937 at 1 percent each for employers and employees on the first $3,000 earned, rising to 2 percent each by 1954. Since then, the tax rate has increased as benefits have grown, reaching 6.7 percent in 1982 (by then covering Disability and Hospital Insurance, *see pp. 18, 20*).

Social Security taxes, first collected in 1937, were placed in a special trust fund account set up in the U.S. Treasury, with the money reserved for payment of pensions to eligible persons.

The Contribution and Benefit Base. Payroll taxes were loosely tied to the payment of benefits in that revenues would be drawn from the same maximum earnings base that was used to calculate benefits. This contribution and benefit base would assure that Social Security provided strictly "supplemental" retirement income, placing an upper limit on the benefit "credit" that could be amassed by any individual or family. Congress periodically hiked the maximum earnings base as average earnings increased over the years, eventually indexing it to average national wages in 1972.

Eligibility. Eligibility for Social Security benefits was to be a matter of right and would not depend on need. An individual would become el-

Social Security Contribution and Benefit Base, Tax Rate and Amount by Income Level, 1937-1990

| Date | Contribution and Benefit Base | Employee/ Employer Tax Rate | Employee/Employer* Annual Tax Payments | | |
			Minimum Wage	Average Wage	Maximum Wage
1937-49	$ 3,000	1.000%	6.44	16.80	30.00
1950	3,000	1.500	22.49	38.16	45.00
1951-53	3,600	1.500	23.40	44.56	54.00
1954	3,600	2.000	31.20	63.11	72.00
1955-56	4,200	2.000	35.53	68.34	84.00
1957-58	4,200	2.250	46.80	82.30	94.50
1959	4,800	2.500	52.00	96.39	120.00
1960-61	4,800	3.000	63.96	121.41	144.00
1962	4,800	3.125	74.75	134.11	150.00
1963-65	4,800	3.625	92.57	164.72	174.00
1966	6,600	4.200	109.20	207.41	277.20
1967	6,600	4.400	126.98	229.39	290.40
1968	7,800	4.400	144.89	245.16	343.20
1969	7,800	4.800	159.74	282.90	374.40
1970	7,800	4.800	159.74	296.94	374.40
1971	7,800	5.200	173.06	337.85	405.60
1972	9,000	5.200	173.06	370.96	468.00
1973	10,800	5.85	194.69	443.44	631.80
1974	13,200	5.85	227.16	469.80	772.20
1975	14,100	5.85	255.53	504.91	824.85
1976	15,300	5.85	279.86	539.75	895.05
1977	16,500	5.85	279.86	572.10	965.25
1978	17,700	6.05	333.48	638.64	1070.85
1979	22,900	6.13	369.76	703.69	1403.77
1980	25,900	6.13	395.26	767.08	1587.67
1981	29,700	6.65	463.37	915.91	1975.05
1982	32,400	6.70	466.86	971.38	2170.80
1983	35,700	6.70	466.86	1016.14	2391.90
Projected:					
1984	37,500	7.00	506.26	1101.90	2625.00
1985	39,300	7.05	537.56	1170.02	2770.65

	Contribution and Benefit Base	Employee/ Employer Tax Rate	Employee/Employer* Annual Tax Payments		
Date			Minimum Wage	Average Wage	Maximum Wage
1986	40,800	7.15	575.77	1253.20	2917.20
1987	42,900	7.15	608.41	1324.24	3067.35
1988	45,300	7.51	673.68	1466.30	3402.03
1989	48,000	7.51	710.38	1546.17	3604.80
1990	50,700	7.65	764.26	1663.45	3878.55

* Figures in combined years are averages.

Source: Report of the National Commission on Social Security Reform, January 1983; OASDI Trustees' Annual Reports, 1982, 1983.

igible for a monthly cash payment at age 65 if he had worked a specified amount of time in employment subject to the payroll tax and had thus contributed to the costs of his own pension.

Charity vs. Insurance

Because Old Age Insurance trust fund operations were based on actuarial principles, requiring many years before the system built up reserves and a large number of workers became eligible, the first monthly benefits were not scheduled to be paid out until 1942. Amendments added in 1939, however, changed the effective date to 1940.

In the interim years the main burden of providing income for the aged fell on the traditional charity approach. Congress, in the 1935 act, created a separate public assistance program for the aged, called Old Age Assistance, which provided matching grants to the states to enable them to give charity aid to the indigent elderly. Need, as determined by the states through a "means test," was the sole criterion of assistance. Payments were meant to be adequate to sustain the indigent person only at or near subsistence levels. Financing came from general revenues at the federal, state and local levels.

President Roosevelt and members of Congress emphasized that once the Old Age Insurance system was in full operation, that program was to be the primary government method of providing supplemental income for the aged. The public assistance program was only a secondary safeguard to protect those who were ineligible for insurance benefits or those whose insurance benefits were extremely low. It was expected that eventually, as more individuals built up insured status, the number of elderly requiring public assistance charity would decline proportionately.

These expectations proved correct. In 1940, the first year of monthly retirement insurance benefits, nearly 223,000 retirees received Social Security benefits, while more than 2 million persons received Old Age Assistance aid. By 1964 the number of beneficiaries under the expanded Old Age, Survivors and Disability Insurance (OASDI) program had swelled to close to 20 million for an increase of nearly 18 million. Of these, about 15 million were age 62 or older; the rest were dependent children, disabled persons and other dependents. Meanwhile, the number of persons receiving Old Age Assistance benefits in 1964 had climbed by a scant 200,000. In 1982 OASDI beneficiaries numbered 36 million, while recipients of public assistance, by then a federal program known as Supplemental Security Income (SSI), were only 4 million. Of that group, fewer than half received benefits due to old age.

Financing Concepts

To achieve the long-term financing required for the Social Security Old Age Insurance system, Congress sought initially to employ a reserve method of financing. Contributions from the payroll tax were to be paid into a fund on a regular basis according to mathematical projections of future need.

Optimistic legislators were convinced that an accumulation of reserve monies would make the Social Security system relatively impregnable to fluctuations in the economy. A reserve system would permit benefit costs to be balanced against income over several decades and payroll taxes to be imposed at a more or less level rate covering the whole period.

Moreover, it was believed that, just as the adoption of a self-financing program would circumvent periodic appropriations battles in Congress, reserve financing would eliminate political fights over the rate of the payroll tax.

However, the Old Age Insurance system as actually set up in 1935 and amended in 1939 adopted somewhat relaxed reserve requirements. Under a strict scheme of reserve financing, large reserves would have to be built up so that the retirement fund at all times would have enough cash available to pay out all current and future benefits earned by individuals on the basis of work already performed. While the system was intended to build up large reserves, there was no real attempt to accumulate reserves great enough to meet all accrued liabilities, only a sizable portion.

In subsequent amendments, Congress generally raised benefit levels and expanded the program's coverage without providing adequate additional financing. This, along with strains on the program's trust funds caused by unforeseen developments in the national economy, made Social Security more of a pay-as-you-go financing system, under which, in its most extreme form, revenues would be provided only in amounts sufficient to meet current obligations, with no allowance for future requirements. Payroll tax rates simply would be adjusted each year to bring in enough funds to pay for benefits expected to be paid out that year.

The Benefits Explosion

As established, the Old Age Insurance program provided retirement benefits for the insured worker only. Over the years, however, Congress increased benefits and made more people eligible for them. Greater emphasis was placed on assuring an adequate retirement income to an ever-increasing proportion of the population. Even before any benefits had been paid out, Congress was already broadening Social Security coverage to include beneficiaries who had never paid into the system.

The first major amendments to the Social Security Act were voted in 1939, when Congress made important structural changes in the Old Age Insurance program, broadening its scope. The most significant change authorized monthly benefits to be paid both to the dependents of an insured retiree while he was living and drawing Social Security benefits and to his survivors after his death. As a result, the program was renamed Old Age and Survivors Insurance (OASI).

To make benefits available in 1940, rather than in the original target date of 1942, the 1939 changes adopted a system of eligibility by quarters. Since then, and subject to a number of qualifications, potential Social Security beneficiaries have had to show minimum earnings for a requisite number of quarters after 1936 — six in 1940 — in order to become fully covered.

In 1983 the minimum earnings per quarter required to become eligible were $340, down from the equivalent of $568 ($50) in 1940. However, those retiring in 1983 had to have accumulated 31 quarters, or just under eight years, for full coverage. The requirement for full coverage was scheduled to increase to 40 quarters early in the 1990s.

The 1939 amendments also introduced the concept of basing the amount of a worker's monthly Social Security payment on the worker's average monthly wage during his entire working career. Congress directed that lifetime earnings be averaged — and in later years, indexed to inflation — to yield a worker's average indexed monthly earnings (AIME). In turn, the worker's monthly benefits would be calculated by application of the formula to his or her AIME.

Postwar Era

Because of the long-range method of financing and other factors, the Old Age Insurance program was just hitting its operational stride when World War II ended. Relatively few people by then had become eligible for benefits, and coverage still was confined largely to urban blue collar workers. Only about $274 million was paid out in benefits in fiscal 1945.

As it began to mature, the retirement system had an ever greater impact on society. By the late 1940s there was a rapid increase in the number of beneficiaries and a corresponding rise in benefits. Whereas in 1940 fewer than a quarter of a million people received Social Security benefits totaling close to $4.1 million, by 1950 approximately 3.5 million beneficiaries were receiving monthly payments amounting to $126.9 million.

Keeping Pace With a Growing Economy. Despite substantial increases in wages and the general standard of living, the OASI system in 1950 still operated under 1939 benefit formulas and coverage rules. As a result, the system no longer was able to fulfill its anticipated role as the primary mechanism for providing supplemental income after retirement. That led Congress to overhaul and update the entire program in 1950.

A new payroll tax schedule and a higher taxable wage base of $3,600 per year were established to bring in more revenues. In turn, the earnings ceiling upon which initial Social Security payments would be calculated also was boosted to $3,600. To compensate for increases in the cost of living, benefit levels already established by the formula would again be increased by an average of 70 percent.

The amendment substantially eased eligibility requirements for many currently aged persons and extended the basic reach of the system beyond urban employees. The self-employed (except farmers and professionals), many agricultural and domestic service workers, and state and local government workers — about 9.2 million persons — became eligible for participation in the social insurance system.

These and later changes clearly established a benefit bias in favor of persons receiving the lowest retirement benefits. For them, increases in benefits were proportionately higher than for those persons receiving the maximum benefits.

Other changes during the 1950s continued to expand the retirement system by increasing benefits and easing eligibility requirements. In 1952 benefits were raised slightly but the increases were not substantial. In 1954, however, the taxable wage and benefit base was increased to $4,200 a year, a new, higher tax schedule was set and benefits were increased further. Some 7.5 million more persons were brought under Social Security coverage, including self-employed farmers, additional farm and domestic workers, and additional government and non-profit organization employees. After the 1954 amendments, about 80 percent of the paid labor force was covered by the retirement system.

Disability Insurance/ Early Retirement. In 1956, Congress made two major changes in the Social Security law. In the postwar years, the question of whether the system should assume responsibility for supporting disabled persons below retirement age was a controversial issue. A public assistance program, Aid to the Permanently and Totally Disabled, had been set up for the disabled in 1950. Congress linked that program to the Social Security system in 1956, establishing a separate Disability Insurance (DI) trust fund to provide benefits to long-term and permanently disabled workers aged 50 to 64. The Social Security program was renamed Old Age, Survivors, and Disability Insurance (OASDI).

The 1956 amendments also reduced the minimum benefit age for women from 65 to 62, with actuarially reduced benefits in some cases.

Two years later benefits again were raised slightly, the taxable wage base was increased to $4,800 a year and a new Social Security tax schedule, set at 2.5 percent, took effect in 1959. Dependents of workers receiving monthly Disability Insurance payments also were made eligible for monthly dependents benefits.

The 1960s: A Broadening Constituency

During the economic prosperity of the 1950s and 1960s, workers' wages increased at a relatively rapid rate compared to price increases. Between 1950 and 1972, wages increased by an average of 4.7 percent annually, while prices rose only 2.5 percent. As a result, the Social Security trust funds built up a heavy cushion of reserves from the payroll tax lev-

Social Security Benefits and Beneficiaries, 1940-82

| | **OASDI Beneficiaries**
(In Millions) | | | Average
Monthly
Benefits; Re- | | |
	Retired Workers, Dependents & Survivors	Disabled Workers	Total	tired, Depen- dents and Survivors	Covered Workers (In Millions)	Workers per OASDI Beneficiary
1940	.2	—	.2	$ 23	35.4	177.0
1945	1.3	—	1.3	24	46.4	35.7
1950	3.5	—	3.5	44	48.3	13.8
1955	8.0	—	8.0	59	65.2	8.2
1960	14.1	.7	14.8	74	72.5	4.9
1965	19.1	1.7	20.9	84	80.7	3.9
1970	23.6	2.7	26.2	118	93.0	3.5
1975	27.7	4.3	32	207	100.2	3.1
1980	30.9	4.7	35.6	341	114.3	3.2
1982	31.9	3.9	35.8	419	116.0	3.3

Source: Social Security Administration

ied on the relatively higher earnings. Congress continued to expand benefits under Social Security, which was becoming an increasingly popular and politically appealing program for winning votes back home.

Although there were no general benefit increases in 1960, Congress did remove the minimum age of 50 for receipt of Disability Insurance benefits and loosened general eligibility requirements for Social Security benefits. In 1961 eligibility requirements were eased again, a higher schedule of tax rates replaced the one set up in 1958 and benefits were increased for some groups of workers. In addition, the minimum age at which men could receive benefits was dropped from 65 to 62, with actuarially reduced benefits if a worker chose to retire at the earlier age instead of waiting for "full" retirement at 65.

The Largest Entitlement Program. By the end of 1964, about 90 percent of all employment in the nation was covered by the expanded Old Age, Survivors and Disability Insurance program. Approximately 76 percent of the nation's aged were receiving benefits under the program, with another 8 percent eligible but not drawing benefits because they either had not yet retired or had not applied for them. The total amount paid out by the Social Security system in fiscal 1964 to approximately 20 million people was nearly $16.2 billion, compared with the $274 million paid to beneficiaries in fiscal 1945. The average monthly benefit for a retired worker had climbed from $22.60 when benefits were first distributed in 1940 to $83.92 in 1965.

In short, the Old Age, Survivors and Disability Insurance program had become the nation's single most important entitlement program by the early 1960s, accounting in fiscal 1964 for 37 percent of all welfare expenditures compared with only 6 percent in fiscal 1950.

Hospital Insurance. The U.S. social insurance system carved out a yet deeper niche in the federal budget when Congress in 1965 established a major medical care program for the aged under the Social Security system. The health care issue had come up repeatedly in the postwar years. President Harry S Truman had proposed a health insurance program covering a large portion of the population. President John F. Kennedy began in 1960 to press for a federally operated health insurance program for the elderly.

Legislation passed in 1965 provided a new payroll tax (applied equally to employers, employees and the self-employed) and a taxable earnings base to finance the new Medicare program enacted that year. Federal tax revenues were expected to finance the plan for persons not covered by Social Security. The payroll taxes and general revenues earmarked for the plan were placed in a new Hospital Insurance (HI) trust fund, separate from the system's OASI and DI trust funds. *(Medicare, Chapter 3, p. 77)*

The 1965 law also made other significant changes in Social Security, including a 7 percent increase in retirement benefits. These were followed by new expansions of the Social Security Act during the Lyndon Johnson administration. Congress raised retirement benefits again in 1967, this time by 13 percent, and continued to ease Social Security eligibility requirements.

Cost-of-Living Increases. Rising inflation in the late 1960s — due in part to expanded government programs and increasing federal deficits as the Johnson administration's Great Society programs took hold — led Congress to raise OASDI benefits three times between 1969 and 1972: 15 percent in 1969, 10 percent in 1971, and 20 percent in 1972.

In addition, various eligibility requirements for the OASDI program were considerably eased. To finance the increased benefits, the amount of earnings subject to the Social Security tax was substantially increased. The taxable earnings base jumped from $4,800 in 1965 to $10,800 in 1973. Increases in the tax rate itself, which caused greater hardship for lower-income workers, were not as great, rising from 3.625 to 5.85 over the same period. (Part of this increase was necessary to put the Medicare trust fund on a more stable basis.)

All of these benefit and tax rate changes were added piecemeal to bills dealing with other subjects. It was not until 1972 that Congress approved a comprehensive revision of the Social Security Act itself.

Social Security Overextended

In 1972, the large trust fund reserves resulting from the relative buoyancy of wage levels — and therefore of payroll tax receipts — in the 1950s and 1960s led Congress to make basic changes in the way benefit increases were calculated.

Rather than increase benefits on an ad hoc basis, often involving intense political fights, Congress in 1972 decided to tie future increases in Social Security benefits to the Consumer Price Index (CPI). Some members maintained that benefits from Social Security still were relatively low and that a healthy economy and rising wages would generate adequate revenues to cover future increases. Conservative members of Congress — perhaps the most important advocates of indexing — saw it as a way to keep benefits down by insulating the process from the pressure of benefit-hungry constituents.

Congress provided for automatic benefit increases beginning in 1975, when the cost of living rose at an annual rate of more than 3 percent. In years of price inflation above 3 percent, both the initial benefit formula and the rate of subsequent benefit hikes would be increased accordingly. In addition, Congress tied the wage base on which Social Security taxes were levied to a wage index that also was expected to increase.

The 1972 legislation also made a revolutionary shift in the structure of Social Security. A new program of assistance to the aged poor — Supplemental Security Income (SSI) — was set up as a replacement for the original Old Age Assistance program. Unlike the OAA, the new program was to be fully financed by the federal government from general tax revenues and would set uniform national eligibility requirements. Old Age Assistance had been a jointly funded federal-state program. The SSI program provided benefits in 1975 to more than 4 million persons, compared with 3.2 million under the entire federal-state public assistance program that had preceded it. In 1979 between 8 percent and 9 percent of the population age 65 and over received Supplemental Security Income, while approximately 90 percent received Social Security payments.

The First Deficits

These developments caused a greater intermingling of welfare policies with the insurance principle conceived in the original Social Security Act. They also precipitated a multitude of financial problems for the benefit-heavy social insurance program.

The price indexing of benefits made Social Security even more dependent on the economy's performance. Although indexing seemed logical in the context of 1950s and 1960s prosperity, the relationship between wages and prices — in which the former had outpaced the latter — changed drastically during the 1970s as the national economy took a series of sharp downturns.

The cost of rising benefits outpaced the tax increases provided by the 1972 amendments, and by the mid-1970s the first signs of Social Security's financial troubles had become apparent. After 1975 the OASI trust fund consistently paid out more to Social Security beneficiaries than it collected from payroll taxes. By relying on its reserves between 1975 and 1981, the system was able to keep delivering benefits. By 1981 the reserves had been cut into by more than $15 billion for that purpose.

In its 1977 annual report, the Social Security Board of Trustees — the secretaries of the Departments of Labor, Treasury, and Health, Education and Welfare (since 1979, Health and Human Services) — projected that the Social Security system's Disability Insurance fund's reserves would be exhausted by 1979 and that the retirement and survivors' benefits fund would run out of money in the early 1980s. Although there were other contributing factors, the main cause of these shortfalls was the combination of prolonged inflation and recession, which caused Social Security benefit costs to rise and which reduced revenues from the payroll tax. Government actuaries and other experts predicted grave financial strains for the Social Security system.

1977: Correcting an Error

The Carter administration in May 1977 proposed a Social Security rescue plan based on gradual increases in employer, but not employee, tax contributions into the system. The proposal also included transfers of general revenues to the dwindling trust funds to make up for revenues lost during the 1970s periods of relatively high unemployment when fewer workers were paying into the retirement system.

Carter's plan was designed to provide an additional $83 billion to the funds by 1982. The president said that his proposals would achieve that goal without raising payroll taxes for low- and middle-income workers, thus fulfilling a 1976 election campaign pledge. However, Carter's plan made little headway in Congress.

Burden on Future Beneficiaries. After considering some innovative financing schemes, Congress in 1977 decided to rely exclusively on traditional payroll taxes to replenish the shrinking reserves in the trust funds. The 1977 Social Security tax increase — intended to yield $227 billion over a 10-year period — was the nation's largest peacetime tax increase ever. The measure set new, steeper tax schedules that steadily increased both the tax rate and the taxable earnings base for both employee and employer equally, from 1979 through 1990.

Taxed at the maximum rate, a worker's Social Security taxes would more than triple by 1987. In 1977, with payroll taxes set at 5.85 percent each for employer and employee on a worker's earnings up to $16,500, the maximum Social Security tax paid by a worker and his employer was $965 each. In 1987, when the tax rate was set to rise to 7.15 percent on a projected earnings base of up to $42,900, each could expect to pay more than $3,000 a year into the Social Security system. *(Table, pp. 13-14)*

Congress Plugs a Benefit Leak. The 1977 Social Security changes also took a modest step toward reducing Social Security expenditures by including an important administration-backed measure to correct a technical flaw in the formula for computing the starting benefit levels of future retirees.

The 1972 amendments had permitted increases in both wage levels and prices to influence the formulas for calculating the initial benefits of new retirees. This meant that when the Consumer Price Index rose, it affected overall benefit levels in two ways: by increasing certain factors in the formula for calculating initial benefits and by boosting the annual amount of subsequent benefit hikes. Depending on the performance of the economy, the resulting overcompensation for inflation could have allowed recipients' benefits to exceed their pre-retirement wages and threatened to send benefits skyrocketing over the next several decades.

To correct the problem, Congress in 1977 separated ("decoupled") the process of granting annual cost-of-living Social Security increases to already retired persons from the computation of their initial benefit levels. Under the 1977 law, the formula used for intitial benefits would be affected only by changes in the average level of wages, not prices.

Further Belt Tightening

The 1977 law also eased the earnings test, allowing elderly persons to earn more money without losing a portion of their benefits, and liberalized the treatment of divorced and widowed beneficiaries. The Carter administration had criticized those changes as too costly.

It soon became evident that the 1977 amendments would not restore the system to financial health. Carter in 1979 urged Congress to eliminate a number of "unnecessary" Social Security benefits.

That Carter would even mention the possibility of reducing benefits reflected a major shift in thinking about Social Security, since Congress historically had done little but increase benefits. Among the changes Carter proposed were a phase-out of education benefits for dependent children age 18 and over, a cut-off in surviving parent benefits after the youngest child had reached age 16, and elimination of the minimum benefit guarantee.

Acknowledging that the system was becoming too expensive, Congress in May 1980 attempted to roll back Social Security payments slightly by reducing Disability Insurance benefits to workers who became disabled after July 1 of that year. Provisions of the 1980 law were expected to reduce Social Security and welfare spending by $2.6 billion in fiscal 1981 through 1985.

Later in 1980, Congress opted for a politically appealing "stopgap" solution to the system's impending financial crisis. Under election-year pressures, members agreed to reallocate funds from the Disability Insurance fund to the OASI fund in 1980-81 to assure that there would be sufficient revenue to pay beneficiaries. However, by this action, Congress merely postponed the financial crisis for a few more years.

Partisan Deadlocks Under Reagan

In the first year of the Reagan administration, talk of lopping off benefits and adopting cost-cutting policies intensified. However, Social Security had developed a vast constituency over the years, and any efforts to change the system — particularly cuts in benefits — had become highly politicized. The funding crisis required urgent action, but the partisan labels that accompanied suggested changes in Social Security caused the president and Congress to abandon comprehensive reforms in 1981.

Minimum Benefits. Outlining his program for economic recovery in February 1981, President Reagan proposed short- and long-term approaches to Social Security's problems.

The main component of Reagan's short-term strategy was a proposal to eliminate as of July 1981 the minimum benefit program, which provided a payment of $122 a month to anyone eligible for Social Security, regardless of the person's employment and wage history. The administration sought particularly to cut off the windfall available to certain beneficiaries — often retired government workers with generous federal pensions — who worked only a short time in employment covered by Social Security. (Federal civil service workers were not covered by Social Security.) While the House and the Senate went along with this plan in their 1981 budget bills, both houses reversed themselves later that year, voting to restore the minimum monthly benefit.

Long-term Plans. Meanwhile, President Reagan set off a firestorm of controversy by proposing drastic changes in the Social Security system to protect it from financial insolvency. His plan included a reduction in benefits for early retirement at age 62, a one-time three-month delay in the annual cost-of-living allowance (COLA), tougher eligibility requirements for disability payments, and an altered benefit formula that would have reduced initial benefits for future retirees.

Reaction on Capitol Hill and across the nation ranged from skepticism to outright anger. Congressional critics including House Speaker Thomas P. O'Neill Jr., D-Mass., House Select Aging Committee Chairman Claude Pepper, D-Fla., and Sen. Daniel Patrick Moynihan, D-N.Y., charged the plan was unnecessary. They saw it as a backdoor attempt to reduce the federal budget deficit. Not surprisingly, groups representing the elderly immediately voiced their opposition to the Reagan package and predicted a major outcry when the American people became aware of what the impact of the proposals would be.

Compromise Falls Through. Acknowledging the political sensitivity of the issue, Reagan backpedaled on his reform plan within a week of its announcement. Administration officials insisted that almost everything in the proposals was negotiable. Against this backdrop, congressional leaders on the Social Security issue — Senate Finance Committee Chairman Robert Dole, R-Kan., Sen. William Armstrong, R-Colo., and

Rep. J. J. Pickle, D-Texas — sought to accommodate the president to some degree in the belief that bipartisan support would be necessary to push comprehensive Social Security reforms through Congress.

But the issue had become so politicized during the year that major changes were not feasible. Dole's committee was unable to reach agreement on a comprehensive reorganization package and instead approved a short-term funding solution to tide the system over through the mid-1980s. The final legislation, approved by Congress in December 1981, restored the minimum benefit payment for those already eligible, but eliminated it for those retiring after Dec. 31, 1981. The bill also allowed the financially troubled Old Age and Survivors Insurance (OASI) trust fund to borrow from the somewhat healthier disability and hospital insurance trust funds through the end of 1982.

Perhaps the most important development of 1981 was Reagan's request that Congress form a bipartisan task force to address long-term funding problems. Congress complied, and Reagan asked the commission to submit a report by Dec. 31, 1982, after the midterm congressional elections.

The National Commission on Social Security

The National Commission on Social Security Reform proved to be the right vehicle for getting comprehensive Social Security reforms through Congress. The commission consisted of five members appointed by the House Speaker, five appointed by the Senate majority leader and five by the president himself. Eight of the 15 members were Republicans and seven were Democrats.

A conscious effort was made by Chairman Alan Greenspan (chairman of the Council of Economic Advisers under Richard Nixon) to avoid controversy until after the November 1982 elections. Thus, for most of 1982, the volatile Social Security issue was buried in the commission's private meetings. The panel reserved all decision making until a three-day brainstorming session that was held Nov. 11-13.

Funding the Deficit. After a somewhat faltering start during its November meetings, the commission in January 1983 approved a set of recommendations that paved the way for quick congressional action to keep the retirement system afloat for the rest of the century. The compromise was most specific on the question of raising revenues, recommending that the system raise $168 billion for calendar years 1983-89. This would be accomplished by a variety of controversial and innovative mechanisms, including a six month COLA delay, a higher payroll tax schedule, the inclusion of federal employees under Social Security and the taxation of a certain percentage of benefits.

The commission was divided on how to solve a projected Social Security shortfall in the 21st century when the so-called "baby boom" generation would begin to retire and there would be insufficient workers paying into the fund. Generally, Republicans favored increasing the retirement age while Democrats preferred to increase the payroll tax yet further.

Rescue Legislation. The widespread endorsement of the commission package gave members a relatively easy way to take the necessary, but politically difficult, steps for keeping the system from going broke.

In March 1983, Congress finally approved a massive overhaul of Social Security (PL 98-21), ending almost two years of partisan wrangling and congressional stalemate. Congress was able to resolve the long-term funding dispute after accepting Republican demands that the retirement age be pushed back from 65 to 67 by the year 2027. Otherwise, the basic parameters of the Social Security revisions largely conformed to the January recommendations of the Greenspan commission. Key provisions of the legislation delayed the annual COLA six months — beginning in 1984, COLA payments would be made in January, not July, of each year — and increased payroll taxes periodically throughout the 1980s for both employees and employers.

Congress also made a fundamental change in the Social Security concept by taxing benefits of high-income recipients and by using transfers from the general Treasury to help bolster the system's trust funds. It also voted to bring new federal employees, members of Congress, the president, the vice president and federal judges under the Social Security system.

Financing Problem: A Potent Time Bomb

When the Greenspan commission submitted its report in January 1983, the Social Security system's Old-Age and Survivors Insurance trust fund was on the brink of insolvency. The interfund borrowing authority granted by Congress in 1981 had expired in December 1982, and, as the conference report had specified, would insure "benefit payments for a period [no] more than six months beyond the date of such determination." If Congress had not honored the commission's recommendations later that year and passed a new Social Security law, the OASI trust fund would have run short of funds in June 1983 and benefit payments would have ceased.

The new law was also intended to meet a large discrepancy between expenditures and revenues that threatened to plague the funds for the rest of the decade. Even if Congress had allowed OASI to continue relying on loans from the system's two other funds, all three likely would have run out of money sometime in 1984. If this happened, not only would the retirement fund have dried up, but Medicare and disability payments — financed by the system's other trust funds — would have stopped as well. *(Medicare background, see Chapter 3.)* The commission's January report estimated that $150 billion to $200 billion would be required to tide the trust funds over between 1983 and 1990, when the payroll tax increase mandated in 1977 would start to ease some of the revenue shortage.

For the long term, halfway into the next century, the commission warned that the funds would continue to pay more than they would take in by a margin of 1.80 percent of the total taxable payroll in the United States ($1.6 trillion), so measured as to ease comparison with the payroll tax. Later in 1983, the long-term shortfall was re-evaluated at more than 2 percent of the taxable payroll ($1.8 trillion).

As if these problems were not enough, there was another — albeit less talked about — reason why Congress and the administration were under increasing pressure to get the Social Security system under control in 1983. The Congressional Budget Office (CBO) projected budget deficits of about $150 billion for each of fiscal years 1984 through 1986. If Congress wanted to get these deficits under control, CBO Director Alice M. Rivlin said in 1982, it would be "difficult to achieve without reductions in Social Security."

Evolution of a Crisis

When it passed the 1977 amendments, Congress thought it had settled the Social Security financing problem. But the system's money troubles apparently had only just begun. Unforeseen economic difficulties — double-digit inflation, economic recession and stagnation, low productivity and sustained high unemployment — reduced the revenues needed to replenish the Social Security trust funds.

Even with the steep increases in the tax rate and the wage indexation of the taxable earnings base set up in the 1977 amendments, revenues expected from the payroll tax dropped as a result of high unemployment in the late 1970s and the long-term trend toward early retirement. Meanwhile, payments to beneficiaries rose unexpectedly due to inflation.

Runaway Benefits. Congress' 1972 decision to index Social Security benefit payments to the Consumer Price Index (starting in 1975) turned out to be much more costly than anticipated. In 1975 the indexing formula gave retirees a 14.3 percent cost-of-living increase in benefits. And while the 1977 changes corrected the gross excesses in the calculation of initial benefits that had occurred in 1972, they left the indexation of subsequent benefits intact.

Cost-of-living increases after 1977 continued to outstrip the projections of the OASDI trustees — reaching 14 percent instead of an anticipated 5 percent in 1980 and 11 percent instead of 4 percent in 1981. They increased 7.5 percent in July, 1982.

Perhaps the greatest short-term damage was wrought by the relationship between wages and prices caused by inflation. The indexation of benefits to prices would serve the system well as long as wages rose as fast or faster than prices, and, correspondingly, as long as payroll tax revenues exceeded the cost of Social Security payments. Wages had grown faster than prices for more than 20 years before 1972 and Congress assumed that they would continue to do so. While the 1977 amendments made some adjustments for the magnitude of benefits being paid out after 1972, they did not alter the fundamental economic assumptions upon which the indexation scheme was based. When the relationship between wages and prices was reversed after 1977, the system's trust funds suddenly were burdened with unanticipated strains.

A Shrinking Tax Base. Unemployment also cost the system revenues. For every one million workers who were laid off for a single month in 1980, approximately $100 million in anticipated employee and employer taxes to the Social Security trust funds were lost. Most experts agreed that heavy unemployment, on top of high inflation, might also act as an impetus for an increasing number of workers to retire earlier than actuaries originally projected, thus reducing anticipated Social Security revenues and increasing benefit payments sooner than expected. As retirees seemed to be better protected against rampant inflation than workers paying into the system, it was little wonder that there was an increase in the number of persons retiring before age 65.

Other social and economic trends — including low birth and

mortality rates, increased participation of women in the work force and the slow rate of economic growth — also contributed to the financial strains burdening the Social Security system.

Gauging the Damage. Social Security's assets began their decline in 1974. At that time the OASDI fund amounted to $45.6 billion. By 1977 a cumulative shortfall of $10 billion had developed. Contrary to the projections of the 1978 OASDI Trustees Report, benefit costs to the OASDI fund totaled $471.3 billion during the period 1978-81 while revenue from the payroll tax and other sources came to $460 billion for a further depletion of the funds on the order of $11.3 billion. The funds' total assets had plummeted to $24.5 billion in 1981. *(OASDI Fund Operations, see table, p. 33.)*

Throughout the 1970s, presidential advisory groups made up of economists, government officials and other Social Security experts warned of the growing budgetary problem. The National Commission on Social Security, a congressional study group created under the 1977 Social Security amendments, said in its March 1981 final report that the financial and actuarial estimates used in the 1977 law were overly optimistic and alarmingly outmoded. Milton S. Gwirtzman, chairman of the commission, told the House Ways and Means Subcommittee on Social Security in February 1981 that by the end of the year "we will be coming very close to the margin of safety."

Losses in the OASI fund were responsible for more than 75 percent of the system's overall decline. Disaster for OASI recipients was averted, explained Robert J. Myers, executive director of the Greenspan commission in 1983, only because funds were transferred from the disability fund to the old age fund through loans and reallocations of the payroll tax during 1980 and 1981.

Earlier, the Carter administration had predicted for fiscal 1982 that $150 billion would be paid into the Social Security system from payroll taxes and other receipts — with expected outlays totaling $160 billion — for a shortfall of $10 billion. President Reagan's revised projection for that year set outlays at $157.7 billion.

The fund did in fact experience a decline of $12.2 billion for a balance of $12.3 billion in 1982. The Social Security system was paying out more than it was bringing in at the rate of approximately $17,000 a minute. Again, the OASI fund received loans from the DI and HI funds, this time to ensure adequate retirement payments through the first six months of 1983.

Disputed Assumptions

The debate over remedies for the Social Security system's impending financial crisis often was complicated by widely varying economic and demographic assumptions about inflation, unemployment, fertility, mortality and other factors that were used to project the financial health of the trust funds. There was considerable disagreement over exactly when, and by how large a margin, benefit payments ultimately would exceed revenues generated from the payroll tax. Depending on whose statistics were used, the urgency of the retirement system's financial troubles ranged from manageable to critical.

In 1981 the array of economic assumptions included the "worst-case" economic assumptions on which the Reagan administration based its Social Security proposals, more moderate economic assumptions projected by the Congressional Budget Office and the Social Security Board of Trustees' 1981 report, and optimistic assumptions used by the administration for its fiscal 1982 budget requests.

The administration decided to base its Social Security proposals on "worst-case" assumptions in May 1981 because, it said, past administrations had been overly optimistic. As a result, they had been forced to return to Congress repeatedly for additional help in rescuing the funds. Under the administration's pessimistic outlook, the combined Social Security trust funds were expected to have a $111 billion budget deficit by 1986. However, under the assumptions the administration used in its fiscal 1982 budget request, the funds were expected to face only an $11 billion deficit over that period.

Some members charged that the administration's ulterior motive was to use larger-than-necessary cuts in Social Security benefits to reduce the federal budget deficit. While the administration pointed out that Social Security funds could not be used for anything but Social Security payments to beneficiaries, general revenue deficits in the so-called "unified" budget would be offset by trust fund surpluses in determining the total federal deficit. Sen. Bill Bradley, D-N.J., challenged the administration in early 1981 for using one set of assumptions for its Social Security request and another, more optimistic set of assumptions, for its fiscal 1982 budget and tax program. "You can't have it both ways," he told HHS Secretary Richard S. Schweiker.

The Reagan administration's fiscal 1983 forecast for factors affecting Social Security was consistent with the second most optimistic set of economic assumptions used by the Greenspan commission. These assumptions led to deficit projections of $9.9 billion in the OASDI funds between 1983 and 1986.

Adequate Reserve Ratios

When expenditures from any of the Social Security funds exceed revenues, reserves must be used to make up the difference. For this purpose, policy makers must decide what the system's "reserve ratio" should be. The reserve ratio is the amount of money in the trust funds at the beginning of the year expressed as a percentage of that year's anticipated expenditures. Generally, a reserve ratio of between 9 and 13 percent is considered necessary at any one time, and many Social Security experts maintain that a ratio of about 20 to 25 percent is the bare minimum needed to cushion the funds against unexpected economic conditions. This means that a safe margin of reserves is about one-fourth of anticipated benefit payments for the year — or enough to pay benefits for three months in the absence of additional income to the funds.

While Social Security reserves were thought of as contingency, rather than operating, funds, the OASDI trustees became alarmed as the old age fund's reserve ratio dropped steadily throughout the 1970s. The OASI reserve ratio had declined to a level of 15 percent at the beginning of 1982. According to a statement by Myers accompanying the January report of the Greenspan commission, had OASI not been bailed out by the DI and HI funds in 1980 and 1981, its reserve ratio would have dropped to 4 to 6 percent in 1982. At these levels, the fund would not have been able to meet its obligations.

The Reagan administration's 1981 proposals had called for a 30 percent reserve ratio by 1990 and a 50 percent ratio by 1995, an amount some critics maintained was too large too soon, especially if it was accumulated through substantial cuts in benefits. While Myers agreed in 1983 that a desirable reserve ratio might fall between 50 and 100 percent, the Greenspan commission did not seek a ratio anywhere near this level, recommending instead that the funds maintain a 15 percent reserve through 1988, and thereafter, 20 percent.

Short-Term Troubles

No matter what set of economic assumptions were used, most experts believed that the combined Old Age, Survivors and Disability Insurance trust funds would be severely tested in the 1980s. The more negative assumptions indicated that the old-age fund balance could drop

OASDI Fund Operations, 1970-1982

Year	Income	Outgo	Fund Increase	Fund at Year-end	Reserve Ratio at Beginning of Year
			(in billions)		
1970	$ 37.0	$ 33.1	$ 3.9	$ 38.1	103%
1971	40.9	38.5	2.4	40.1	99
1972	45.6	43.3	2.3	42.8	93
1973	54.8	53.1	1.6	44.4	80
1974	62.1	60.6	1.5	45.6	73
1975	67.6	69.2	−1.5	44.3	66
1976	75.0	78.2	−3.2	41.1	57
1977	82.0	87.3	−5.3	35.9	47
1978	91.9	96.0	−4.1	31.7	37
1979	105.9	107.3	−1.5	30.3	30
1980	119.7	123.6	−3.8	26.5	25
1981	142.5	144.4	−1.9	24.5	18
1982	147.9	160.1	−12.2	12.3*	15

* Balance not counting loans from Health Insurance (HI) trust fund.

Sources: Report of the National Commission on Social Security Reform; OASDI Trustees' Annual Report, 1982.

by $20 billion in 1983 alone.

In its recommendations, the Greenspan commission chose to take into account a range of economic assumptions, including the most pessimistic ones. Under the worst conditions, Myers' report anticipated that the OASDI fund would show a deficit of around $20 billion early in the 1980s, growing to $36 billion by 1989. Even with the hike in the tax rate (scheduled to reach 7.65 percent in 1990), the combined fund was projected to show a deficit of $14 billion for that year.

According to the Greenspan commission's pessimistic figures, the OASDI funds would need $175 billion between 1983 and 1989 to remain solvent. If the funds were going to attain the reserve ratio recommended by the commission — 15 percent by the end of 1988 — a buildup of the fund's reserves of at least $200 billion would have to be achieved between 1983 and that year. The shortfalls would be lower under the commission's next most pessimistic assumptions — $50 billion to balance the books and $75 billion to reach the 15 percent reserve ratio. The commission praised the virtues of planning for the worst.

The Social Security Board of Trustees' 1982 Annual Report and the CBO concurred that remedial legislation would be necessary in the near future, noting that the financing problem had become worse since 1981.

Beggar Thy Neighbor. The interfund borrowing authority approved by Congress in 1981 would have kept the old age fund functioning through the first six months of 1983. However, there was little leeway left in the other two trust funds to bail out the OASI fund again. While the Disability and Hospital Insurance funds were not suffering, at least in the short term, as badly as the old age fund, the two of them together were less than one-third its size and could hardly be expected to support it indefinitely. Even if Congress took what commission member Sen. Robert Dole, R-Kan., sarcastically called the "courageous" step and extended interfund borrowing authority, experts believed that the big OASI fund would drag the others down and the entire system would run out of funds in 1984 or 1985.

Meanwhile commission members such as Dole, Rep. Barber Conable, R-N.Y., and Sen. William Armstrong, R-Colo. echoed the president's rhetoric of 1981, expressing their hope that any future legislation be based on more realistic — in this case pessimistic — assessments of future economic performance than had prevailed in 1977.

How Serious a Problem? Not all observers adopted such pessimistic views. Like opponents of Reagan's proposed Social Security cuts in 1981, they argued that the cost of excessive gloom could be painful, unnecessary cuts in benefits for Social Security recipients.

In 1981 the House Select Committee on Aging heard testimony to the effect that the trust funds would be actuarially secure through the early 21st century provided interfund borrowing was allowed. Experts — including Alicia Munnell, an economist with the Federal Reserve Bank in Boston and author of a book on Social Security reform — argued that large cuts in benefit payments were not necessary. "We have a short-run problem of reasonable and solvable magnitude," Munnell maintained. Even the CBO's Alice Rivlin told the Senate Finance Committee in September 1981 that recent CBO figures indicated interfund borrowing possibly could tide the system over until 1990.

In a March 1983 rebuttal to a series of articles in the *New York Review of Books* by Peter G. Peterson, a commerce secretary in the Nixon administration, Munnell sought to dampen the hysteria surrounding Social Security's troubles. She maintained that the financing problem could quickly be eased by a new procedure for indexing benefits.

Assuming that the near-term shortfall of funds would be reversed in some way, some experts — including Munnell in 1983 — predicted the Social Security system would be in good shape through the medium term, from 1990 through 2010 or 2015. This would be due to certain demographic factors: In this period, the number of retirees born in the Depression years would be low compared with the number of active workers born during the post-World-War-II "baby boom." While the influx of new workers probably would only stabilize the number of workers in relation to retirees — which had declined almost since the beginning of the program — analysts expected the scheduled payroll tax increases set up in the 1977 amendments to bring in enough money to put the OASDI trust funds in the black with safe margins through the early years of the next century.

A Long-Term Problem

Even if the economy could be stabilized and Social Security costs contained through the end of the century, a much more serious crisis looms in the long run for the retirement income system. The basic problem is that, by about the year 2020, significantly fewer workers will be supporting more retirees, which eventually could result in considerably higher Social Security costs per worker.

While unexpected economic developments caused the short-term cash-flow problems of the system, unforeseen demographic trends have altered the statistical basis on which the system was founded and promise to plague Social Security in the future. The growing percentage of the U.S. population over 65 has skewed the population as a whole so that the number of workers paying into the Social Security system has been shrinking in relation to the number of individuals receiving benefits since the system was first set up. The strain has been compounded by the fact that, with increased longevity, more benefits are paid over the lifetime of each retiree. Following what is likely to be a slack period between 1990 and 2020, the demographic imbalances resulting from the post-World War II baby boom, plus a decline in the national birth rate, will join with these factors, threatening to put nearly intolerable burdens on pension systems — both public and private — by the early 21st century.

Most experts in 1982 conceded that Social Security revenues certainly would be unable to cover anticipated costs by the early 21st century when the baby-boom generation would begin reaching retirement

35

age. The Greenspan commission in its 1983 report projected an average annual deficit of 1.82 percent of the total taxable payroll — equal to $25 billion in 1982.

The Demographic Factors

As Peterson observed in his series of articles, "demographics will hold very few surprises since almost every new worker by the year 2000 has already been born and can be counted." Thus the number of retirees in the next century also can easily be determined. Policy makers know pretty well what to expect in terms of Social Security benefit payments. It remains to be seen, however, how other factors, such as the fertility rate and immigration, will affect the size of the contributing population of 2020.

More Retirees/Fewer Workers. At the beginning of the 20th century, the average life expectancy was 47 years; only 4 percent of the U.S. population lived beyond age 65. A child born in 1935, when the Social Security system was created by Congress, could expect to live to age 61. By mid-century, however, the average life span had increased to 68 years. Life expectancy for a child born in 1980 was more than 74 years.

According to a May 1981 Census Bureau report, there were 25.5 million Americans over age 65 in 1980 — a 28 percent increase over 1970. In 1981 nearly 25 million people in the United States were over age 65 — about 11 percent of the total population.

These numbers were expected to grow steadily through the end of the century, with the population over 65 accounting for 12 percent of the total population by the year 2000, according to Dr. Beth J. Soldo of the Center for Population Research in Washington, D.C. By the year 2020, when the postwar baby-boom generation is retiring, she calculated that there would be 45 million persons over age 65 — 16 percent of an expected U.S. population of 290 million.

In addition to the greater longevity of the present U.S. population, there has been a sharp decline in the birthrate. Consequently the median age of the population has been increasing steadily. It was 29 years in 1940 when the Social Security program was gearing up and reached 30 years in 1980. By the century's end it is expected to climb to 36. In subsequent decades, as the postwar generation reaches retirement age, the median age is expected to pass age 38.

Steadily decreasing birthrates resulted in the so-called "baby bust" of the 1970s and early 1980s. Contributing factors included improved

Dependency Ratio, Selected Years 1940-2030

	1940	'50	'60	'70	'80	'90	2000	'10	'20	'30
OASDI Beneficiaries (in millions)	.2	3.5	14.8	26.2	35.6	40.5	45.0	52.1	65.1	76
Covered Workers (in millions)	35.4	48.3	72.5	93.0	114.3	132.4	142.2	149.5	149.8	151.7
Workers Per OASDI Beneficiary	177	13.8	4.9	3.5	3.2	3.3	3.2	2.9	2.3	2.0

Source: Social Security Administration

methods and increased use of contraceptives and postponement of child-bearing until women reach their late 20s or 30s. Moreover, a larger percentage of couples wanted only one or two children compared with parents of earlier generations.

The birthrate at the height of the postwar baby boom in 1957 was 25.3 births per 1,000 persons; by 1976 it had fallen to 14.8, only four points above the all-time low during the 1930s Depression. While there have been some indications of an increase in fertility trends recently — the birthrate was 16.2 in 1980 — there is no evidence of a future explosion in birth rates above the current low trends.

The Dependency Ratio. Barring unforeseen developments in U.S immigration policy and other demographic trends, the plummeting birthrate means there will be far fewer numbers of young people entering the work force. Decreasing numbers of active workers will have to support a much enlarged retired population in the years ahead.

Whereas more than 100 workers were paying into the Social Security system to support each retiree when the program was getting started in the early 1940s, the ratio of contributors to beneficiaries had dropped to about 3 workers for each retiree in 1980. This "dependency ratio" — the number of workers paying into the Social Security system in proportion to the number of retirees and dependents receiving benefits out of the trust funds — was expected to decrease steadily through the middle of the 21st century. Soon after the baby-boom generation, born in 1945 through 1959, retires, the dependency ratio is expected to drop dramatically, to approximately two workers supporting each retiree.

Early Retirement/Effects of Longevity. This gloomy forecast is complicated by two other factors. First, more and more American workers have been opting for early retirement. In 1977 about 77 percent of the recently retired men and 79 percent of the recently retired women took reduced early retirement Social Security benefits, available before age 65. Although some evidence suggests the trend might be changing in the face of continued inflationary pressures, the early retirement factor has accelerated the decline in the Social Security trust funds.

Second, medical advances, better nutrition and other changes in lifestyles have resulted, as noted earlier, in greater longevity. Americans are living in retirement longer than in the past. When Social Security was enacted in 1935, the average person who retired at age 65 spent 12.8 years in retirement. According to the February 1981 final report of the President's Commission on Pension Policy, that statistic had jumped to 16 years and presumably would continue growing. The 1982 OASDI Trustees' annual report projected an average life expectancy for 65 year-old men and women in the year 2020 of 19.8 years.

The Pension Policy Commission in 1981 summed up the alternatives that the members of Congress would face over the next two years:

> Only under the optimistic demographic and economic assumptions will the trust funds accumulate to very high levels and then decline when the baby boom retires. If the more unfavorable, but more likely alternatives develop, more revenue from higher payroll taxes or other revenue sources must be found or benefits must be reduced.

Assessing the Problem

An article published in 1982 by the Federal Reserve Bank of New York observed that the "basic problem is that . . . average retirees both now and in the future can expect to receive benefits that, by any measure, are far in excess of lifetime contributions. . . . The difficulties of Social Security are almost entirely the result of the fact that a self-financed system cannot continue to pay out subsidies forever."

What makes the situation especially alarming is that today's workers have been forced to subsidize today's retirees at rather high rates *and* at the same time build up reserves for their own retirement. This is because the dependency ratio is expected to further deteriorate when the baby-boom generation retires.

Whether the burden is bearable or not will depend on a number of long-range factors that cannot be predicted with any great certainty. These include the evolution of political attitudes toward Social Security, economic growth rates and demographic trends, among others. Demographic trends, in particular, are volatile, and many developments in the U.S. population — the baby boom, for example — were not predicted by professional demographers.

If fertility rates rise more sharply than expected in the next two decades, then the burden of supporting the baby-boom generation in retirement could be lighter than currently anticipated. However, fertility rates also could turn out to be even lower than expected, and in that case the problems facing the system after the year 2020 will be even more serious than the pessimists now predict.

Another unknown factor is the role immigrants will play in the coming decades. Since immigrants tend to be younger than the population as a whole, many of them could still be in the work force when the baby-boom generation retires. Moreover, illegal immigrants may never claim the benefits for which they have contributed via the payroll tax, either because they are afraid to disclose their identities to authorities or because they have left the country.

In her 1983 *New York Review of Books* article, Alicia Munnell was optimistic about the long-term future. She projected a larger and wealthier tax-paying generation — resulting from a higher fertility rate and high rates of legal and illegal immigration — that she thought could bear the burden of future benefits. Peterson, on the other hand, predicted that if the system went unchanged, workers in the next century could be paying 44 percent of their paychecks to the Social Security system.

In any event, as one expert pointed out, as long as Social Security is "financed by intergenerational transfers instead of by the contributions of the recipients themselves, the system will be vulnerable to demographic shifts that legislation cannot fully anticipate."

Lane Kirkland, president of the AFL-CIO and member of the Greenspan commission, warned in 1982 against characterizing the Social Security crunch as an intergenerational dispute. Young people benefit from survivor and disability payments, he pointed out, and they live more happily in the knowledge that their parents will be provided for. Wilbur J. Cohen, a founding father of Social Security and secretary of health, education and welfare in the Johnson administration, said in much the same vein that short- and long-term problems should not be lumped ɔgether. "It doesn't seem to me that we have to worry so much about the crunch of 2015 right this year or this month," he said. "We've got to solve the problem of 1984 first."

Courting Public Opinion

Other than the funding exigencies of the Social Security system, the American public's lack of confidence in its soundness has been a factor in provoking remedial action on behalf of the retirement funds. In an April 1981 survey conducted for the National Federation of Independent Business, 68 percent of those persons interviewed said they felt the Social Security program was in trouble financially; only 18 percent expressed confidence that the system was financially sound.

A May 1980 nationwide poll ordered by the National Commission on Social Security found that most U.S. workers under age 55 feared that the system would not have enough money to pay their benefits when they retired. A staggering 73 percent of those interviewed between the ages of 25 and 44 expressed little or no confidence in the system's ability to pay future benefits. Of persons aged 45 to 54, 56 percent lacked confidence in the system. On the other hand, 58 percent of those between the ages of 55 and 64 — and 74 percent of the elderly — had a great deal of faith in it.

Growing Public Concern. In a similar survey conducted by CBS News and *The New York Times* in mid-1981, after President Reagan had announced his proposed cutbacks in the program, approximately 73 percent of workers age 18 to 29 felt the retirement income system would not have sufficient funds to pay their benefits. In the 30- to 44-year-old age group, 67 percent said the Social Security system would not be able to pay their benefits. About 40 percent of those age 45 to 54 felt the same way. In marked contrast to the 1980 survey, only 54 percent of persons over age 65 showed confidence in the Social Security system; 13 percent indicated the system would not be able to pay their benefits and 33 percent expressed no opinion.

Any talk of radically restructuring Social Security touched raw nerves, as Republicans found out in the 1982 congressional elections. The week before the November election, the National Republican Congressional Committee found it advisable to withdraw a controversial fundraising letter in which contributors to the party were asked to choose between different options for reforming the Social Security system, among them a proposal to make the system voluntary.

Speaking for the Democratic Party just before the election, Sen. Edward M. Kennedy, D-Mass., charged that the administration was "waiting to spring a November surprise — a secret post-election plan to slash Social Security and tarnish the golden years of the elderly."

President Reagan's efforts to defuse the issue with promises to "protect the solvency" of the system were apparently not completely effective. A *New York Times*/CBS survey of voters leaving the polls on Nov. 2 indicated that concern about Social Security was an important factor in Democratic House victories. Even among business-oriented groups, proposals to slash Social Security benefits or make the system voluntary did not necessarily meet with enthusiasm. A November 1982 article in *Industry Week* pointed out that many companies would have to compensate for cuts in Social Security benefits because most "have chosen to integrate their pension plans with Social Security — that is, they rely on formulas that adjust company-paid benefits to reflect the amount a retiree receives from Uncle Sam."

Can We Afford Social Security? With the failure of Congress to rectify Social Security's finances in the late 1970s and early 1980s in mind, many experts argued that Congress needed to address the "fundamental" problems confronting the system and not just "tinker around the edges." Peterson asserted in his *New York Review of Books* article that Social Security's "financial problems are not minor and temporary, as most politicians, at least in election years, feel compelled to insist. . . . To put the matter bluntly, Social Security is heading for a crash. . . . The Social Security system has become a high-risk gamble on economic progress and population growth."

Drawing on work done in the early 1970s by Martin Feldstein, chairman of the Council of Economic Advisers under Reagan, and A. Haeworth Robertson, chief actuary of the Social Security Administration from 1935 to 1978, Peterson argued that the growing burden of Social Security taxation was retarding the country's rate of investment and economic growth. Comparing the United States to Japan, where rates of investment in new plant and equipment, public infrastructure and civilian research and development have been much higher, Peterson attributed the difference partly to the fact that "pensions in Japan — both public and private — are meager, forcing workers to save for their retirement."

Not all economists have agreed with this line of reasoning. In a book published in November 1982, Henry Aaron, a senior fellow at the Brookings Institution in Washington, D.C., asserted that the evidence was inconclusive as to whether Social Security has had significant detrimental effects on the level of U.S. savings and labor supply. On the other hand, Aaron cited strong evidence that Social Security had greatly improved the economic status of the aged. Aaron found that Social Security provided 39 percent of the total money income of the elderly in 1978 and 76 percent of the income of the elderly poor.

A Responsive Commission. Under pressure by the public and in a highly partisan atmosphere, members of the Greenspan commission sought a realistic compromise solution that would transcend the failed remedies of the past.

"I think everybody on the commission wants to have, as a result of what we do, a credible and sound Social Security system that people can believe in — both young and old," said Rep. Bill Archer, R-Texas. "That binds all of us together." He and others pointed to polls that showed a dramatic decline in preceding years of the public's confidence in the system, especially among younger people.

Chairman Alan Greenspan was pushing for the use of realistic economic assumptions in the commission's deliberations to prevent further erosion of public confidence. "We don't have another four shots at this," he warned commission members. "We have to solve it in the context of the real world."

National Commission on Social Security Reform member Lane Kirkland, Executive Director Robert J. Myers and Chairman Alan Greenspan deliberate Social Security reform.

Chapter 2

RESCUING SOCIAL SECURITY

There has been no shortage of official reports and studies on why the Social Security program was having money troubles and how they could be solved. In December 1979 the Advisory Council on Social Security — which was required by law to report every four years on the status of the Social Security system — supplied Congress with a long list of proposals for strengthening the system. In 1981 numerous study panels, including President-elect Ronald Reagan's Social Security Task Force, the President's Commission on Pension Policy and the National Commission on Social Security (chaired by Milton S. Gwirtzman), all offered alternatives for making the retirement income system financially sound.

Many of these proposals for basic changes in the Social Security system, such as funding some benefit payments through general tax revenues, had been recommended to Congress as early as 1938. Although Congress over the years put many recommendations into law, significant changes failed to win approval.

Three basic alternatives had been suggested: raising payroll taxes steeply, reducing benefits substantially or letting the federal deficit increase. Any of these adjustments in such a massive and popular program as Social Security would be painful — both politically and economically — and would affect virtually every citizen in one way or another. Increased taxes or large federal deficits would hinder economic growth; cuts in benefits could devastate elderly persons who relied on Social Security as their sole source of retirement income. When difficult choices were made, as in 1977 when substantial tax increases were approved, their effects were negated by the institutional bias toward increasing benefits that had become entrenched in times of prosperity and program growth. *(1977 tax hikes, benefit adjustment, see p. 22.)*

Each time a Social Security crisis arose after 1977, Congress responded with a "band-aid" solution, juggling funds from one trust fund to another. Many members recognized that while these transfers may have saved the day, they were courting disaster in the long run.

By contrast, the January 1983 recommendations made by the bipartisan National Commission on Social Security Reform (Greenspan commission) were unprecedented in their comprehensive treatment of Social Security issues. *(See p. 26.)* Just as the commission provided a badly needed vehicle for compromise among divergent political views, its suggested reforms attempted to apportion the heavy burden of resuscitating the system evenly among the presently employed and current beneficiaries, the rich and poor and later generations of participants in the system.

The Search for Solvency

Many parts of the commission's delicately balanced plan had been suggested in earlier years. Of the prospective remedies, those raising revenue were the most numerous. Policy makers, fearful of the political repercussions of cutting Social Security benefits, were searching for new sources of revenue for the troubled social insurance system. This spawned a wide variety of schemes.

Payroll Tax Hike

Although it presented a politically distasteful move, some Social Security experts had recommended raising the payroll tax rate even higher than those increases already scheduled under the 1977 amendments. The April 1981 final report of the Gwirtzman commission recommended changing the tax rate schedule so that the trust funds would be adequately financed with a contingency reserve of at least one year's benefit payments (a reserve ratio of 100 percent). *(Social Security trust funds, see pp. 11-20; reserve ratio, see p. 32.)* Others suggested changing the Social Security law so that a covered employee's income exempt from the payroll tax — interest, rents, profits or other unearned income — would be subject to Social Security taxes, thus generating additional revenues.

Taxes Politically Unpopular. However, additional taxes were not considered a real policy option in 1981 because members of Congress feared they would result in a further undermining of public support for the Social Security system. Furthermore, experts generally conceded that any additional revenues derived from increases in the payroll tax alone would not be sufficient to make up the projected Social Security deficit of billions of dollars by the mid-1980s.

Critics of a tax hike pointed out that, with scheduled increases in the payroll tax totaling 15 percent between 1981 and 1990, the average worker's tax burden was too heavy already. Raising Social Security taxes any higher to finance current benefit payments would be unfair to those workers who had to bear the tax burden. Because the tax rate is regressive, increases affect low-income persons disproportionately. On the other hand, since lower-paid workers receive a higher percentage of their past earnings out of the system than better-paid workers, increases in the wage base disproportionately affect the wealthy.

In 1982 there was growing congressional concern about the regressive nature of the Social Security payroll tax because of its great impact on low-income individuals. To relieve the burden of a payroll tax hike, some Democrats proposed an income tax credit for the additional tax paid by low-income individuals.

Another reason commonly given against a payroll tax hike was that it would only serve to slow down the hoped-for economic recovery. Since employers paid half of each employee's Social Security tax, higher tax rates would add to an employer's labor costs and eventually result in increased prices for consumer goods. Some businesses also might be reluctant to hire new workers.

Therefore, higher tax rates might discourage further economic growth. Critics pointed out that this "extra" money eaten up by Social Security taxes perhaps could be used more efficiently elsewhere in the economy, perhaps as capital investments, to spur new growth.

A Potent Fund Raiser. Despite political and economic drawbacks, an increase in the payroll tax was one of the most talked about rescue plans among members of the Greenspan commission.

Under the provisions of the 1977 Social Security changes, workers paid a 6.7 percent payroll tax in 1983, scheduled to increase in increments to 7.65 percent by 1990. Employers would pay the same percentages, bringing the total to 15.3 percent by the end of the decade. According to a staff memo prepared for the commission in September 1982, only by advancing the 1990 tax rate to 1983 would the combined trust funds become "financially viable." But, Executive Director Robert J. Myers warned that such an advancement would be "difficult, both legislatively and administratively, let alone politically."

The Congressional Budget Office (CBO) had estimated that

moving up the tax increase scheduled for 1990 to 1984 would raise $46 billion. Another possibility was to move up the 1985 and 1986 tax hikes to 1984, which, according to CBO, would raise $17 billion.

Raising taxes had its attractions. As commission member Rep. Barber B. Conable Jr., R-N.Y., pointed out, because there were more than three times as many workers contributing to Social Security as recipients (including disability and Medicare), changes affecting recipients would hit them three times as hard as changes affecting the system's contributors.

Payroll Tax Reallocation. Short of a payroll tax increase, some economists and policy makers suggested that the Social Security payroll tax be reallocated as needed among the three trust funds. One such reallocation — between the DI and OASI funds — was made in 1980. The Greenspan commission was considering another reallocation of the payroll tax so that some taxes earmarked for the DI fund — which was expected to have a $171 billion reserve by the end of 1990 — would go to OASI instead. In 1981, reallocations of HI funds — to be refunded by general Treasury revenues — had been considered. These would not undermine the "earned right" concept of Social Security, because health-care payments were not strictly tied to past earnings.

General Revenue Financing

Most proposals to use general revenues from the Treasury have been contingency plans to bail out the trust funds when they were in trouble. President Jimmy Carter in 1978 proposed using income taxes to supplement the payroll tax whenever high unemployment depleted the income of the Social Security trust funds.

The 1979 Advisory Council on Social Security recommended a similar protection against severe economic fluctuations if reserves in the Social Security funds were less than 60 percent of annual outlays.

The National Commission on Social Security advocated that one-half of the cost of Social Security's Health Insurance fund be financed from general revenues, beginning in 1983. Payroll taxes would be kept at the scheduled rates, with the extra money supporting the troubled OASDI (combined) funds. Again, borrowing from the U.S. Treasury could be used as "an emergency measure only."

General Revenue Welfare? Most other industrial nations use general revenues to pay for some social insurance, but the idea has been hard to sell to the U.S. Congress. The traditional conservative argument against general revenue financing is that it would obliterate the original insurance theory behind Social Security by breaking the relationship between contributions paid into the system and benefits received.

Opponents of this approach maintained that a Social Security system financed with general tax revenues would be perceived by the public as even more of a welfare program than it already had become. In addition, some lawmakers argued that once general Treasury funds were made available for Social Security financing, it would become very difficult for Congress to resist proposals to increase benefits, thus driving up program costs further.

The main obstacle to all general revenue financing proposals, however, has been the federal deficit. Particularly at a time of fiscal austerity, extra money has not been available for a transfer of funds to finance anticipated Social Security deficits.

Separate Insurance Systems. Some general revenue proposals would take Hospital and Disability Insurance out of the Social Security system entirely and fund them with general Treasury revenues to lessen pressure on the payroll tax.

Removing these programs from the payroll tax would put the OASI fund — for which benefits bear greater relationship to past contributions — on more solid actuarial footing. Such a separation of the welfare and insurance aspects of the Social Security system — with the welfare portions funded from general tax revenues — would allow health and disability payments to be based on need only.

While it would open parts of the system to general revenues, this alternative was designed to overcome the concern that general revenue financing would reduce fiscal discipline in the Social Security program.

No Passing the Buck. While many groups representing the elderly had argued for the use of general revenues in past years, projections about the system's financial condition and the federal budget deficits generally had worsened. In this situation, almost all members of the Greenspan commission agreed that using general revenues was not feasible as a method of rescuing the system. "I think the liberal side would agree that general revenues as a main solution is unlikely to gain acceptance," said Robert Ball, a former Social security commissioner.

CBO's Rivlin added that relying on "general revenue transfers as the sole means of resolving the Social Security financing problem would place the entire burden of deficit reductions on other portions of the budget." She and Ball suggested the possibility of some limited fallback arrangement allowing Social Security to borrow from the general Treasury in certain emergencies.

The commission thus agreed that some "fail-safe" mechanism should be built into the system in case the changes made to keep it solvent proved insufficient. Myers said such a mechanism could include emergency authority to borrow from general revenues or a "triggered" increase in payroll taxes or cost-of-living-allowance (COLA) cuts if trust fund reserves fell below a certain level.

Increasing Retirement Age

A number of economists and government officials argued that raising the retirement age for full Social Security benefits to 68 or older would resolve to a large extent the system's financial problems. They suggested gradually phasing in the higher age requirement to coincide with the retirement of the baby-boom generation when higher taxes would be needed to pay benefits. According to C. Peter McColough, chairman of the President's Commission on Pension Policy in 1981, raising the retirement age to 68 would boost the Social Security dependency ratio to four workers to one beneficiary, compared with the projected 2-to-1 ratio by the year 2030.

Advocates of raising the eligibility age argued that 65 was an arbitrary age limit, set at a time when life expectancy was considerably shorter. As a result, the burden placed on the system in the 1980s was far beyond what its founders ever imagined. Congress in 1978 raised the mandatory retirement age for most private sector workers to age 70 and abolished the age limit for federal employees. These experts maintained that some adjustment in eligibility for full retirement benefits also was necessary to preserve the integrity of the Social Security system.

The Greenspan commission considered several proposals to slowly increase the retirement age from 65 to around 68. Generally, such proposals called for a hike in the retirement age over a 10-12 year period early in the 21st century. A gradual increase, it was argued, would give today's workers enough time to take the change into account when making retirement plans. Ultimately, however, the commission took no position on the retirement age question.

Another approach to the budgetary advantages of a higher eligibility age was to encourage longer working careers by phasing out the limits in the Social Security program on outside earnings for retired workers age 65 to 71. This would provide the system with additional payroll taxes since workers would be paying into the system for longer periods of time and would take out less in benefits later.

The Reagan administration advocated such a policy in 1981. Legislation considered by the House Ways and Means Social Security Subcommittee that year would have eliminated the "earnings test" in 1983 for persons 68 and older. The idea was buried in the general failure of Social Security legislation in 1981, but it was revived in the Senate's 1983 debate on Social Security, eventually becoming law.

Interfund Borrowing

With the idea of general Treasury financing of Social Security benefits so distasteful to so many members of Congress, some experts suggested that the Social Security Administration be given permanent authority to borrow among the three Social Security trust funds. This was a less painful, short-term means of relieving some of Social Security's payment troubles.

This method allowed a fund with a deficit to borrow from a fund with a surplus, easing temporary cash-flow problems. For example, between 1980 and 1982, Congress reallocated some money in the Disability Insurance fund to prop up the ailing OASI fund. Some observers in 1981, including the CBO, indicated that it might tide the system over for 10 years or so.

Others, however, including the Social Security Board of Trustees, maintained that interfund borrowing would not provide adequate short-range financing under adverse economic conditions. Any notions of interfund borrowing as the primary remedy to the financing problem were discredited by the time the Greenspan commission issued its report in January 1983. Yet while the commission and Congress were reluctant to extend interfund borrowing too long because it would threaten depletion of the whole trust fund system, there was some sentiment for allowing OASI to continue borrowing from the healthy DI fund (in addition to the payroll tax reallocation).

Extension of Coverage

Another suggestion for raising new revenues to bail out the Social Security system was through extending coverage to the approximately 2.8 federal workers and 12 million state and local employees who were not participating in the program before 1983. This group constituted about 10 percent of U.S. workers in 1981.

According to this argument, universal coverage would greatly increase the system's cashflow in the short run, although most of the anticipated extra revenue eventually would be paid out to a larger number of people drawing benefits. In the long run, according to most analysts, the system probably would not be any better off with the extended coverage.

Legislating universal coverage would prove difficult. Federal workers were regarded as one of the most formidable Washington lobbies. And they obviously had something to fight for: The government pension system was considered far superior to the Social Security system. Initial benefit levels under the federal pension system usually were much higher than those under Social Security or most private pension systems. Federal retirees had the additional security of knowing that — as a matter of routine — their benefits were backed by general Treasury revenues.

However, some thought civil service employees might be amenable to a merger of the two systems if Social Security could be used to supplement certain coverage gaps in their own plans. In 1982, Myers estimated that $21 billion could be raised for the Social Security system during 1983-89 if all new federal employees (including those with less than five years of service) and employees of non-profit organizations were required to participate.

Although no specific details were discussed on how such a change would be made, Rep. Conable said some procedure could be worked out so that federal employees would still receive supplemental civil service retirement benefits. "No one in the current system would lose out," he vowed.

Left for Congress to consider was a proposal that state and local government employees be required to join the system. While some commission members favored the idea, it was thought likely to lead to a troublesome constitutional dispute. *(State and Local Government Pensions, see Chapter 5, p. 186.)*

Taxing Benefits

Some experts called for a tax on Social Security benefits as one more method of making the system financially secure. Money derived from such taxes could be channeled back into the trust funds to cover the deficit. Before 1983, Social Security benefits were not subject to federal taxes.

The 1979 Advisory Council on Social Security recommended that 50 percent of benefits be considered as taxable income for federal tax purposes. The advisory council pointed out that instead of a gift, the "right to Social Security benefits is derived from earnings in covered employment just as in the case with private pensions." Private pensions are, of course, subject to federal income tax. Due to the income tax exemptions for the elderly, the council pointed out that even if benefits were subject to taxation, few persons or couples over the age of 65 would pay any income tax if Social Security were their only source of income.

The advisory council estimated that, based on 1978 data, taxing half of Social Security benefits would affect 10.6 million tax filings out of the 24.2 million persons who were receiving benefits that year. It was estimated that the average additional tax would be $350, and the total increase in federal tax collections would be $3.7 billion.

Prospects were slim that Congress would approve the taxation of Social Security benefits. One reason was the obvious political fallout; another was that taxation would change Social Security from a contribution-based to a need-based system. Its critics pointed out that such a tax would be biased against low-income workers, who received a proportionately higher amount of their retirement income from Social Security than those in higher income brackets.

By fall 1982, however, the Greenspan commission was again examining the possibility of taxing some portion of Social Security benefits. There was general agreement that any taxing scheme would be imposed only on recipients with incomes above a certain level, easing any burden on low- and middle-income recipients.

According to a CBO study in 1982, if half of all benefits were taxed for individuals with total annual incomes above $20,000, $5.2 billion could be raised over three years. The proposal, not unexpectedly, was extremely unpopular with the public. Pollster Louis Harris told the Senate Finance Committee in September 1982 that 86 percent of those interviewed in a poll had opposed any taxation of Social Security benefits.

Other Tax Proposals

Other suggestions for raising additional revenue for the Social Security system through taxation received comparatively little attention. A plan offered by Sen. John C. Danforth, R-Mo., would have added a 10-cent tax to a package of cigarettes to raise revenues for the Hospital

Insurance trust fund. Others suggested easing the burden of future Social Security costs with a "value-added tax (VAT), " which essentially was a national sales tax levied on manufacturers at each stage in the production and distribution of a particular product.

Efforts in the 97th Congress to bolster the Social Security system through revenues derived from the tax on oil industry profits resulting from the 1981 deregulation of oil received little support. Moreover, the Reagan administration was adamantly opposed to increasing taxes for Social Security.

In 1982 proposals resembling those of Sen. Danforth to increase the excise taxes on products such as alcohol and tobacco for the HI and DI trust funds again came under consideration. The rationale was that since such products are considered health risks, users should pay additional fees to fund the government programs that pay benefits for health and disability care. One drawback, however, was that tobacco taxes had just been raised earlier in 1982, and plans for additional levies were sure to face heavy industry and congressional opposition.

Spending Cuts

The alternative to increasing revenues was to cut outlays. Expenditures for administering the trust funds could be reduced somewhat, or benefit payments could be decreased by either cutting them across-the-board or tightening eligibility requirements.

Some observers maintained that one way to reduce spending was to reduce waste and fraud in the administration of the Social Security program. The Social Security Administration had been criticized for its heavy case backlog and chronic computer problems.

The investment policies of the Social Security trust funds also had been blamed for the shortfalls. Sen. William Proxmire, D-Wis., charged that Social Security "needlessly" lost $2 billion in 1980 by investing in securities that yielded low — 8.3 percent — interest. He introduced a measure in the 97th Congress to require the system's Board of Trustees to maximize its investments.

New Benefit Formulas. In the 97th Congress there was strong support for changing the formulas by which Social Security benefits were indexed. One Reagan administration proposal that received widespread attention would have cut benefits for future retirees. The plan entailed a revision of the formula used to determine the monthly payment for a retiree.

Again in 1982, a change in the indexing formula was proposed so that workers would have a lower "replacement rate." *(Replacement rate, see p. 12.)* Benefits would not actually be cut, rather they would not increase by as much as they had under prevailing law. This plan eventually was superseded by proposals to adjust cost-of-living allowances as the main benefit reduction considered by the Greenspan commission.

COLA Changes. Many experts had called for changes in the indexing of annual cost-of-living increases in Social Security benefits. Under the pre-1983 law, Social Security benefits were increased each July by 100 percent of the rise in the Consumer Price Index (CPI) during the previous year. The Reagan administration proposed in 1981 that the annual cost-of-living increases be moved to October of each year, to coincide with the beginning of the government's fiscal year. Expected savings for the three-month delay for fiscal 1982-86 would be about $6.3 billion, according to the administration.

For members of the Greenspan commission, the attraction of a COLA cut was that its effects would be cumulative. If the COLA was reduced by a few percentage points one year, for example, then increases in subsequent years would be smaller as a result. There were a number of COLA-adjustment options available to the commission. A one-time move of the COLA payment from July to October would result in a savings of $7 billion through 1985, according to CBO. Another proposal before the commission was to cap the increase at a certain percentage, such as 4 percent, for a savings of $7.7 billion over the same period.

Opponents of the COLA proposals, however, pointed out that, while some retirees no doubt were well off, millions were on the verge of poverty. Each reduction in COLA increases, they said, could have profound financial effects. According to a study commissioned by the American Association of Retired Persons (AARP), capping the COLA at two-thirds of the increase in prices, beginning in 1983, would force 500,000 elderly below the poverty line by 1985 and 1.3 million by 1990.

The CBO's Rivlin suggested that such problems could be accommodated in part by liberalizing benefits and eligibility requirements of the welfare-oriented Supplemental Security Income (SSI) program.

Insulation from Inflation. Many economists maintained that the CPI distorted the real level of inflation and that fluctuations in the economy had disproportionate effects upon the Social Security trust funds. The increase in prices relative to wages was the main factor behind this imbalance.

A number of Social Security advisory groups, along with Senate Budget Committee Chairman Pete V. Domenici, R-N.M., and economist Martin Feldstein, chairman of the President's Council of Economic Advisers since late 1982, proposed various mechanisms to insulate Social Security from movements of the CPI in 1981. These ranged from the indexation of benefits to the lower of annual average increase in prices or wages to capping COLA increases at some point below increases in the CPI.

Myers developed a proposal for the Greenspan commission that tied future benefit increases to wages rather than to prices, as they had been since 1977. His plan called for a formula in which the COLA benefit would reflect an increase in the wage level minus 1.5 percent — a figure actuaries used for their long-term projections of price increases when calculating future COLAs. "If in 1977 we had geared benefit increases to the lesser of wages and prices, we wouldn't be sitting here talking today," he said. "What it [the proposed formula] does is ask beneficiaries to have a share in the economy. If it's bad, you have to suffer a little; if it's good you can benefit."

Eventually, the commission recommended automatic COLA adjustments to wages or prices — depending on which of the two had increased less in the preceding year — if the funds' reserve ratios dipped below 15 percent.

For Every Plan a Constituency

Anticipating congressional action on Social Security, many groups and individuals in 1982 issued proposals for a fundamental restructuring of the system that reflected their own interests and preferences. Groups ranging from the Heritage Foundation, a conservative Washington, D.C., think tank, to the Gray Panthers assembled to make their views known via press conferences and demonstrations as the Greenspan commission met for a three-day brainstorming session in November 1982.

Right and Left

What particularly irked conservatives was the absence of any direct relationship between the amount one paid into Social Security and the amount one drew out in benefits. The Heritage Foundation called for greater reliance on private retirement plans and for separation of the "insurance" and "welfare" portions of Social Security. It proposed that the welfare portion be financed out of general revenues.

The foundation's proposal was similar to a "family security plan" that had been prepared by Reagan White House adviser Peter J. Ferrara. Ferrara proposed that, starting in 1986, individuals be allowed to deduct 20 percent of their Social Security contributions and invest them in individual retirement accounts (IRAs). *(IRAs and Keoghs, see Chapter 6.)* He also suggested that their employers contribute up to 20 percent of the employer share of the tax to IRAs. More investment in IRAs, according to Ferrara, would help stimulate the economy, ultimately assuring individuals a higher return on their contributions than they would get from Social Security.

Another group, The National Taxpayers Legal Fund, promoted a proposal that also called for the separation of Social Security's welfare and insurance functions and for greater reliance on private retirement accounts. The group had argued against a hike in what it called the regressive payroll tax. Under the Legal Fund's plan, the Supplemental Security Income (SSI) program, which provides benefits for the elderly poor and which is funded from general revenues, would take over responsibility for the welfare functions. According to that plan, benefits from "future security individual retirement accounts" would be tax-exempt.

Liberals, on the other hand, generally preferred to explore new options for strengthening Social Security's main trust funds. Congress Watch, a branch of Ralph Nader's Public Citizen Inc., suggested taxing Social Security benefits received by the wealthy, funding Medicare out of general revenues and including all government employees in Social Security.

House Majority Leader Jim Wright, D-Texas, suggested earmarking revenues from offshore oil leases for Social Security and providing persons of retirement age with tax credits to encourage them to keep working.

Protecting Benefits

Perhaps the most numerous and shrill were parties with a direct stake in possible Social Security reforms. Proposals to cut benefits faced strong opposition from groups representing the interests of the elderly — whose ever-increasing numbers exerted powerful political pressure — and public employees would not easily accede to plans including them in Social Security.

A coalition of 100 national elderly and other groups called Save Our

Security (SOS) — representing between 35 and 40 million members and headed by Wilbur J. Cohen — insisted that cutting benefits would amount to a breach of faith with today's workers and would seriously undermine the already-troubled Social Security system.

The Gray Panthers and the National Council of Senior Citizens, two lobbying groups for the elderly, called for some general revenue financing of Social Security, no penalty for early retirement and increased employment to boost payroll tax revenues.

The AARP suggested that revenues could be raised by means of special excise taxes on such products as alcohol and tobacco or by delaying President Reagan's tax cut scheduled for mid-1983.

Arguing against any benefit cuts, the National Council of Senior Citizens (NCSC) claimed that an infusion of general revenues and borrowing between the system's three trust funds would make Social Security as "good as new." "Social Security may have hit a bump in the road," said NCSC President Jacob Clayman, "but its motor is still going strong."

On a similar note, the Leadership Council of Aging Organizations vowed opposition to all benefit cuts. It called instead for better investment of Social Security funds, emergency general revenue financing and work incentives for the elderly. Said a council statement: "Social Security is not going bankrupt, nor is it in danger of doing so; scare tactics suggesting impending doom frighten older people unnecessarily and undermine young people's confidence in the system."

Representing public employees, the Organization for the Preservation of the Public employees retirement industry and Opposition to Social Security Expansion to such industry (OPPOSE) warned against proposals to require that state and local government employees participate in Social Security, arguing it would be unconstitutional.

Crafting a Better System

Congress and the White House had moved in 1981 to solve Social Security's immediate financing problems. But intense public opposition to President Reagan's proposals for long-term reform of the system forced the president to put aside those suggestions and propose that the Greenspan commission take the issue out of the partisan arena.

Congress was quick to fall in with that plan. Public pressure already had forced legislators to overturn the one major action that Congress took in 1981 to hold down Social Security costs. It restored a $122 minimum monthly benefit program under Social Security that Congress had eliminated earlier that year.

The prospect that the elderly population would be more than willing to vent its anger at the polls in November 1982 inhibited Democrats and Republicans alike from voting on major changes in the Social Security system, which would require either benefit cuts or tax increases.

Partisan Offensives

Members of Congress and others assailed plans proposed by Reagan in 1981 to make cuts in the Social Security system. House Select Aging Committee Chairman Claude Pepper, D-Fla., called the proposals "the most fundamental assault" ever on Social Security. House Speaker Thomas P. O'Neill Jr., D-Mass., said they were "despicable. . . . I for one will be fighting this thing every inch of the way."

A plan to reduce benefits for those who elected to retire early, beginning in January 1982, was the most criticized provision of the president's package. President Reagan wanted to further reduce those early benefits — already less than the full benefits received at age 65 — to encourage people to remain in the work force longer.

A proposed delay in the 1982 cost-of-living increase — which the administration estimated would save at least $6.3 billion through 1986 — also came under attack. Jerry Wurf, president of the American Federation of State, County and Municipal Employees (AFSCME), called the Reagan proposals a "fiscal hoax." He accused the Reagan administration of using the money saved through Social Security reductions to finance its proposed tax cut.

The lobbying group Save Our Security (SOS) argued that the long-term financial stability of the system's trust funds could be ensured without reducing benefits at all. The group advocated funding part or all of Medicare benefits with general revenues, increasing the payroll tax with an offsetting income tax credit, and allowing borrowing among the system's three trust funds until a solution could be found.

The real danger to the elderly, said former Social Security commissioner Robert Ball, was not the Reagan proposals themselves — "they're so horrendous, it's unlikely they'll be adopted," — but the compromises on Capitol Hill that could result from them. "They'll end up with something that's still terrible," he predicted.

House and Senate Democrats made the most of initial unfavorable reaction to the president's proposals. In the Republican-controlled Senate, Democrats pushed through a nonbinding resolution promising that the Senate would not cut early retirement benefits immediately or unnecessarily. Similarly, the House Democratic Caucus adopted a resolution calling the proposed changes an "unconscionable breach of faith." The caucus vowed not to "destroy the program for a generation of retirees."

The atmosphere became yet more highly charged in the course of bitter legislative fighting and maneuvering over Reagan's proposal to eliminate minimum benefits.

Last-Ditch Efforts Fail. While accepting the Reagan plan as a foundation for markups, Sen. Dole attempted to get broad support for at least some Social Security measure by eliminating the most controversial of the Reagan proposals, including the immediate curtailment of benefits for retirement before age 65. In the House, Rep. J. J. Pickle, D-Texas, chairman of the House Ways and Means Subcommittee on Social Security, also proposed an overhaul of the system less drastic than that of the administration. It would gradually raise the retirement age to 68 by the year 2000, use general revenues to fund part of the Hospital Insurance trust fund and reduce benefits for those opting for early retirement.

However, these attempts were eclipsed as Congress was able only to come up with stopgap legislation to allow interfund borrowing. Recognizing his political miscalculation in proposing drastic cuts in Social Security benefits, Reagan acquiesced in the short-term fix and left a long-term solution on the issue to the Greenspan commission.

A Catalyst for Action

While Reagan's appointment of the Greenspan commission had been criticized by Democrats as little more than a diversion from the public uproar over his proposals to cut benefits, observers thought the panel could be a most promising catalyst for congressional action.

Unlike Social Security study commissions before it, the membership of the commission included most of the key characters in the congressional debate. It consisted of seven members of Congress, powerful labor and business leaders as well as former officials in the Social Security Administration. "Never have there been on a Social Security commission important legislators who could carry out its recommendations if they want to. If it's at all possible to get some agreement, it will carry immense weight," said Robert Ball.

Members of the National Commission on Social Security Reform

Appointed by the President

Alan Greenspan — Chairman and President, Townsend, Greenspan and Company, New York, N.Y. (Chairman of the president's Council of Economic Advisers 1970-74).

Robert A. Beck — Chairman of the Board and Chief Executive Officer, Prudential Insurance Company of America, Newark, N.J.

Mary Falvey Fuller — Management Consultant, San Francisco, Calif. (Member of the 1979 Advisory Council on Social Security).

Alexander B. Trowbridge — President, National Association of Manufacturers, Washington, D.C.

Former Rep. Joe D. Waggonner, D-La. (1961-79) — Consultant, Bossier Bank and Trust Company, Bossier City, La.

Appointed by the Senate Majority Leader

Sen. William Armstrong, R-Colo. — Chairman of Finance Subcommittee on Social Security.

Sen. Robert Dole, R-Kan. — Chairman of Finance Committee.

Sen. John Heinz, R-Pa. — Chairman of Special Committee on Aging.

Lane Kirkland — President, American Federation of Labor-Congress of Industrial Organizations (AFL-CIO).

Sen. Daniel Patrick Moynihan, D-N.Y. — Ranking minority member of Finance Subcommittee on Social Security.

Appointed by the House Speaker

Rep. William Archer, R-Texas — Ranking minority member of Ways and Means Subcommittee on Social Security.

Robert M. Ball — Visiting Scholar, Center for the Study of Social Policy, Washington, D.C. (Social Security Commissioner, 1962-73).

Rep. Barber B. Conable Jr., R-N.Y. — Ranking minority member on Ways and Means Committee.

Former Rep. Martha E. Keys, D-Kan. (1975-79) — Director of Educational Programs, The Association of Former Members of Congress, Washington, D.C. (Assistant Secretary of HHS, 1980-81).

Rep. Claude D. Pepper, D-Fla. — Chairman of Rules Committee.

During its meetings in November and December 1982 and January 1983, the commission operated with surprising harmony, despite the ideological divergencies of its eight Republican and seven Democratic members. President Reagan, Senate Majority Leader Howard H. Baker Jr., R-Tenn., and House Speaker O'Neill each appointed five members of the bipartisan board.

Greenspan was widely credited for this cohesion. "He really has gone out of his way to accommodate all the factions on the commission," said Laurie Fiori, a legislative representative of the National Retired Teachers Association/American Association of Retired Persons (NRTA/AARP).

Toward an Agreement

By the end of the Greenspan commission's November 1982 meeting — at which the group began to assemble a prototype solution for Social Security — commission members were able to agree on the scope of the problem: The shortfall through the 1980s could reach $200 billion and the long-term deficit could be as high as 1.8 percent of the payroll tax (recalculated in 1983 at more than 2 percent by the Social Security Administration). The panel decided not to recommend major structural changes in the Social Security system, but instead called for some adjustments in financing and benefit increases.

However, the commission decided that it needed the involvement of both Reagan and O'Neill before it could make a specific recommendation on how to save the ailing system. Ironically, it was the inability of Reagan and O'Neill to reach agreement on appropriate changes that had led to appointment of the commission in the first place.

Signals from Congress, Reagan. The commission, aware of its advisory relationship with Congress and of the delicacy of any compromise it might reach, had to time the announcement of its views with care. While Greenspan said he would seek a December consensus on a specific plan, members cautioned that without some agreement between O'Neill and Reagan, such a consensus was unlikely. "Clearly, we are not all the people who are going to be downstream in the political process," said commission member Sen. John Heinz, R-Pa. "The president has only one vote, but it's a very big vote."

Meanwhile, key members of Congress avoided any premature actions that might jeopardize an agreement. Commission members were bolstered during their deliberations by the release of a letter from House

Ways and Means Committee Chairman Dan Rostenkowski, D-Ill., urging House members to "keep their powder dry" on the volatile issue. Rostenkowski called for a balance in any Social Security legislation between the interests of those receiving benefits and the interests of taxpayers.

Attempted Compromise. While the commission was unable to reach agreement on a specific plan to save Social Security, some progress was made in behind-the-scenes negotiations with Congress. Five liberal Democrats appointed by O'Neill submitted a proposal that marked the first concessions in a fundamental split among participants in the Social Security debate: Whether tax hikes or benefit cuts should be the major ingredient in a new funding package.

The plan was a bid for compromise in that it would allow COLA delays in return for accompanying payroll tax increases. Robert Ball, the commission member who developed the plan, said that the COLA change was a "major concession" for liberals and "about the limit that we could possibly go."

However, the 10 members appointed by the president and Senate Majority Leader Howard H. Baker Jr., R-Tenn. were opposed to heavy reliance on tax increases to help the system through its short-term crisis. Armstrong charged that an acceleration of the 1990 tax hike could exacerbate unemployment over the coming decade and would have other damaging effects on the economy. Commission member Robert A. Beck, chairman of the Prudential Insurance Company, said tax hikes were of "great concern, especially to the young."

This time it was Greenspan's turn to be cautious. Rather than attempt to force a premature compromise, Greenspan made it clear he would prefer to reach a consensus that embraced a cross section of commission views. Only then, aides said, could the commission's final product become the framework for a congressional compromise.

As the commission's December reporting date drew near, it appeared unlikely that any specific set of recommendations would be adopted on time. However, Greenspan asked the administration for, and received, a 15-day extension of the commission's deadline.

A Plan of Action

The Greenspan commission finally reached a delicate compromise — endorsed by Reagan and O'Neill — in January 1983. As a comprehensive solution to Social Security's woes, the commission's recommendations could only be challenged piecemeal; no other group had been able to assemble a comparable package.

The compromise was intended to raise $168 billion for calendar years 1983-89 by a variety of controversial and innovative mechanisms, including a six-month COLA delay, a new, higher payroll tax schedule, the inclusion under the system of federal employees and the unprecedented taxation of certain benefits.

The balance between benefit cuts and tax hikes was the main issue among commission members, although the final plan called for both. Of the amount to be raised, about $40 billion was to come from a one-time, six-month delay in the July 1983 cost-of-living adjustment (COLA) and a January payment date for all future COLAs.

Revenue Raisers. The greater part of the revenue would come from various tax hikes and the inclusion of new federal employees under the system. An increase in the basic payroll tax would yield $40 billion by 1990. The rate would be raised an extra .3 of a percentage point in 1984 to 7 percent and another .36 of a point in 1988 to 7.51 percent. A one-time income tax credit — effectively a transfer from general Treasury revenues — would be allowed in 1984 to offset that year's higher payroll tax.

Tax Rates Before and After 1983 Social Security Law

Year	Prior Law	New Law
1983	6.70%	6.70%
1984	6.70	6.70/7.00*
1985	7.05	7.05
1986	7.15	7.15
1987	7.15	7.15
1988	7.15	7.51
1989	7.15	7.51
1990	7.65	7.65

* In 1984, employees will continue to pay taxes at the 6.7% rate, with an additional 0.3% provided from general revenues; employers will pay taxes at the 7.0% rate.

Source: Democratic Study Group, U.S. House of Representatives.

Self-employed individuals would be required to pay 33 percent more in payroll taxes to equal the total combined tax paid by employees and employers. However, as with the employee/employer payroll tax hike, an income tax deduction would be allowed.

The commission also recommended that, for the first time, Social Security benefits be taxed for retirees with high incomes. Under the plan, retirees with $20,000 a year or more in adjusted gross income other than Social Security benefits would have half of their benefits taxed. The threshold would be $25,000 for those filing joint returns.

Also proposed was mandatory Social Security coverage for all new federal employees and all workers in non-profit organizations. The commission plan forbade state and local employers to drop out of the system. Despite earlier discussions, the commission did not recommend that members of Congress or their staffs be covered by Social Security.

Additional revenues would be raised by crediting the Social Security trust funds with certain military service credits and uncashed Social Security checks.

Long-term Solutions. Disagreement similar to that between liberals and conservatives on short-term solutions impeded any agreement on how to solve the projected Social Security shortfall in the 21st century.

Republicans preferred a gradual increase in the retirement age. They proposed that after the turn of the century the age be raised one month a year from 65 to 66 by the year 2015. Democrats, however, called instead for an additional .46 of a percentage point increase in the payroll tax in the year 2010, with an income tax credit for employees.

The commission, therefore, left much of the long-term problem for Congress to decide, observing that "it is, of course, highly uncertain what the economy and the labor market will look like in the next century. . . . The best medicine for Social Security is full employment and economic growth, not benefit cuts."

A Fragile Compromise

The commission's compromise agreement was termed an "extraordinary event" by Chairman Greenspan. After nearly a year of study and days of difficult last-minute negotiating between the White House and key members of the panel, the commission report had won the assent not only of Reagan and O'Neill but of politically diverse members such as AFL-CIO President Lane Kirkland, National Association of Manufacturers President Alexander Trowbridge, Rep. Pepper, and Sen. Dole. "Each of us recognizes that this is a compromise solution," Reagan said of the plan. "As such, it includes elements which each of us could not support if they were not part of a bipartisan compromise."

On the negative side, James Hacking of the AARP observed that the commission's compromise was "a very fragile one. If any one component is knocked out, it will fall like a house of cards." While legislation remained to be crafted, criticism mounted from outside interest groups and commission members themselves continued to debate the merits of their own work.

Reaction to Commission Proposals. The 14-million-member AARP was one of several groups, including federal employee unions, the National Federation of Independent Business (NFIB) and the National Taxpayers Union, that were prepared for an all-out grass-roots campaign against the commission plan. AARP and the NFIB already were mobilizing members to defeat the package in January 1983. "This is just something we cannot under any circumstances support," said AARP's Hacking.

The group objected to the payroll tax increase and taxation of Social Security benefits, which Hacking criticized as a "fundamental change" in the Social Security program. He pointed out that the amount beneficiaries would be allowed to earn without having their benefits taxed would not be indexed to reflect inflation. As a result, while only about 10 percent of current beneficiaries would have to pay the tax, the number probably would grow dramatically. "This will convert Social Security into much more of a welfare system," he said.

NFIB's director of federal legislation, Mike McKevitt, complained that higher payroll taxes would prove a disincentive for the creation of new jobs the economy desperately needed.

The National Council of Senior Citizens attacked the proposed six-month COLA delay. Removing the provision's protection against inflation "even for a limited period — is to take a step backward and to abdicate federal responsibility to the aged," the group said.

Federal employee unions joined forces to defeat the proposal requiring new federal employees to enroll in the system. The unions charged that it would have only minimal long-term advantages for the Social Security system and would seriously damage the Civil Service Retirement Fund, which paid federal employee pensions. "We're very concerned about the stability of the Civil Service Retirement Fund, because no one will be paying into it if younger workers are taken out," said Jane McMichael, legislative director of the American Federation of Government Employees.

Commission Doubts. Some members of the commission regarded their report as far from being the last word. "When the president and the Speaker agree, they usually get their way — but not always," said Armstrong. "We have not yet heard from Middle America. If they howl out enough, there is some chance of amending the package."

Armstrong and Rep. Archer attacked the plan for its high dependence on tax hikes to fund the system's projected deficits and for its reliance on what they called optimistic economic assumptions. "The agreement reached continues to leave in doubt, in my opinion, the future stability of the Social Security system," Archer said in his minority views accompanying the report.

Armstrong added that Congress would "only be repeating the same basic mistake" it made in 1977, when it projected that new payroll tax increases would keep the system solvent well into the next century. He argued that higher payroll taxes would put a drag on the economy, worsening the prospects for economic growth.

He and Archer also criticized the plan for relying on large sums from general Treasury revenues to solve the system's shortfall. Some estimated that approximately one-third of the plan's $168 billion would come from the Treasury, either through income tax credits and deductions or direct infusions into the trust funds.

Another "fundamental principle" violated by the plan, alleged Armstrong, was the traditional parity between employer and employee contributions to the system. The 1984 payroll tax credit would be available only to employees.

Major Issues Before Congress

In previous years, Congress had shown little inclination to take action as drastic as tackling Social Security unless pushed against the wall. Legislators found it easier to follow the Greenspan commission's lead in 1983.

Many observers were confident that the bipartisan compromise would survive essentially intact in Congress. Boosting their optimism was the announcement by a wide range of groups during hearings of the House Ways and Means Committee in February that they would support the package. Endorsements included those from the Business Roundtable (made up of the heads of America's largest corporations), almost the entire executive board of Save Our Security and the National Council of Senior Citizens.

Major Provisions in . . .

Enhanced Tax Revenues

● Increase employer and employee payroll taxes. Would be .3 percent less for employees than for employers in 1984. Difference to made up by income tax credit.

● Increase payroll taxes for the self-employed individuals by 33 percent to equal the combined tax paid by employers and employees.

● Tax as regular income the Social Security benefits of individuals with adjusted gross income over $25,000; $32,000 for a married couple filing joint return.

COLA Cuts, Adjustments

● Delay the July, 1983 cost-of-living allowance (3.5 percent) six months until January, 1984.

● Adjust the annual COLA indexation to lesser of wages and prices whenever OASI or DI reserve ratios fall below 15 percent (20 percent after 1988).

Increasing Retirement Age

● Gradually increase the retirement age from 65 to 67 by the year 2027. To 66 by 2009; to 67 by 2027.

● Liberalize the penalty currently placed on retirees with outside earnings.

● Increase the benefit bonus individuals receive for delaying retirement.

● Require the secretary of health and human services to study the effects of the retirement age change on those who are forced to retire early because of physically demanding work.

Extension of Coverage

● Require Social Security coverage of all new federal civilian employees, current and future members of Congress, the president, the vice president, sitting federal judges, top political appointees and civil servants by Jan. 1, 1984.

● Require Social Security coverage of non-profit organization employees.

● Prohibit state and local governments already under Social Security from withdrawing.

...1983 Social Security Law

Accounting

● Require the Treasury to credit the Social Security trust funds at the beginning of each month with all payroll taxes expected that month.

● Allow the three Social Security trust funds — OASI, DI and HI — to borrow funds from each other through 1987.

● Permanently reallocate payroll taxes from the DI trust fund to the OASI trust fund.

● Remove the Social Security system from the "unified" federal budget, beginning in fiscal year 1992.

● Require the Social Security Board of Trustees to inform Congress in its annual report if the system is in danger of falling short of funds (before general Treasury revenues can be tapped).

● Require state and local governments to turn over payroll taxes to the Treasury more rapidly. Before the law, such employers could hold the funds for 30 days.

Miscellaneous

● Add two public members to the Social Security Board of Trustees.

● Require a study by April 1, 1984, on how to turn the Social Security Administration into an independent agency.

● Reduce the so-called "windfall benefit" some retirees — most often former government employees — receive when they work under Social Security for only a short time by cutting base retirement benefit.

● Change the investment procedures of Social Security trust funds to address criticisms that past investments have yielded low returns.

● Credit the Social Security trust funds with certain military benefits and uncashed Social Security checks.

● Restrict benefits for survivors and dependents of non-resident aliens and for convicted felons.

● Include certain elective fringe benefits in the wage base subject to Social Security payroll taxes.

● Eliminate a credit now allowed certain individuals under age 65, who collect government pensions, to compensate them for the fact that their pension income does not include tax-free Social Security benefits.

● Liberalize benefits designed especially to help widowed, divorced and disabled women; eliminate certain sex distinctions in the law.

Few Congressional Options

Public sentiment and the immediate financial crisis in the system largely predetermined the direction Congress would take. It was tantamount to political suicide for members of Congress to propose benefit cuts for those already on the rolls. And with the high federal budget deficits projected for the rest of the decade, there was not much likelihood of siphoning off general revenues to help bail out the Social Security system.

In the short run, that left Congress with few choices apart from finding new revenues, in conjunction with other smaller changes, to get the system back on its feet. "Because we have delayed, we now face the inevitable fact that we must rely on the government directly or indirectly to meet benefit payments," Rep. Pickle observed as early as August 1982.

At the same time, some members recognized that certain groups of retired persons had been getting more than they really needed from Social Security. Speaker O'Neill said he might support the commission's recommendation that the benefits of persons with more than a specified level of income be taxed.

Certainly there was strong incentive for members to steer clear of any drawn-out fight over the plan. Without some resolution of the Social Security issue, the system's largest trust fund, OASI, would be unable to distribute its 36 million retirement checks after June 1983.

The urgency was exacerbated by one of the commission's major proposals — a six-month delay in the July 1983 cost-of-living payment — which would have to be enacted by early May 1983 when the Social Security Administration would start to process the July checks. Under this time pressure, the Ways and Means Committee headed by Rostenkowski labored to ready a bill for the full House in early March.

However, before Congress passed the new Social Security law late in March 1983, a number of adjustments and additions were made to the commission's recommendations. Most important among these was a provision — raising the retirement age — to deal with that part of the long-term deficit left by the commission for Congress to decide. Members also argued about the proper borrowing powers of the Social Security trust funds and the procedure for including federal workers.

Raising the Retirement Age

In the wake of unofficial recommendations by Republican members of the Greenspan commission that the retirement age be increased,

House Rules Committee Chairman Pepper told Ways and Means he would not support a bill that changed the retirement age or reduced benefits beyond cuts already proposed by the commission. Pepper's backing was considered essential for passage of Social Security legislation in the House, not only because of his strategic position on the Rules Committee but also because of his influence with the elderly community.

To make matters worse, HHS Secretary Schweiker announced to the committee that new actuarial estimates could bring the the system's deficit to more than 2 percent of taxable payroll during the next 75 years.

Social Security Subcommittee Chairman Pickle — who favored an increase in retirement age or some other benefit change — suffered an early defeat as his subcommittee voted to combine a 5 percent benefit cut beginning in the year 2000 with a payroll tax increase of .24 percentage points in the year 2015. The plan's sponsor, Rep. Beryl Anthony Jr., D-Ark., said about 60 percent of the unresolved long-range deficit would be covered by the benefit cut and about 40 percent would be covered by the additional payroll taxes.

Pepper denounced the benefit cut and threatened to bring an amendment to the House floor that would call instead for additional payroll tax increases.

The subcommittee bill, which was unsatisfactory to both Pickle and Pepper for different reasons, precipitated a pivotal legislative battle between the two. Pickle planned for further changes in the full committee and, if necessary, on the House floor. "This is the first step in a long process," said Pickle. "There is significant support for other approaches, but we have tried to reach an agreement on something that will move this process along."

The Ways and Means Committee voted to accept Anthony's scheme. But committee Chairman Rostenkowski deferred action on the choice between raising the retirement age or increasing payroll taxes by asking the Rules Committee to allow votes on both issues on the floor.

In the House debate on the legislation, Pepper's proposal to increase payroll taxes by .53 percent in the year 2010 was pitted against the Pickle amendment to raise the retirement age from 65 to 67 by the year 2027. Pepper's impassioned plea to his colleagues not to cut benefits won him a standing ovation, but it was not enough to convince most members that the "structural" change of a higher retirement age was the best way to restore the confidence of current workers in the retirement system.

The Pickle amendment was approved by a 228-202 vote in the House. It raised the retirement age in two stages. The first was through a gradual increase from 65 to 66 over a six-year period ending in the year 2009. The second stage would raise the retirement age from 66 to 67 over a second six-year period ending in 2027. While individuals still would be able to take early retirement at age 62, their benefits would be reduced gradually from the current 80 percent of full benefits to 70 percent in 2027. (*Major provisions, see box p. 68*)

New Retirement Age and Percentage of Full Benefits Received Under 1983 Social Security Law

Age of Retirement	Current Formula	End of Stage One (2009)	End of Stage Two (2027)
62	80.0%	75.0%	70.0%
63	86.7	80.0	75.0
64	93.3	86.7	80.0
65	100.0	93.3	86.7
66	103.0	100.0	93.3
67	106.0	108.0	100.0

Source: Democratic Study Group, U.S. House of Representatives.

Pepper and other opponents charged this would penalize the millions of workers who had to retire early because of poor health or mandatory retirement. "This amendment assumes people are able to work longer than they are now. This is just not the case," argued Rep. James M. Shannon, D-Mass. "This will simply cut their benefits."

But Pickle defended the age increase as necessary to keep up with changing demographics. He pointed out that life expectancy had increased more than 10 years since the 65-year retirement age was set in place over 40 years ago. Raising the retirement age is "not harsh," he said. "That is just in keeping with the times."

Pickle's amendment also required HHS to make recommendations by Jan. 1, 1986, on how Congress should deal with individuals who cannot retire later because of physically demanding jobs.

A Senate proposal, offered by John Heinz, R-Pa., would have increased the retirement age less drastically, from 65 to 66 between the years 2000 and 2015. This would have been accompanied by a 5 percent cut in initial benefits after the turn of the century. The Heinz proposal was approved by the Senate on March 23. However, House and Senate conferees approved the House version on March 24.

Pickle reported that he felt "bruised as a rodeo mule" after debating an issue that was one of the most troublesome points surrounding Social Security for both Congress and the Greenspan commission. Nonetheless, he was confident that he and his backers had "done the right thing and I think history will prove that."

Accounting Debate

Late in February, Republicans on the House Ways and Means Social Security Subcommittee who were defeated in the early going on the retirement age dispute, also were distressed by a controversial "fail-safe" provision allowing the system to borrow from the general Treasury in emergency cases. *(Fail-safe funding schemes, see p. 50.)* They charged that Democrats had inserted some major changes in the bipartisan commission's report and used their majority strength to push through their own plans. "Let's not play the game that the commission's recommendations are carved in stone tablets," Rep. Bill Gradison, R-Ohio, said after the subcommittee's draft proposal was reviewed. "If they were, the tablets are now broken."

Republicans charged that using Treasury funds — even in an emergency — could open the floodgate to future financing of the system through general revenues. Subcommittee Democrats modified the measure to require congressional approval each time the system's trustees needed to borrow funds and agreed that the Treasury would have to be repaid within two years, with interest.

But the Democrats' gestures were insufficient to carry the measure through the Ways and Means Committee. In order to win bipartisan support for the entire package, the committee agreed to an amendment by Gradison — later incorporated in the final version — requiring the Social Security trustees to report to Congress if it appeared that any of the system's three trust funds (Old-Age and Survivors Insurance, Disability Insurance and Hospital Insurance) were in financial danger. Congress then could approve emergency measures — such as temporary benefit cuts, tax hikes or borrowing from the Treasury — to rebuild trust fund reserves.

One of the House subcommittee's fail-safe provisions that survived

Medway High School
Library

to become law was a new accounting procedure to allow the Treasury at the beginning of each month to credit the Social Security trust funds with all the payroll taxes that were expected to be received during that month. Republicans called the proposal "gimmickry" and charged the measure amounted to little more than a one-month, interest-free loan from the general Treasury to the Social Security system.

Congress amended the commission's recommendation that the three funds be allowed to borrow from each other through 1987, imposing the requirement that the Hospital Insurance fund could not make loans if its reserves fell below a specified level.

New Coverage Requirements

In the course of assembling the Social Security law, Congress made significant additions to the Greenspan commission's recommendation that new federal employees and employees of non-profit organizations be included in the system. When Congress finished with the Social Security reform bill, members of Congress and their staffs, new federal judges, top political appointees, and the president and vice president were subject to the new requirement for Social Security coverage as well. However, extending coverage to members of Congress and to federal employees was achieved with considerable grumbling.

In testimony before the Ways and Means Committee in February 1983, House Majority Leader Jim Wright, D-Texas, said that inclusion of all members of Congress, old and new, would at least be a "symbolic" gesture of congressional commitment to keeping the system solvent.

Chairman Rostenkowski and ranking minority member Conable dissented from this view, warning that Congress might find itself in a bind by taking such a step. Prior to enactment, members of Congress paid Social Security taxes, as self-employed individuals, only on outside earnings, such as honoraria. As a result, some members could actually get a tax cut once congressional salaries were covered, because the employee payroll tax was lower than the self-employed tax on the outside income they earned. "We don't want to appear to be doing one thing and wind up appearing to be taking some special advantage for ourselves under the banner of virtue," Conable said.

A more serious challenge arose in the Senate when Russell B. Long, D-La., ranking minority member of the Senate Finance committee, proposed an amendment to delay coverage of federal employees under Social Security until a supplemental Civil Service retirement system could be established providing them with an additional pension comparable to those offered in private business.

Long's amendment was approved by voice vote, but only after several attempts to block it by the Senate leadership. Ted Stevens, R-Alaska, charged that the Long amendment would give federal employees a chance to escape coverage altogether. That loss would cut the value of the rescue plan by $9.3 billion over the next decade, said Sen. Dole.

Long argued it was unfair to expect federal employees to accept the new plan before they knew what supplemental benefits they would receive. "I do not think it's fair to ask these people to buy a pig in a poke," he said.

The final bill, however, did not defer coverage. New federal employees would come under Social Security as of Jan. 1, 1984.

The Bill Overall

The Social Security bill — after slightly more than a month of debate — was passed by Congress on March 25. President Reagan signed the measure (PL 98-21) on April 21. It was in most respects close to the recommendations made by the Greenspan commission. Like the commission plan, the new law involved an eclectic mix of tax hikes, other revenue raisers, benefit cuts and adjustments, new accounting techniques, and public relations gestures — such as adding two public members to the cabinet-dominated Social Security Board of Trustees — to enhance the image of the system. *(Major Provisions, see pp. 68-69.)* Of the reform package, Rep. Conable remarked that "It may not be a work of art, but it is artful work, . . . It will do what it was supposed to do: It will save the nation's basic social insurance system from imminent disaster."

There are no doubt many perspectives on the degree to which the new law favors one sector of society or another. One rough measure of this might be found in the various sources of the $165 billion in savings the law was intended to raise. Depending on one's definition of revenue-raising and benefit-cutting measures, the former could be considered to have accounted for 60 to 75 percent of the savings, appearing to place the greatest burden on today's wage earners. Because of economic and demographic variables, the long-term implications of raising the retirement age are even more difficult to discern.

Health care is one of the largest expenses faced by the nation's elderly. Medicare and Medicaid programs have attempted to alleviate the costs.

Chapter 3

HEALTH CARE: MEDICARE AND MEDICAID

When Congress established a medical care system for the aged through the Social Security system in 1965, the federal government assumed substantial responsibility for paying the health-care bills of the nation's elderly and poor. Under the system's main component, Medicare, all Americans age 65 and over, regardless of income level, are today entitled to hospital benefits. A voluntary supplementary Medicare policy covers 80 percent of other medical costs, including physicians' fees.

The other part of the U.S. health-care system, Medicaid, is a public assistance program differing from Medicare in that it uses a combination of state, local and federal funds — instead of federal funds alone — to provide medical care for the poor. Each state is required to provide health care conforming to federal standards to those who qualify for public assistance, but sets the amount of benefits on its own.

The Medicare and Medicaid programs have been largely successful over their 18-year history in meeting the health-care needs of the elderly and poor. The elderly have benefited from both programs. Medicare provides hospital protection for 95 percent of that group, while Medicaid specifically helps the elderly poor pay for services not covered by Medicare, such as nursing home care.

In 1981 public funds covered 64 percent of the health bill incurred by elderly Americans, which averaged $3,140 per patient that year. By virtue of the federal health programs, the frequency of physician visits by persons whose family incomes were below $7,000 increased by almost 50 percent between 1964 and 1980, according to a 1982 Public Health Service report.

However, better health care for the elderly and poor has been expensive. The federal programs have been plagued by some of the same problems confronting the private health-care sector, especially rising costs and program abuses.

As with private insurance, Medicare and Medicaid provide payments to health-care providers — hospitals, doctors and skilled nursing facilities — after costs have been incurred. This means there is little incentive on the part of providers or patients to keep costs down. As costs have risen, the share the government pays for health care under the two programs has fallen relative to the amount the patient must pay out of pocket (a phenomenon known as "Medigap").

At the same time, the agencies that run Medicare and Medicaid have been billed by health-care providers for services not rendered or for patients not seen. To a lesser extent, patients have made fraudulent statements about their eligibility.

Enactment of Medicare and Medicaid in 1965, as part of President Lyndon B. Johnson's Great Society program, reflected the view in Congress and in the administration that access to health care was the right of all Americans. Developments in the early 1970s furthered this idea by expanding benefits and loosening eligibility requirements for recipients of government-funded medical assistance.

But almost from their inception the programs proved to be much more expensive than planners had envisioned. The rising costs of health care that accompanied inflation throughout the 1970s led to a number of belt-tightening measures late in that decade. Congress curtailed benefits — increasing the share of health costs beneficiaries had to pay themselves — and tightened eligibility requirements. Congress also took steps to improve program management.

By the 1980s, cost control was the principal issue of the health-care debate. Changes made by Congress in Medicare and Medicaid as part of general legislation to reform the Social Security system in 1983 represented a fundamental reassessment of the federal role in financing medical care.

In a report on the fiscal 1984 federal budget by the Brookings Institution, health-care expert Louise B. Russell argued that the changes "abandon the principle... that medical care should be provided whenever it is needed, that the cost should not be considered when life or health is at stake.... By placing absolute limits on what Medicare will pay for a hospital stay and on how much the federal government will contribute to state Medicaid programs, Congress has implicitly agreed that some medical benefits are too small or too costly." Russell added that the new policy would involve some painful choices in the search for a new balance between the costs and benefits of more federal spending on medical care.

The Nascent Health Plans

In 1798 Congress established a government health-insurance program for the merchant marine, perhaps the first such program in the United States. Sailors were required to contribute a few cents a month to pay for hospital care provided by a marine hospital. It was not until the early 20th century, however, that the idea of compulsory health insurance for the general public gained serious attention. The debate was spurred by the American Association for Labor Legislation (AALL), a group of lawyers, academics and other professionals, which lobbied in several states for enactment of health-insurance legislation.

Meanwhile, after publishing several articles in favor of compulsory health insurance, the American Medical Association (AMA), drafted health-insurance bills that were introduced in the New York and Massachusetts legislatures. In 1917 the AMA's House of Delegates endorsed a health-insurance plan comparable to an earlier bill drafted by AALL.

Opposition to the idea of compulsory health insurance developed almost immediately. The opponents were in large part labor leaders, including Samuel Gompers, who felt that a national health-insurance system would result in government control over the working class. In addition, they feared that such an insurance plan would cause fewer employees to join unions and give management a reason for not granting raises.

Employers also opposed compulsory health insurance for fear they would have to contribute a disproportionate share of funding to the plan. By 1920 the AMA, reacting to pressure from state medical societies, had reversed its position and opposed compulsory health insurance.

The Inspiration of Social Security

Interest in a government-sponsored health program was not revived until the 1930s, when the Depression stimulated greater concern for social welfare. The Social Security Act of 1935 established a broad range of social insurance and public assistance programs. *(See Social Security programs, p. 9.)*

Although the Social Security Act did not include a health-insurance program, the president's Committee on Economic Security had endorsed the principle of compulsory national health insurance. President Franklin D. Roosevelt dropped the idea for fear its inclusion in the 1935 legislation would endanger passage of the entire act.

79

Medical expenses were taken into account in determining an individual's monthly payments under Social Security's public assistance programs. However, financial support for medical services was a small part of welfare assistance since participation by the states in these programs was optional.

From 1935 on, compulsory health-insurance bills were introduced regularly in Congress. One of the most comprehensive was that proposed in 1943 by Sens. Robert F. Wagner, D-N.Y. (1927-49), James E. Murray, D-Mont. (1934-61), and Rep. John D. Dingell, D-Mich. (1933-55). The "Wagner-Murray-Dingell" bill called for a sweeping revision of the Social Security Act, including the creation of a compulsory national health-insurance system for persons of all ages to be administered by the federal government and financed through a payroll tax. No action was taken on the measure in the 78th Congress, and the proposal died.

In 1945 President Harry S Truman, in a message to Congress, proposed a comprehensive medical insurance plan for all persons to be financed through a 4 percent increase in the Social Security Act's Old Age and Survivors Insurance tax. Truman recommended that the plan cover doctor, hospital, nursing, laboratory and dental services.

Lobbying on the Truman proposal reached a peak when the president pushed for congressional action in 1949-50. Labor unions supported national health insurance but could not overcome the opposition of the AMA, the private health-insurance industry and business groups. Ultimately, the AMA's dire warnings that national health insurance would mean "socialized medicine" and government interference in medical practice made Congress wary of the measure and there was no action in either chamber.

The 1950s: Incremental Progress

Although Congress refused to take action on compulsory health insurance, it did move in 1950 to help states provide medical assistance to welfare recipients through amendments to the Social Security law. The amendments provided federal support to the states to cover part of the costs of vendor payments (direct reimbursement to hospitals and clinics) for the health care of persons eligible for any of the following four federal-state programs: Old Age Assistance (OAA), Aid to Dependent Children (ADC), Aid to the Blind (AB) and Aid to the Permanently and Totally Disabled (APTD). Federal sharing of the costs greatly accelerated state efforts in health care for public assistance recipients.

In 1952, after it had become clear that Truman's proposal for compulsory health insurance was not likely to be passed soon, if ever, some of its congressional backers suggested a less comprehensive plan. They proposed that the Social Security Old Age and Survivors Insurance system (OASI) begin paying for the hospitalization costs of retired persons receiving OASI old-age benefits. Their plan was intended to assist elderly persons who had high health-care costs and low incomes, and thus could not afford the high premiums of commercial health insurance.

There was no congressional action on the hospital cost payment plan while Truman was president, and the Eisenhower administration, which came to office in 1953, opposed the concept of compulsory health insurance. But in 1957 legislation was introduced by Rep. Aime J. Forand, D-R.I. (1937-39, 1941-61), that incorporated many features of the 1952 plan. Forand's proposal covered hospital, nursing home and surgical costs of the aged, financed by an increase in the OASI payroll tax. There was little congressional activity on the issue until 1960, but the Forand plan drew considerable public interest.

By 1960 the Forand bill had become an intensely partisan issue, with the chief interest groups taking positions similar to those they had taken a decade earlier on Truman's comprehensive health-care proposals. Backing the bill were organized labor, Democrats and liberal groups. Against the bill were most Republicans, including President Dwight D. Eisenhower, and spokesmen for business and insurance groups.

Once again, the AMA conducted a nationwide lobbying campaign against compulsory medical insurance. The Eisenhower administration responded with its own program to help the needy aged meet the costs of catastropic illness without compulsory national health insurance.

In Congress, however, the House Ways and Means Committee opted for a plan similar to, but less generous than Eisenhower's. Congress eventually amended the Social Security Act along these lines when it passed the Kerr-Mills bill in July 1960. The bill was named for sponsors Wilbur D. Mills, D-Ark. (1939-77), chairman of the House Ways and Means committee, and Sen. Robert S. Kerr, D-Okla. (1949-63).

The Kerr-Mills bill extended the 1950 Social Security amendments by providing additional federal funds to the states for vendor payments under the Old Age Assistance (OAA) program. It also established the Medical Assistance to the Aged (MAA) program, which was a separate federal matching grant program for the needy aged who were not receiving cash assistance. Under this program the government agreed to reimburse states for 50 to 80 percent of the cost of setting up state programs to pay medical costs for needy aged persons.

A Procedural Obstacle

John F. Kennedy, first as a senator (D-Mass, 1953-60) and then as president (1961-63), strongly backed the concept of health insurance for the aged. Shortly after taking office, President Kennedy proposed to Congress a revised version of the Forand plan to be introduced by Rep. Cecil R. King, D-Calif. (1942-69), and Sen. Clinton P. Anderson, D-N.M. (1949-73). The new health-care proposal called for Social Security coverage for 90 days of hospital care (with a small deductible), extensive nursing home care or home health services, but did not provide for payment of surgical costs.

But while the King-Anderson bill was an annual presidential priority from 1961 through 1964, administration efforts were frustrated throughout this period. One factor in these failures was a constitutional rule requiring that any revenue-raising bills — including amendments to the Social Security Act — originate in the House. In practice this meant that Social Security bills had to be reported from the House Ways and Means Committee if they were to have any chance of enactment. Unfortunately for proponents of health insurance, that committee was controlled by its powerful chairman, Wilbur Mills.

Naturally the administration took every opportunity to convince the House leadership to fill Ways and Means Committee vacancies with members who would support health insurance for the aged. In 1963 the margin of opposition on the committee had declined to one member, but Mills stood firm against the plan and administration efforts to get a majority behind the bill failed.

Mills' disapproval of Social Security involvement in medical care for the aged was considered a major stumbling block to such a program by 1964. Mills elaborated his views that year in a speech in Little Rock, Ark.:

> Many of the newspapers have widely reported that, singlehandedly, I have for six or seven years prevented this legislation from being considered. . . . Apparently a majority of the members of the House of Representatives share the deep concern which I have over using the Old Age, Survivors and Disability Insurance [OASDI] system for financing a medical or hospital care program. . . .
>
> I have always maintained that at some point there is a limit to the amount of a worker's wages, or the earnings of a self-employed

person, that can reasonably be expected to finance the Social Security system. . . . The central fact which must be faced on a proposal to provide a form of service benefit — as contrasted with a cash benefit — is that it very difficult to accurately estimate the cost. These difficult-to-predict future costs, when such a program is part of the Social Security program, could well have highly dangerous ramifications on the cash benefits portion of the Social Security system. The American people must be assured of the continued soundness of the OASDI program.

Although the King-Anderson proposals passed the Senate for the first time in 1964 as an amendment to a bill raising Social Security retirement benefits, the bill died in conference when a majority of House conferees opposed any medical care plan.

Assembling a Compromise

Failure of the King-Anderson bill in 1964 was one of President Lyndon B. Johnson's few serious legislative defeats to date. In 1965, therefore, he took no risks. The president's first legislative message to the 89th Congress dealt with health legislation. In it he called 1965 the year "when, with the sure knowledge of public support, the Congress should enact a hospital insurance program for the aged. . . . In this way, the spectre of catastrophic hospital bills can be lifted from the lives of our older citizens."

Johnson's 1965 hospital care bill was very similar to those that had been introduced and debated since 1961. One major difference, however, was that the new bill provided coverage for 60 days of hospital care, instead of 90 days. Other major provisions called for the following benefits: 60 days of nursing home care, 240 home health-care visits and outpatient hospital diagnostic services. The program covered all persons 65 and over, except government workers with federal insurance and certain aliens. It was to be financed mainly by increases in the Social Security tax rate.

The AMA once again mounted a vigorous campaign against the administration proposals, but this time changed its strategy by attacking the bill for not being sufficiently comprehensive. The medical association argued that the elderly needed more than just hospital benefits. They introduced an alternative plan, called "eldercare," which covered doctor bills. The eldercare plan called for a voluntary comprehensive medical insurance program that would be available to persons 65 and over if their state government signed up for the program. The program was to be fi-

---

Terminology Used . . .

Providers — Doctors, hospitals, skilled nursing facilities or home health facilities that provide medical services to Medicare beneficiaries.

Suppliers — Persons or organizations, other than doctors or health care facilities, that furnish equipment or services covered by Medicare insurance. Ambulance firms, independent laboratories and organizations that rent or sell medical equipment are considered suppliers.

Benefit Period — A benefit period begins when a patient covered by Medicare insurance enters a hospital. It ends when the patient has been out of a hospital or other facility providing primarily skilled nursing and re-habilitation services for 60 consecutive days. There is no limit on the number of benefit periods a patient can have.

Intermediaries — Private insurance companies under contract with the government that handle Medicare claims from hospitals, skilled nursing facilities and home health agencies (part A).

Carriers — Private insurance companies that handle claims from doctors and other suppliers of services covered under Medicare's supplementary medical insurance program (part B).

Assignment — A method of medical insurance payment in which reimbursement for services rendered is made by Medicare to a doctor or supplier. When the assignment method is used, the doctor or supplier agrees that his or her total charge for the covered service will be the amount approved by the Medicare carrier.

---

nanced by matching federal-state funds and variable contributions from recipients.

The House Republican leadership also set forth their own bill, introduced by the ranking minority member of the Ways and Means Committee, John W. Byrnes, R-Wis. (1945-73). The Byrnes bill provided a voluntary health-insurance program for all persons 65 and over, which would cover a large proportion of most health-care costs in old age. It was to be administered by the federal government and financed by a graduated premium contribution based on the individual's ability to pay, by contributions from the states, and by an annual appropriations from the federal government.

... In the Medicare Program

Deductible — The initial dollar amount that the patient must pay for medical services before Medicare insurance payments begin.

Co-payment (also called co-insurance) — The dollar amount of services covered under the Medicare program that a patient is responsible for paying (beyond the deductible amount the patient also must pay). The co-payment is calculated from the deductible. For example, the co-payment for covered services for the 60th through the 90th day in a hospital is one-fourth of the deductible.

"Reasonable Charges" (also called approved charges) — The portion of the total cost of a given medical service to be borne by Medicare, as deemed appropriate by the Medicare carrier. The amount of the charge — reviewed annually — is based on whichever is lowest, the hospital or physician's customary charge, the prevailing charge in the region or, in the event of services already rendered, the actual charge.

"Reasonable Costs" — The provider costs for services to Medicare beneficiaries. These costs are determined on the basis of an annual cost report from the provider and are paid only to the provider (not the patient).

Lifetime reserve days (also called hospital reserve days) — A period of covered hospital stay beyond the basic benefit period offered by Medicare hospital insurance. Reserve days are not renewable. Each beneficiary is allowed 60 reserve days in his lifetime.

All three plans — the administration proposal, the Byrnes bill and the AMA's eldercare plan — contributed to the medical care bill that finally was enacted in 1965. Chairman Mills had an influential role in both the shaping and the passage of the legislation.

Mills' change of heart was interpreted as a reflection of his unwillingness to be on the losing side of an issue. Theodore Marmor in *The Politics of Medicare*, published in 1970, said: "Mills' conception of himself as the active head of an autonomous, technically expert committee helps explain his interest in shaping legislation he could no longer block, and his preoccupation with cautious financing of the Social Security system made him willing to combine benefit and financing arrangements that had been presented as mutually exclusive alternatives."

Today's Programs Take Shape

As passed by Congress July 28, 1965, the Health Insurance for the Aged Act (PL 89-97) added two new titles (XVIII and XIX) to the Social Security Act. Part A of Title XVIII was basically the King-Anderson bill; it provided persons over 65 with insurance to cover the costs of hospital and related care. The program was to be financed by a Social Security trust fund, to which employers and employees were required to contribute. Part B of Title XVIII drew heavily on the Byrnes bill and called for a voluntary system of supplemental medical insurance covering doctors' fees and certain other health services.

Title XIX, the Medicaid section of the bill, provided a program of federal matching grants to states that chose to make medical services available to welfare recipients and the medically indigent.

Basic Health Insurance

Most persons age 65 and older became eligible for the basic health insurance program (part A) when the law took effect in 1966. Not eligible were active or retired federal employees enrolled in the federal health benefits program, aliens who had not been lawfully admitted for permanent status or had not lived in the United States for at least five consecutive years and persons convicted of certain crimes.

The plan provided the following benefits:

● Inpatient hospital services for up to 90 days for each period of illness, with the patient paying a deductible amount of $40 for the first 60 days and $10 a day for the next 30 days. Each patient was eligible for 60 non-renewable days of inpatient hospital services (beyond the 90 day period) in his/her lifetime. Excluded from covered inpatient care were the services of radiologists, anesthesiologists, pathologists and physiatrists. Also excluded were private duty nursing and hospital services of physicians, except services provided by dental and medical interns and residents under approved teaching programs. Psychiatric hospital care was subject to a lifetime limit of 190 days, with 60 days per illness.

● Post-hospital care for up to 100 days for each period of illness after at least three days in the hospital, with the patient paying $5 a day after the first 20 days. (Nursing homes were considered post-hospital facilities.)

● Outpatient diagnostic services, with the patient paying the first $20 for diagnostic services provided by the same hospital during a 20 day period and 20 percent of the remaining costs. The $20 deduction was credited against the annual $50 deduction required under the supplementary health plan.

● Up to 100 home health-care visits by a nurse or physician's assistant after discharge from at least a three-day stay in hospital, or from an extended-care facility, and before the beginning of a new period of illness.

The plan defined a period of illness as beginning when the patient entered a hospital or a nursing home and ending when the patient had not been hospitalized for 60 consecutive days.

Part A also provided that deductions required for the various services would be increased if necessary to meet rising health-care costs and that payment to providers of the services would cover the "reasonable cost" of the services. *(Medicare terminology, see p. 85.)*

The plan was to be financed by a payroll tax, which would apply equally to employers, employees and self-employed persons. The tax was fixed at 0.35 percent in 1966, 0.50 percent in 1967-72, 0.60 percent in 1976-79, 0.70 percent in 1980-86 and 0.80 percent in 1987 and thereafter.

The annual taxable earnings base for the health-insurance payroll tax was the same as that for Social Security's old age and disability insurance funds, $6,600. The plan provided that general revenues would finance the plan for persons not covered by Social Security or the Railroad Retirement Act.

Health-insurance payroll taxes (and general revenue funds for those not covered by Social Security) for the plan were to go into a separate Hospital Insurance (HI) trust fund.

The secretary of the Health, Education and Welfare Department (HEW) was to administer the basic health-insurance plan.

Supplementary Medical Care

The eligibility requirements for the supplementary plan (part B) were the same as for the basic plan.

The initial enrollment period for persons age 65 and older was set as a seven-month period beginning three months before the 65th birthday. No person could enroll after three years from the close of the first period in which he/she was eligible to enroll. Persons who dropped out of the plan could re-enroll only once, and it had to be within three years of dropping out. The plan provided that states could enroll and pay the premiums of their public assistance recipients.

The benefits provided that the supplementary plan would pay 80 percent of the patient's costs, after an annual deduction of $50, on the following:

● Services of physicians, surgeons, radiologists, anesthesiologists, pathologists and physiatrists and certain services of dental surgeons, regardless of whether these services were provided in a hospital, clinic, office or home.

● Up to 100 home health-care visits a calendar year.

● Other medical and health services, whether provided in or out of a medical institution, including X-rays, laboratory tests, electrocardiograms, basal metabolism readings, artificial legs, arms and eyes, and rental of certain medical equipment. Payment for out-of-hospital mental disorders would be limited in each calendar year to $250 or 50 percent of the costs, whichever was smaller. Payment would not be made for routine exams, dental care, eyeglasses or hearing aids.

The plan required that payments to institutional providers be based on "reasonable costs" and payments to doctors be based on "reasonable charges." *(Medicare terminology, see box, p. 84.)*

The supplementary medical insurance plan was to be financed jointly by persons enrolled in the plan and by the federal government. Enrollees would pay monthly premiums of $3 each. The premiums would be deducted from the monthly retirement benefits received under the Social Security, railroad and civil retirement systems. The federal government would match from general revenues the $3 monthly premium paid by each enrollee. Individual and government contributions went into a separate trust fund for the supplementary plan.

The plan provided that the premium could be increased as medical costs rose. A higher premium was also levied on those persons who delayed enrollment until after the first period when enrollment was open to them and for persons who re-enrolled after dropping out.

The secretary of HEW would contract with private carriers to perform major administrative functions of the plan, such as determining rates of payments and disbursing funds.

Medicaid

The medical provisions for the needy already covered under the Social Security Act were combined in a new title (XIX) to the act, which became known as Medicaid. The plan also extended the Medical Assistance for the Aged (MAA) program for the indigent aged to needy persons under the dependent children, blind and permanently and totally disabled programs; and made eligible for medical aid needy children who did not qualify for public assistance (if the state so provided). Existing provisions of the act covering medical assistance programs would terminate upon adoption of the new program.

States participating in the program were required to provide inpatient and outpatient hospital services, laboratory and X-ray services, skilled nursing home services and physicians' services. States could provide additional benefits. Needy persons receiving state aid were to be provided with assistance to meet the deductible amounts imposed by the federal basic health plan.

The plan increased the federal share under the existing MAA federal-state matching program so that states with average per capita incomes would receive 55 percent (rather than the existing 50 percent) and states with very low per capita incomes could receive up to 83 percent (rather than 80 percent).

The federal government was required to pick up a 75 percent share of the cost of training professional medical personnel participating in the programs and 50 percent of the other administrative expenses.

States were required to provide a means test to determine eligibility of the needy elderly for the program. The program would not be based on rigid income standards, which could adversely affect persons of some means but with very large medical bills.

Program Adjustments, 1967-1980

From 1967 to 1980 federal expenditures for health care rose with the expansion of the Medicare and Medicaid programs. Congress expanded both eligibility and the variety of services covered. Almost at the start of the programs, it was realized that they were more costly than planners had envisioned. While the Nixon and Ford administrations were concerned about cost containment, Congress did little to curb program expenditures.

During the period 1967-1977, national compulsory health insurance remained a controversial issue and an elusive goal. While the Nixon and Carter administrations paid lip service to some form of national health insurance, their actual proposals were more limited, with an emphasis on catastrophic health insurance.

However, a number of intermediate developments in health insurance occurred in these years. Specifically, certain benefit extensions in the Medicare and Medicaid programs in the 1970s reflected a new emphasis on preventive medicine and less expensive forms of health care, such as health-maintenance organizations (HMOs) and home health services.

New Programs/Physicians' Review. Nixon's 1971 health-insurance proposal had three parts: a national health-insurance standards program designed to fill the gap caused by the failure of many private insurance plans to cover catastrophic illness costs; a federal Family Health Insurance Plan to replace Medicaid; and a proposal to encourage the development of HMOs, which provided prepaid comprehensive health care. Despite extensive hearings in House and Senate committees, Congress did not act on these proposals in 1971 or 1972.

However, major alterations of the Medicare and Medicaid program were included in legislation enacted in 1972 (PL 92-603) revising the Social Security Act. The main provisions of that law extended Medicare eligibility to an additional 1.7 million disabled Social Security beneficiaries; provided federal funding for Medicare beneficiaries to enroll in HMOs that provided federally approved services; brought the services of chiropractors under Medicare; provided coverage under Medicare for most Americans afflicted with chronic kidney disease; and established professional standards review organizations (PSROs) — representing local practicing physicians — to oversee Medicaid and Medicare services.

During the 93rd Congress (1973-74), several measures were enacted that coordinated Medicaid eligibility requirements with the federal Supplemental Security Income (SSI) program, which provided federal assistance to the needy aged, blind and disabled. One part of Nixon's 1971 national health-insurance program, federal assistance to HMOs, was passed by Congress in December 1973, in a more limited form than the original proposal. *(HMO details, see p. 103.)*

In 1975 legislation was passed (PL 94-182) that extended the time limit for local medical groups to set up PSROs. That law also provided that prevailing charges for physician services under Medicare could not be lowered. HEW regulations had tied increases in Medicare reimbursement rates to an economic index, and the 1975 measure represented a legislative victory for medical groups.

Management Reforms. Originally, a number of different HEW bureaus and divisions administered the Medicare and Medicaid programs. In 1977 their functions were consolidated and transferred to the Health Care Financing Administration, which was established in March 1977 as part of HEW. (HEW officially went out of existence May 4, 1980, and was replaced by two departments: the Department of Health and

Human Services (HHS) and the Department of Education.)

In 1976 and 1977 Congress moved to correct mismangement in the two programs when it passed legislation (PL 95-142) increasing penalties for fraud and abuse, strengthening the oversight responsibilities of PSROs and requiring more ownership information from providers. The bill was the result of three years of congressional study that followed disclosure by federal and state investigators that kickbacks, fraudulent billings, unnecessary medical treatment and other problems were occurring in the federal health programs. (Congress in 1976 also established an Office of Inspector General for HEW, now HHS.)

In 1977 Congress approved legislation (PL 95-210) that extended Medicare and Medicaid reimbursement to services provided by nurse practitioners and physicians' assistants in rural clinics. The measure was designed to encourage the development and utilization of rural health clinics in medically underserved areas. In 1978 legislation was enacted (PL 95-292) that amended the kidney disease program under Medicare to provide incentives for patients to conduct kidney dialysis treatments in the home as an alternative to more costly hospital-based dialysis.

Carter Plan Stymied. President Jimmy Carter had made a comprehensive health-insurance proposal one of his campaign pledges, but his 1979 proposal was limited to a catastrophic health-insurance program. Carter's plan was not approved by Congress due in part to concern about the costs of the plan.

Perhaps more importantly, the White House and its allies — the insurance industry, organized labor and groups representing the elderly — were out-lobbied. While catastrophic health insurance was one of many priorities for those groups, the AMA and the hospital lobby worked against the plan without distraction.

The following year, however, a number of changes were made in Medicare and Medicaid as a part of the fiscal 1981 budget reconciliation bill (PL 96-499). (The 1974 budget act provided for a "reconciliation" procedure for bringing the overall spending by the federal government into conformity with the spending decisions made by Congress.) The bill expanded coverage of home health services under Medicare and payment for minor surgery or tests done outside hospitals. Existing law ordinarily covered these services only if the patient was hospitalized.

Other changes made by the reconciliation bill were meant to encourage physicians not to charge their elderly patients more than Medicare would pay for certain services, but these provisions were not made mandatory. Under existing law, doctors could, and often did, charge well above what the program considered a "reasonable" fee, and patients had to pay the difference. *(Medicare terminology, see box, p. 84.)*

Reducing the Government's Role

President Ronald Reagan, in his 1980 campaign, endorsed the concept of health insurance in the event of a catastrophe, but flatly rejected a national health-insurance plan. Reagan subscribed to a "free-market" or "competition" health policy based on a theory advocated by Alain C. Enthoven, a Stanford University economist specializing in the study of health care. The idea behind a free-market health plan was that if individuals spent their own health dollars, they would demand and get better and cheaper services. Cost and quality would largely be controlled by market forces, not government regulators.

The Reagan administration began drafting complex legislation based on the free-market theory. Its proposals included taxing insurance premiums; replacing Medicare with a "voucher system" (by which enrollees would purchase their own health insurance); and restructuring hospital reimbursement systems so that hospitals would be paid according to preset limits instead of after the costs were incurred. *(Free-market theory and accompanying plans, see p. 104.)*

Most changes in the Medicare and Medicaid programs during Reagan's first two years were part of a larger administration effort to cut spending for social programs and to reduce the federal deficit. However, administration officials also sought to create pressure for a future overhaul of health-care financing in the United States. Ultimately, said HHS Secretary Richard S. Schweiker, the administration wanted to "use the marketplace to hold down these costs," rather than relying on spending limits and other regulations imposed by Congress.

Medicaid Cuts/Local Autonomy. Congress agreed to cut federal Medicaid spending in 1981, but rejected a Reagan administration proposal to set a rigid ceiling on federal Medicaid contributions to the states. The Economic Recovery Tax Act of that year (PL 97-35) required reductions in spending for Medicaid (3 percent in fiscal 1982, 4 percent in fiscal 1983 and 4.5 percent in fiscal 1984). Those cuts were expected to reduce federal spending on the programs by $5.8 billion.

The 1981 bill also broadened the independent authority of the states under Medicaid, modifying a provision of the 1965 act allowing

Medicaid recipients to choose their own health-care providers (doctors, hospitals, and skilled nursing facilities), and giving states the option of restricting physicians and facilities available to recipients in certain cases. States would also be able to arrange for laboratory services or procure medical devices through competitive bidding.

Perhaps the most important provision was one that gave the states the opportunity to waive restrictions on the types of services the federal government would fund through Medicaid reimbursements. Previously, Medicaid insurance had been restricted to hospital stays. The Medicaid waivers provided a mechanism by which states could be reimbursed for providing home- and community-based health services to recipients who otherwise would have had to seek more expensive hospital care in order to qualify for federal payments.

According to the Intergovernmental Health Policy Project (IHPP), a university health-research project funded by the Health Care Financing Administration, 40 states applied for waivers between October 1981 and May 1983.

Meanwhile, more than 30 states cut back on types of benefits, eligibility groups and payments under Medicaid in 1981, according to the IHPP.

Additional savings would come from increases in the deductible payments required of Medicare beneficiaries for both the basic (part A) and supplementary (part B) insurance programs, and from other limits on reimbursements.

A Second Round of Cuts. Congress made a number of further changes in Medicare and Medicaid in the Tax Equity and Fiscal Responsibility Act of 1982 (PL 97-248) — President Reagan's tax increase measure — in an effort to reduce federal outlays for health programs in fiscal 1983-85. The changes would cut spending for the programs by an estimated $14.4 billion over the three years, nearly two and one-half times the amount pruned from the programs in 1981.

The bulk of the spending reductions made by the 1982 act came in Medicare ($13.3 billion). The principal cost-cutting measures revised limits on payments to hospitals and doctors. One provision imposed new caps on the percentage of costs for ancillary services, such as X-rays and laboratory services, that Medicare would pay each year. Payments for such services could not exceed 110 percent of the preceding year's expenditure. Previously, only payments for routine services were so restricted. Another change set limits on how much Medicare payments could rise each year for various types of hospitals.

The bill also required employers to offer workers eligible for Medicare comparable coverage under their company health plans. This provision was inspired by the administration view that Medicare was an "unwarranted subsidy" of private business. The plan would make Medicare a secondary source of health benefits for those 65 and older and covered by a company plan. Employees who chose not to join their employer's health plan would continue to receive their primary coverage from Medicare.

Federal government employees also were made eligible for Medicare coverage and were required to pay the 1.3 percent payroll tax for their coverage beginning in January 1983.

Premiums for Medicare supplementary medical insurance (part B) were boosted from a level covering just under one-fourth of the program's costs to a full 25 percent. Under the new law, the monthly premium for supplementary medical insurance would rise from $12.20 in 1982 to $13.70 (instead of $13.10) in July 1983, and to $15.30 (instead of $14) in July 1984.

The bill also expanded benefits to cover less expensive forms of care, a move sponsors said would save money over the long run by encouraging reliance on such care. Added were Medicare coverage for hospice care of terminally ill patients and a new payment system to promote the enrollment of Medicare beneficiaries in HMOs.

As requested by the administration, the bill also repealed the Professional Standards Review Organization (PSRO) program, substituting peer review of Medicare and Medicaid by physician review boards under contract with HHS.

Congressional critics of the cost-cutting changes warned that reducing federal spending on the programs would simply shift costs onto others — hospitals, state and local governments, private insurers, and the poor and elderly beneficiaries of the programs themselves.

The remaining $1.14 billion was cut from projected Medicaid costs. The states would be allowed to charge beneficiaries nominal fees for medical services and to take such steps as placing liens on the property of institutionalized beneficiaries in order to facilitate the recovery of Medicaid costs after death. Other cost-saving moves were administrative in nature and did not require congressional action.

Prospective-rate Plans. Also in 1982, there appeared to be a gradual shift among state Medicaid programs from short-term cost containment strategies to longer-term structural reforms. Cost-control schemes for Medicaid included setting up agencies to review hospital budgets and rates as well as plans to regulate hospital reimbursements before the costs were incurred (prospective payment plans). Six states (Connecticut, Maryland, Massachusetts, New Jersey, New York, and Washington) had introduced prospective payment plans in 1976 or earlier. According to IHPP, more than two-thirds of the states sought federal approval in 1982 to direct Medicaid recipients to more cost effective health-care systems. *(New Jersey DRG experiment, see box, p. 106.)*

As part of a major bill (PL 98-21) to overhaul the Social Security system in March 1983, Congress altered the way the federal government reimbursed hospitals through Medicare to resemble the prospective reimbursement plans for Medicaid tried in the states.

The old reimbursement system was replaced with a prospective system in which inpatient hospital costs were determined in advance and paid on a per case basis, according to rates established for specific medical conditions or combinations of illnesses (called diagnosis-related groups, or DRGs).

To ease the transition between the two reimbursement systems, there would be a three-year phase-in of the DRG program, with an increasing portion of hospital costs reimbursed under the new system. In the fourth year, 100 percent of hospital costs were to be covered by DRGs. The new plan would be "budget neutral" for two years, meaning that federal expenditures for this period would be the same as they had been under the previous system, based on spending limits on Medicare and Medicaid enacted in 1982.

Other Proposals. A number of administration proposals for Medicaid were not addressed by Congress in its Social Security legislation of 1983. One of these was a new block grant to the states for Medicaid administrative costs, ending separate funding in this area.

Also, in a marked departure from prevailing Medicaid policy, the administration sought to allow states to require the adult children of Medicaid recipients to share the cost of their parents' nursing home care. The law had prohibited states from holding relatives (other than spouses) financially responsible for the costs of Medicaid services to patients since 1965.

By contrast to Medicaid, most of the administration's fiscal 1983 budget requests for Medicare were addressed by Congress and found their way into law, albeit in altered form.

Bearing Health-Care Costs

When Congress established Medicare and Medicaid in 1965 under the Social Security system, it specified that Medicare's HI trust fund remain separate from the Old Age, Survivors and Disability Insurance (OASDI) trust funds — the Social Security funds from which retirement benefits are paid. A House committee report on the Medicare legislation said the HI fund would in no way impinge upon the financial soundness of the Social Security trust funds. The independence of the two systems would be assured through such devices as separate trust funds and a separate statement of the hospital insurance tax on individuals' W-2 income tax forms. Like the payroll tax for the OASDI funds, the hospital insurance tax would be levied upon an adjustable taxable earnings base to keep pace with rising earnings levels. However, both the OASDI and HI funds faced bleak financial prospects in 1983.

In February 1983 the Congressional Budget Office (CBO) estimated that the HI fund would run out of money by 1987. While Congress had passed legislation allowing the financially troubled Social Security funds to borrow from the HI fund in 1981, the main reason for the projected deficits, according the the CBO, was the fact that "hospital costs are growing much more rapidly than the earning[s] to which the Hospital Insurance tax is applied."

From 1982 to 1995, costs incurred by Medicare recipients were projected to increase by an average of 13.2 percent, while covered earnings taxed for Medicare benefits were projected to rise by an average of only 6.8 percent over the same period.

Factors in Rising Medical Costs

The federal health-care financing system today has been ravaged by the inflationary nature of health care. While the Consumer Price Index (CPI) rose 134 percent between 1970 and 1981, health-care costs nationwide rose 284 percent over the same period, according to the Health Care Financing Administration.

In 1981 the national rate of spending for medical services grew by 12.5 percent, compared with an overall inflation rate of 8.9 percent, as measured by the Labor Department. This inflation rate for health-care costs was the highest since the department began tracking those costs in 1935.

Federal health outlays in the fiscal 1983 and 1984 (proposed) federal budgets were the fourth largest expenditures after Social Security and

National and Federal Health Expenditures
Selected Years 1950-1990

Year	National Health Expenditures Amount (billions)	Federal Health Expenditures			Federal Expenditures as % of National Health Expenditures
		Amount (billions)	Per Capita	% of GNP	
1950	$ 12.7	$ 1.6	$ 10.50	.6	12.8
1960	26.9	3.0	16.35	.6	11.2
1970	74.7	17.7	84.85	1.8	23.7
1971	83.3	20.3	96.14	1.9	24.4
1975	132.7	37.1	168.52	2.4	27.9
1979	215.0	61.0	266.39	2.5	28.4
1980	249.0	71.1	306.38	2.7	28.5
1981	286.6	83.9	358.93	2.9	29.3
Projected					
1983	362.3	104.2	438.05	3.0	28.8
1985	456.4	131.5	542.02	3.1	28.8
1990	755.6	231.6	915.47	3.7	30.7

Source: Adapted from *Health Care Financing Review*, March 1983, Health Care Financing Administration.

related programs, national defense, and interest on the public debt. Health Care Financing Administration figures showed that federal spending on health care in 1970-1981 rose 374 percent. As a portion of the nation's gross national product (GNP), these costs rose from 1.8 percent in 1970 to 2.9 percent in 1981. Per capita federal health expenditures, $358.93 in 1981, were projected to reach $915.47 by 1990.

Medicare and Medicaid costs grew each year by 19 percent from 1973 to 1981, a period in which most other entitlements grew at an annual rate of 14 percent. Left unchanged, the programs' costs were expected to double between 1981 and 1986, according to the CBO. The Health Care Financing Administration anticipated a 340 percent increase in hospital care costs between 1978 and 1990.

Third-Party Payment. The Medicare and Medicaid systems, along with private health insurance, have been responsible for much of the skyrocketing costs of health care. Health insurance has encouraged policy holders to make fuller use of health services because they do not pay directly for their medical expenses. Instead, they are shifted to a "third party" (private insurance companies or Medicare and Medicaid). The patient pays indirectly for health-care costs through taxes or insurance premiums.

According to the Health Care Financing Administration, the federal agency within HHS that administers the Medicare and Medicaid programs, patients paid only 29 cents out of every dollar spent on health care in 1981. The federal government paid 29 cents, private health insurance and other third-party payers paid 29 cents, and state and local governments paid the remaining 13 cents. *(Nation's Health Dollar in 1981, see fig. p. 100.)*

Because third parties were responsible for 71 percent of medical costs in 1981, patients were cushioned from the full impact of rising costs. Louise Russell, in the Brookings budget report for fiscal 1984, pointed out that this was exactly what third-party payments were designed to do. They put into practice the principle that access to health care should not be based on ability to pay for it.

The particular types of health care the federal government and private insurance companies are willing to cover also have been a factor in making health care more expensive. Medicare, Medicaid and private insurance plans emphasize reimbursement for hospital costs. With the exception of some new coverage of HMOs and hospice care under Medicare and home and community health services under Medicaid allowed in the 1970s and 1980s, less costly home health care and routine and preventative health services have not been covered by these programs. *(Program adjustments, see p. 89.)*

"The increase in costs to the individual has created a situation which deters preventative medicine and stimulates the use of more expensive services," said Lawrence Lane, spokesman for the American Association of Retired Persons. The patient, given a choice between being reimbursed for hospital services or having to pay out-of-pocket for home health care, has been forced to choose the more expensive care.

The means by which government and private insurance plans traditionally have reimbursed doctors and hospitals also has contributed to the inflationary nature of health-care costs. Both private and public insurance plans have reimbursed health-care providers on a fee-for-service basis for "reasonable costs" incurred in treatment. This system has given little incentive to hospitals and doctors to control costs.

Other Cost Factors. Expensive equipment and procedures, highly paid personnel and the growth of the elderly population have pushed up charges for a broad range of treatments and health services.

Advances in medical technology have entailed the use of sophisticated and expensive X-ray equipment such as the computerized axial tomography (CAT) scanner and complicated surgical procedures such as coronary bypass operations and organ transplants.

Hospital workers' wages increased significantly when hospitals came under the minimum wage law in 1967. Since then, the threat of malpractice lawsuits has caused doctors to pass the extra cost of malpractice insurance on to their patients and sometimes to overtreat them — increasing medical care fees — in an effort to protect themselves.

The proportion of the U.S. population 65 and over has increased significantly since the Medicare system was set up in 1965. With the growth of the elderly population there came a steady increase in the number of persons eligible for Medicare. A big jump in enrollment occurred in 1973 when disabled persons under 65 and those with end-stage kidney disease became eligible for Medicare coverage. According to the Health Care Financing Administration, Medicare enrollees in the United States numbered about 28.9 million as of July 1982: 26.0 million 65 and older, and 2.8 million disabled recipients under 65. Between 95 and 98 percent of all Americans 65 and older were enrolled in the Medicare program in 1982.

A less-recognized factor in increased Medicare expenditures has been the extent of the care received by the elderly population. According to a 1983 CBO study, the elderly have a higher hospital admission rate and more resources committed to them per hospital stay than other segments of the population. The elderly also require more sophisticated and expensive health-care services, such as organ repair and replacement, rehabilitation aids, surgery and cancer treatments. A November 1980 *New England Journal of Medicine* article reported that the per capita hospital expenditure for the population 65 and older was three and a half times

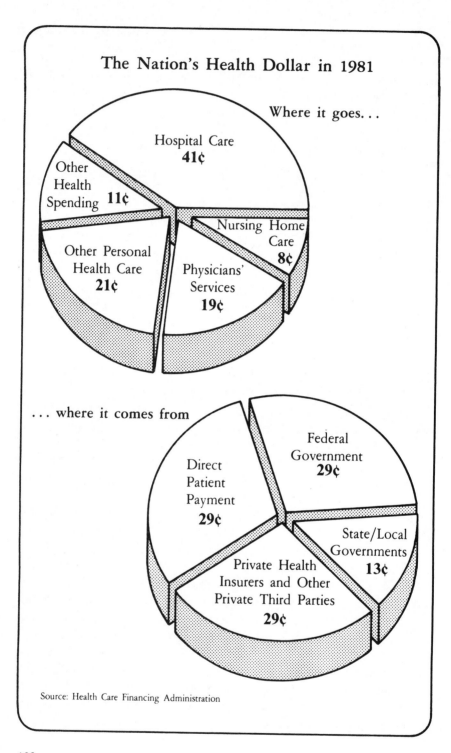

The Nation's Health Dollar in 1981

Where it goes...

Hospital Care
41¢

Other
Health
Spending **11¢**

Nursing Home
Care
8¢

Other Personal
Health Care
21¢

Physicians'
Services
19¢

... where it comes from

Direct
Patient
Payment
29¢

Federal
Government
29¢

State/Local
Governments
13¢

Private Health
Insurers and Other
Private Third Parties
29¢

Source: Health Care Financing Administration

that for persons under 65.

Efforts to sustain life contribute disproportionately to rising Medicare costs, wrote James Fallows, Washington editor of the *Atlantic Monthly*, in a November 1982 article. Approximately one-fourth of all Medicare payments are made in the last year of a patient's life.

Individual Costs. Although patients paid only 29 percent of the nation's health-care bill in 1981, many elderly patients still found their out-of-pocket expenses excessive. As health-care costs have soared, Medicare beneficiaries have had to pay greater deductibles, co-payments and monthly premiums for supplementary medical insurance. *(Medicare terminology, see box, p. 84.)*

Between 1965 and 1983, the hospital insurance deductible increased from $40 to $260 and the annual deductible for supplementary medical insurance rose from $50 to $75.

Co-payments under Medicare hospital insurance have grown dramatically as well. The daily co-payment for hospital services from the 61st through the 90th day under Medicare rose from $10 in 1965 to $65 in 1983. And the co-payment rate for 100 days of care in a skilled nursing facility (post-hospital), after the first 20 days, rose from $5 to $32.50 during the same time period.

In 1965 the premium for the monthly supplemetary medical insurance paid by enrollees was $3. In July 1983 it was scheduled to rise from $12.20 to $13.50.

"Medigap." Along with the deductibles and co-payments a patient must bear under Medicare's basic insurance plan, beneficiaries are responsible for 20 percent of the "reasonable cost" of covered medical services (and any costs over that amount) under supplementary medical insurance. Medicare coverage is not available at all for a number of medical services including prescription drugs used outside the hospital, routine physical examinations, eyeglasses, hearing aids and dental care. *(Medicare terminology, see box, p. 84.)*

Because Medicare covers only part of an individual's medical costs, many elderly persons have bought "Medigap" (supplementary insurance) policies from private insurance companies to supplement Medicare coverage.

Congressional investigations in the late 1970s by the House Select Committee on Aging, chaired by Claude Pepper, D-Fla., disclosed that many Medigap policies included coverage that duplicated Medicare. Investigations into alleged widespread fraud in the Medigap insurance

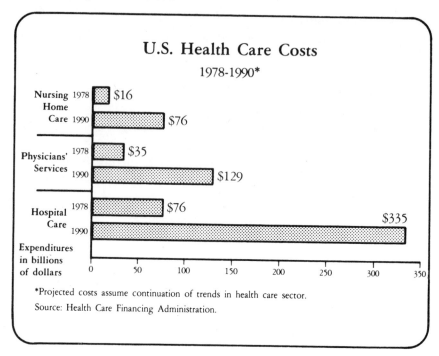

U.S. Health Care Costs
1978-1990*

Nursing Home Care 1978: $16
Nursing Home Care 1990: $76

Physicians' Services 1978: $35
Physicians' Services 1990: $129

Hospital Care 1978: $76
Hospital Care 1990: $335

Expenditures in billions of dollars: 0, 50, 100, 150, 200, 250, 300, 350

*Projected costs assume continuation of trends in health care sector.
Source: Health Care Financing Administration.

industry led to the enactment of a Medigap voluntary federal certification program in 1980. The new program set federal standards for Medigap policies.

Cost Control Strategies

Most remedies proposed for the problems of health-care costs have included one or both of two basic options for reducing expenditures. Louise Russell has defined these as "cost sharing" and the imposition of "budget limits."

Cost sharing is any method that makes individuals responsible for part or all of the costs of the medical services they receive. The amount an individual pays is linked to the quality and price of medical services provided, either directly through service fees or indirectly through insurance premiums. Cost sharing options are effectively built into Medicare in the form of deductible requirements and co-payments for hospital fees as well as supplementary medical insurance premiums for doctors' services.

However, the possibility of reducing medical costs in this way has raised difficult questions: How much should an individual be expected to pay? In what form should payments be made? What effects do cost-sharing schemes have upon access to medical services?

Critics of cost-sharing plans are concerned about their effect on the health of the elderly. A 1983 report of the National Council of Senior Citizens observed that cost sharing may prevent elderly people from receiving necessary medical care or impoverish them when they require hospitalization.

Setting budget limits, as defined by Russell, is a method of placing a limit on the amount paid for a package of medical services by Medicare, Medicaid or private health-insurance plans. The diagnosis-related groups (DRG) reimbursement system for Medicare, enacted into law in March 1983, uses a budget-limit approach to cost control, setting charges in advance for medical treatment.

Health maintenance organizations (HMOs) also provide a budget-limit approach to medical cost containment in that they offer a variety of medical services to members for a fixed annual fee.

Like an insurance company, an HMO pays for health care in return for a monthly premium. And like a doctor or hospital, it provides health care to those that enroll in the plan. However, because an HMO both pays for and provides health care, there is strong incentive on the part of HMO personnel to avoid unnecessary costs.

An HMO physician is unlikely to keep a patient in the hospital longer than necessary for adequate treatment. In addition, HMOs offer a preventive approach to health care, because they provide both routine health care and hospitalization.

The 1972 amendments to the Social Security Act gave those enrolled in the Medicare and Medicaid programs the option of joining an HMO. In 1973 Congress passed the Health Maintenance Organization Act, which offered federal assistance for establishing both non-profit and profit-making HMOs. That law also required businesses with over 25 employees to offer the option of membership in qualified HMOs in addition to regular insurance plans. The number of HMOs in the country rose from 30 in 1971 to 268 by mid-1982.

In 1983 Medicare reimbursed HMOs on a per capita basis for 95 percent of the cost of services. As of March 1981 approximately 2 percent of Medicare beneficiaries participated in an HMO plan, according to the Health Care Financing Administration.

HMOs have reduced health-care costs primarily by providing a cheaper alternative to hospital services. However, while they are effective in the communities where they exist, HMOs have yet to make a significant impact on the national health-care system. Only 5 percent of the U.S. population was enrolled in this type of program in 1983.

Implementing Reforms

Underlying the free-market theory, upon which the Reagan administration's policies were based, was an assumption that Americans received more health services, and at a higher cost, than they needed. Neither patients nor doctors and hospitals were cost conscious because the full cost of medical care was shielded by private or public health insurance.

In addition, proponents of the theory regarded the method by which doctors and hospitals traditionally had been paid (*after* providing their services) as a temptation to prescribe more and more treatment.

In support of the theory, they cited the accelerating pace of health-care costs after the enactment of Medicaid and Medicare in 1965. Private health-insurance plans also proliferated during this period. A competitive system, its advocates said, would reverse these trends. Providers and patients would become more interested in controlling expenses to keep rates down.

The free-market plan, however, appeared to ignore another factor in the health-care industry — the rapid growth of investor-owned hospital chains and other profit-making medical services. In 1982 they accounted for a quarter of total U.S. spending on personal health, according to Dr. Arnold S. Relman, editor of *The New England Journal of Medicine.*

As in any business, the goal of those organizations was to foster the use of their services, not to restrict them, Relman said. Prices might decline to encourage consumption, but "the fact remains that they are in business to increase their total sales," he stated.

Features of a Free-Market System. To create a competitive health-care system, its proponents contended in 1983 that four major changes — combining budget-limit and cost-sharing features — were needed in the national health-care system:

● The cancellation of regulations, such as health planning, peer review, federal antitrust laws and minimum standards for prepaid health plans (HMOs), in order to stimulate the growth of new types of health-care organizations.

● The further encouragement of competing medical plans by the provision of a variety of such plans to workers.

● The conversion of Medicare and Medicaid to a voucher system, allowing recipients to spend a predetermined level of their health dollars where they wish.

● The requirement of more cost sharing on the part of insured patients in both private plans and the public programs. Schweiker suggested in a January 1983 speech that Medicare patients might at some point have to pay as much as several thousand dollars a year themselves in deductibles. Individual payments would be made more proportionate to benefits through higher taxes and premiums for generous health-insurance plans and tax-free rebates for less costly coverage.

Preset Charges under Medicare. The major Reagan proposal that won approval in Congress in March 1983 was the prospective reimbursement system for Medicare that set medical charges in advance.

Under the new system, Medicare would pay hospitals on the basis of preset prices for each of 467 specific medical conditions or combinations of illnesses that had been categorized as distinct diagnosis-related groups (DRGs). Rates would be derived from existing Medicare data and then updated to reflect hospital cost increases during fiscal 1983-85. These rates would be the same for all patients in a given DRG regardless of the particular services used or duration of hospital stay.

The plan had been inspired by state-level prototypes. According to IHPP, there were prospective rate-setting programs in 12 states as of April 1983. However, the state programs differed widely in the composition of medical service packages for which rates were set. There were additional differences in the calculation of rates as well as in the inclusion of carriers (Medicaid and private health-insurance plans) in each reimbursement plan. Seven state programs applied prospective reimbursement only to Medicaid. Five states applied their prospective reimbursement systems to all types of payors.

The state programs appeared to succeed in controlling hospital costs. Russell in 1983 cited a CBO study in which per capita hospital expenses in seven rate-setting states rose by 11 percent annually compared to 14 percent in all other states between 1976 and 1981. New Jersey implemented a prospective reimbursement system based on DRGs in 1980 that served as the primary model for Medicare's new reimbursement system in 1983.

Advocates of the DRG reimbursement system, including major segments of the hospital industry, said it would pave the way for a radical restructuring of Medicare. However, the so-called "payment-by-diagno-

Preset Charges for Medical Care. . .

A September 1980 issue of *State Health Notes* — a publication of the government funded Intergovernmental Health Policy Project (IHPP) — outlined the experimental prospective-reimbursement system for hospitals that served a model for the Medicare reimbursement plan approved by Congress in 1983.

The plan was implemented in New Jersey in 1980 and incorporated the diagnosis-related groups (DRGs) concept. The basic idea behind DRGs was that patients with similar medical conditions should receive similiar hospital treatments at comparable costs, unaffected by regional practices or institutional quirks.

For this reimbursement system to work, DRGs had to have the following characteristics: 1) each DRG had to be medically distinct from other DRGs; 2) the groups had to be statistically valid; and 3) the number of groups had to be manageable. The DRG concept was developed at Yale University by a team of medical researchers. The New Jersey experiment developed 383 diagnosis-related groups.

Reimbursement rates under the New Jersey DRGs were derived from three types of data: the patient's medical discharge abstract summarizing the illness, treatment received and length of hospital stay; the bill corresponding to the abstract; and financial and statistical reports from the hospital. The DRG rate had two components: direct costs, which were an adjusted average of a patient's total hospital costs, and a percentage mark-up to cover indirect costs. The adjusted average, also called the "incentive

sis" plan applied only to Medicare.

Opponents of the DRG legislation, including the American Association of Retired Persons and the Health Insurance Association of America, a trade association of health and life insurance companies, said that to be effective, the DRG-based prepayment system also should apply to Medicaid and private health-insurance plans. Otherwise, hospitals might shift the cost of providing services for Medicare recipients to private insurance companies or other programs, which then would pass on the higher charges to their subscribers through higher premiums. "Until we can solve the cost-shifting problem," said John Kittredge, executive vice president of The Prudential Insurance Co., "we will not

. . .The New Jersey DRG Experiment

standard," took into account regional differences in wage rates and differences in service costs between teaching and nonteaching hospitals.

There were two significant differences between the New Jersey DRG system and the DRG system to be used under Medicare. The New Jersey DRG plan applied to all payors — patients, insurance companies, the federal government — and it required that the cost of uncompensated care be spread among all payors. The federal system applied only to Medicare.

Proponents of the New Jersey system pointed out that it was sensitive to the costs of treating different illnesses. For example, cancer patients usually cost more to treat than maternity patients. Reimbursement was made equitable among hospitals by basing the level of payment on the particular "case mix" — the variety of illnesses — treated by each hospital. The system, according to proponents, encouraged efficiency and cost consciousness. It also provided hospital administrators with management tools to evaluate performance.

The New Jersey program also drew criticism for a variety of shortcomings. The system required complex and detailed reporting. Some questioned the wisdom of implementing the system statewide without adequate analysis of its impact on hospitals, patients, Medicaid and insurance companies. Because the DRG system was based on average costs, some patient groups could be under- or overcharged for certain medical services. For example, Blue Cross patients, on the average, had a shorter hospital stay than Medicare patients.

have cost containment." Government officials in 1983 were not sure exactly how much money would be saved by implementing the DRG reimbursement system. However, they did not expect it to solve Medicare's mounting financial problems.

Even if fully realized, the savings would delay the projected depletion of the HI trust fund by only one year, until 1988 instead of 1987, according to a February 1983 CBO report.

Proposals Deferred/Problems Wait. A number of health strategies promoted by the administration in 1983 were opposed by Congress and various health lobbying groups.

One of the more controversial administration plans to curb health costs would have involved the taxing of insurance premiums. Health-insurance plans often are provided as a fringe benefit of employment. Employers who pay all or part of a worker's health-insurance premiums can deduct them as a business expense, and employees do not pay income or payroll taxes on them. The administration contended that under such circumstances, neither employees nor employers had much incentive to hold down medical costs.

Reagan administration officials thus proposed to put a ceiling on the amount of the insurance premium paid by employers that would continue to receive preferential tax treatment. The administration plan would have required employees to pay taxes on employer contributions to their health-insurance premiums if the cost exceeded $175 a month for family coverage or $70 a month for individual coverage. The administration maintained this would encourage employees to ask employers for less comprehensive insurance coverage or alternative coverage.

The average annual revenue from each of the 16.5 million Americans paying taxable premiums would be about $140, according to administration estimates.

The Reagan plan faced stiff resistance from organized labor. The AFL-CIO Executive Council said the proposed tax would constitute "an unprecedented intrusion in collective bargaining" that would "turn back the clock on decades of progress by workers in winning comprehensive health care protection." Organized labor was not alone in its opposition. Representatives of about 50 groups, ranging from the Chamber of Commerce of the United States and the National Association of Manufacturers to the National Council of Senior Citizens, met in January 1983 with Sen. Bob Packwood, R-Ore., a member of the Joint Taxation Committee, to voice their opposition to the plan. Packwood assured them that there was "no constituency" for the tax scheme and predicted it would not happen. He agreed that such a plan would erode the health of working Americans and set a precedent for taxes on other fringe benefits.

Another Reagan administration proposal would have replaced the Medicare program with a voucher system. Each enrollee would be given vouchers, worth roughly the projected per capita Medicare expenditure for a given year, to purchase his own health-insurance coverage at the best rate he could find. Enrollees would receive a bonus if they purchased a plan costing less than the face value of the vouchers; they would have to pay extra if they wanted a more expensive plan.

Vouchers would work like a fringe benefit in that the employer would pay the same insurance contribution regardless of which medical plan the employee adopted. The voucher plan would assure a basic level of care within a specified cost, and the beneficiary would be free to choose the plan that best met his or her preferences and needs.

The theory behind the voucher system plan was that, given the choice, beneficiaries would purchase the most cost efficient plan, encouraging competing insurers to keep their costs down. However, the voucher system had never been tried on a broad scale.

Interest in the voucher plan waned with enactment of the 1983 Social Security law, perhaps because it did not apply to institutions beyond those already covered by the DRG reimbursement system. As Prudential's John Kittredge pointed out with regard to DRGs, a financial solution for one part of the U.S. health-care system could mean new costs in another.

A major challenge to policy makers of the future would thus be to stem the flow of health-cost burdens from one group of institutions to another. And just as some objected to certain reforms proposed and enacted in 1983 for being insufficiently comprehensive, others believed that unless health policy was formulated for all segments of the population and not just the elderly, cost containment would not be achieved.

The 1974 Employee Retirement Income Security Act (ERISA) divided responsibility for regulating private pension plans among three government agencies.

Chapter 4

PRIVATE PENSION PLANS AND
RETIREMENT INCOME

Private pension plans are an important part of America's complex system of providing retirement benefits to workers. Although the private pension plan system has come to be viewed generally as a supplement to Social Security, its scope nonetheless is vast. In 1980 private pension plans accounted for 20 percent of total retirement benefit payments. Although less than half of the private labor force is covered by the system, according to latest government estimates, that includes between 36 million and 43 million workers, with well over nine million persons actually receiving benefits. Total private pension payments in 1981 amounted to more than $35 billion (by comparison, Social Security payments amounted to more than $171 billion). Altogether, there are about 500,000 private pension plans, with assets totaling between $500 billion and more than $650 billion, according to various estimates.

Private pension plans vary widely in terms of structure, scope of coverage, financing and benefit provisions. However, most participating workers belong to a broad category of plans financed by employer contributions and providing "defined benefits." Those plans promise a specific benefit at retirement or spell out a method of determining such benefits, usually taking into account age, years of service and salary. Defined-benefit plans are regulated by the 1974 Employee Retirement Income Security Act (ERISA), which established criteria for funding and participation and established a government insurance corporation to guarantee benefits. About 27.7 million workers participate in approximately 132,399 defined-benefit plans, according to 1982 Department of Labor estimates.

A much smaller number of private sector employees, about 14.8 million, are members of "defined-contribution" plans. Under those plans the amount of the contribution, either by the employer alone or jointly by employer and employee, usually is fixed as a percentage of the employee's current salary, with the benefit determined by the amount of contribution. Money market, profit sharing and savings and thrift plans are among the more common kinds of defined-contribution plans. For tax treatment purposes the Internal Revenue Service (IRS) has classified defined-contribution plans into 13 types. Altogether, there are about 319,362 such plans. *(Glossary, p. 118)*

The task of sorting through the variety of private pension arrangements — determining how to resolve conflicts, make the system more equitable, improve benefits and establish sound funding principles — is a difficult one. But by the late 1970s and early 1980s most observers and pension experts agreed that tackling the problem was becoming urgent.

When ERISA was signed on Labor Day 1974, after more than a decade of study, the act was hailed as a landmark piece of legislation. The bill for the first time gave the federal government a role in regulating private pension plans. While the new law did not require companies to provide pensions to their employees, those that did or were planning to had to adhere to the federal rules.

But, like any complex law, ERISA proved difficult to implement. At the same time, the continuing lack of a cohesive national retirement income policy raised a number of more complex, broader concerns. Among the most pressing were the lack of pension coverage for many workers in the private sector, low benefits for many workers who were covered and excessive benefits for a minority of others, inequitable treatment of women, inadequate provision for survivors of plan beneficiaries, insufficient funding of many plans and the erosion of benefits due to inflation.

Recognizing that the problems needed comprehensive study, President Jimmy Carter named an 11-member Presidential Commission on Pension Policy to review the nation's retirement, survivor and disability programs and to analyze the role of private pensions now and in the future. In announcing the commission's establishment in July 1978, the White House cited the enormous growth in the number and cost of pension systems. "Although almost 20 percent of the population receives benefits from public or private programs, no comprehensive, coordinated national pension policy has ever existed," it said. "While some systems reflect careful planning, the general lack of coordination among them has caused both costly duplication and gaps between programs that leave some participants with no coverage at all."

Among the disturbing statistics cited by the administration and analysts was the fact that only one elderly person out of four ever receives any private pension. Most lose out because their employer does not have a pension plan, they do not stay in a job long enough, or their benefits are reduced or even eliminated by integration with Social Security benefits.

Even receiving a pension is not a guarantee of economic security in old age because four out of 10 pensioners receive benefits of less than $200 a month. Tax-deferred retirement savings programs are geared toward upper-income workers. Only 1 percent of workers earning under $15,000 a year have retirement savings, while more than half of workers with incomes over $50,000 have special tax-deferred Individual Retirement Accounts (IRAs). *(IRAs and Keoghs, Chapter 6)*

During the 1980s and 1990s, retirement income problems will be magnified as the number of people age 65 and over increases dramatically in proportion to the younger people entering the work force. After the turn of the century, the demographic shift will become even more striking as the baby-boom generation of the 1940s and 1950s retires. And pension payments will need to be stretched out as a greater number of retirees live longer and longer in retirement. A report prepared in 1982 for the American Council of Life Insurance by ICF Inc., an economic consulting firm, projected that between 1979 and 2004 the proportion of Americans age 65 to 69 drawing private employer pensions would increase from 53 percent to 85 percent for married couples and from 33 to 66 percent for unmarried persons.

"If you look at the year 2000, the demographic changes will scare you to death," said Raymond Schmitt, a pension expert with the Library of Congress. "We've got to start developing a policy now."

"Just as people must plan for retirement 20 to 30 years ahead of time, so must the country," said C. Peter McCollough, chairman of the President's Commission on Pension Policy and chief executive officer of Xerox Corp., in presenting the panel's findings to the House Select Committee on Aging Feb. 26, 1981. Warning that Social Security was overburdened, he noted that the "uneven distribution of retirement savings and employee [private] pensions among American workers ... has prevented these two types of retirement income from becoming reliable income sources. ... This uneven distribution of employee retirement income benefits has already caused serious difficulties and promises to create further problems in the future."

Development of the Private Pension System

The beginning of pensions in the United States can be traced to a plan established by the American Express Co. in 1875 that provided pensions for permanently disabled workers with 20 years of continuous service. The railroad industry soon followed suit, and coverage reached 50 percent of railway workers by World War I. Nonetheless, the private pension idea caught on very slowly until well into the 20th century. *(Chronology of pension plan development, Appendix, p. 223)*

The early rationale behind pension plans was that they were rewards by employers to workers for "long and faithful service." The plans usually had no hard-and-fast provisions for funding and were viewed as discretionary. There were probably fewer than 10 private pension plans in operation in the United States by the turn of the century. Then in the early 1900s labor unions began to show an interest in providing a retirement income for their elderly members.

Originally, union plans were completely financed by the members. Organized labor approved of this arrangement because it viewed employer-financed plans as a threat to unions' independence. In 1927, however, the American Federation of Labor reversed its position and began to push for pension plans supported by employer contributions. Today, the majority of private plan participants are covered by systems in which the employer contributes the full amount.

By 1929, 397 of the 421 plans established since 1875 were still in operation. They covered approximately 3.7 million employees, about 10 percent of the non-agricultural labor force. As business activity declined sharply during the Depression, many companies as well as unions began to cut back on pension plans. At the same time, with the unemployment rolls standing at 13 million persons, there was growing awareness of the need for worker income protection. That concern culminated in enactment of the Social Security Act in 1935. *(Details, see history of Social Security, Chapter 1.)*

Postwar Growth of Plans

Private pensions soon rebounded, spreading dramatically in the early 1940s. The economic upswing brought about by World War II, wartime wage controls, changes in tax laws favorable to pension plans and union activism all spurred pension growth. Many companies decided to grant their employees pensions in lieu of salary increases, because the government was controlling wages. Wartime profits were used to fund the plans. Between September 1942 and December 1944, the Internal Revenue Service approved 4,208 pension plans as qualifying for favorable tax treatment, compared with 1,360 plans approved during the entire preceding 12-year period.

The number of private pension plans continued to grow during the postwar years. By 1949-50 there were more than 12,000 private pensions in existence covering about 9.8 million employees, or 15.5 percent of all workers in private industry.

In a 1972 study for the Library of Congress, Schmitt reported that from 1925 through 1949 retirement plans evolved from relatively simple arrangements into the more complicated plans of today. Three events of that period shaped the future development and role of retirement plans, he wrote. "These events were the granting of tax exemption to private pension plans, the passage of the Social Security Act, and the refusal of the U.S. Supreme Court to review an earlier decision that required employers to bargain with labor unions on the issue of pensions. . . ." Besides ruling that pensions were a bargainable labor issue, the courts in 1948-50 held that during the term of an applicable labor agreement no employer could install, alter or terminate a pension plan for organized workers without the union's consent.

Federal tax incentives to qualified plans were a powerful force behind the growth of defined-benefit and profit-sharing plans. Until 1950 almost all private pension funds had been placed in standard life insurance, fixed-interest investments, such as government bonds and mortgages. That year, however, General Motors, under the chairmanship of Charles E. Wilson, began to operate its pension plan as an "investment trust" and became one of the first companies to invest pension funds in the stock market. The plan was quickly and widely copied; within a year, 8,000 new pension plans had been written along those lines. By 1960 an estimated 18.7 million employees, representing 21.6 percent of the work force, were enrolled in private pension plans. Participation had grown to 30.3 million by 1975.

The number of beneficiaries also grew considerably. In 1950 only 450,000 workers were retired on private pensions. By 1975 pension plans were making payments to more than 7 million workers.

Contributions totaled $29.9 billion in 1975, including $27.6 billion by employers and $2.3 billion employees. Benefit payments were estimated to total $14.8 billion in 1975, almost double the 1970 figure. Assets, which had been estimated at $137 billion in 1970, reached $213 billion five years later.

Statistics compiled by the President's Commission on Pension Policy showed that in 1978 non-married individuals received an average of $2,919 annually from private pensions, compared to $7,700 for beneficiaries of military retirement. The average Social Security payment was about $2,800.

Reforms in the 1950s and 1960s

Along with the postwar growth of pension funds came complaints of mismanagement and even occasional embezzlement by fund managers. In an attempt to correct such abuses, Congress in 1958 passed the Welfare and Pension Plans Disclosure Act, requiring fund managers to report on their operations annually. But the information obtained under the act was limited, and there was no provision for audits or enforcement.

Moreover, the act did not deal with other issues that were surfacing. Many plans contained no provisions guaranteeing participants receipt of their benefits (vesting), and eligible recipients also were not protected when improperly capitalized pension funds went bankrupt.

Convinced that disclosure alone was insufficient to ensure proper management of funds, Congress in 1962 authorized the Labor Department to investigate the truthfulness of reports and made it a federal crime to steal from employee welfare and pension funds. However, the new law still did not provide for the vesting of pension rights or protect eligible recipients if a fund went bankrupt.

Pension plans again came under public scrutiny two years later when Studebaker-Packard went out of business, leaving thousands of automotive workers jobless at its South Bend, Ind., plant. Only employees aged 60 and older with 10 years of service received full pension benefits. Younger but fully vested workers were given only 15 percent of the retirement benefits they had earned under the Studebaker plan. Many other employees received nothing.

A committee that President John F. Kennedy had appointed in 1962 to study pension funds recommended in January 1965 that federal regulations be instituted to require fuller funding of private plans and minimum vesting standards. A comprehensive pension reform bill was introduced in the Senate in 1967 but lay dormant. From 1969 through 1972, however, extensive hearings were held in both the Senate and House. As witnesses voiced their grievances, public interest in pension reform picked up and constituent mail increased in Congress. Pension reform was becoming a popular issue, particularly after Ralph Nader and other consumer advocates publicized pension plan abuses.

Meanwhile, the administration of Richard Nixon in 1971 proposed minimum vesting standards for private pension plans. The Senate Labor and Public Welfare Committee in 1972 reported a bill providing for the first comprehensive regulation of private pension plans and requiring vesting of rights after eight years of service. But the measure died in a jurisdictional dispute between two committees. Then in 1974, after seven years of effort, Congress passed legislation establishing minimum standards to ensure a worker the right to at least part of his pension.

Lobbying on the measure was intensive. The bill was supported by the AFL-CIO, the United Auto Workers and the United Steelworkers of America. The U.S. Chamber of Commerce led many business interests in opposition to some of the proposed standards. The American Medical Association and the American Bankers Association successfully pushed for an increase in the maximum tax-deductible amount to be taken by self-employed persons for their retirement.

The Employee Retirement Income Security Act

Born out of frustration over pension benefits lost due to bankruptcies, mergers and occasionally unscrupulous employers, the Employee Retirement Income Security Act, or ERISA, aimed to correct basic shortcomings in the private pension system. The law (PL 93-406) did not require all private employers to establish pension plans. But it did require employers who were operating or intended to set up plans to meet minimum federal standards.

ERISA's Safeguards

The major provisions of ERISA covered vesting, funding, fiduciary standards, insurance against plan terminations, tax changes and new reporting and disclosure regulations. In general, the act required employers to contribute to their pension plans at an orderly rate so that adequate funds would be on hand to meet pension obligations. Plans in existence before 1974 had to amortize their unfunded liabilities in no more than 40 years. Those created after 1974 had 30 years. (Immediate

Pension Terminology . . .

A pension plan in its simplest terms is a legal promise by an employer to pay a periodic benefit (usually for the life of the retiree) to employees who meet the requirements set forth in the plan. Both the benefits payable to the employees and the contributions required of the employer must be determinable by actuarial principles. The means of funding of a pension plan must assure that there are adequate resources or assets available to pay benefits as employees retire.

Defined-benefit plans — These are the most common type of private plans. In defined-benefit plans, the benefit level and structure are defined in advance (according to such factors as flat amounts or salary, length of service and age). The employer must contribute necessary amounts to ensure that these benefits will be paid at retirement. The employees' benefits are not affected by any investment gain or loss on the plan's assets.

Defined-contribution plans — Plans in which an employer pays a specific amount (usually a percentage of wages) into the fund. Benefits are a function of the amount contributed per employee, age, sex and normal retirement age under the plan (usually age 65), the earnings of the fund and its actuarial experience. Profit sharing, money purchase or stock bonus plans fall into this category. Defined-contribution plans are less common than defined-benefit plans and are also designated by the 1974 Employee Retirement Income Security Act as *individual account plans.*

Contributory plans — These require contributions by the employee as well as the employer. Usually, employee contributions remain the employee's property (that is, the employees are vested). In non-contributory plans, the employer makes all the contributions in behalf of the employee. Contributory plans comprise only 6 percent of private pension plans in the United States.

Insured funds — Plans in which the contributions essentially purchase an annuity guaranteed by an insurance carrier who does the investing and bears some of the risks associated with fluctuations on the return of the investments.

Self-insured plans — Those that bear the above risk themselves (through trustees), although they may entrust the investment function to the trust department of a bank or seek investment advice from the outside.

Integrated plans — Also called "excess" or "offset" plans, these are private plans whose contributions are related to Social Security. Under

. . . In the Private Sector

excess plans, the employer provides contributions or benefits only on earnings in excess of some level specified by the plan, above the Social Security taxable wage base. Under offset plans, a more common way of integrating Social Security and private pension benefits, the pension provided by the employer may be reduced in response to increases in Social Security benefits.

Multi-employer plans — Plans established and maintained through collective bargaining agreements between unions and a number of companies in an industry.

Fiduciary or trustee standards — Standards establishing regulations for proper management of pension funds.

Miminum-funding standards — Standards requiring pension managers to put aside enough money (adequate actuarial reserves) to ensure payment of workers' pensions.

Vesting — Guarantees a worker the right to at least some benefits after he has completed the term of service required by his pension plan, regardless of whether he continues to work for the sponsoring company until retirement.

Past-service liabilities — Claims against the fund by persons who were covered when the plan began for work performed before the plan began, even though no contributions were made on their behalf during that time. Such retroactive coverage is common.

Plan-termination insurance — Protection of workers' benefits if companies go bankrupt or have underfunded their pension plans. The program is administered by the Pension Benefit Guaranty Corporation (PBGC).

Portability — The degree to which a worker may transfer his pension benefit credits from one employer to another. Multi-employer plans are more likely to have this provision than single-employer plans.

Roll-over — An arrangement enabling a worker who moves to a company whose plan has a reciprocal agreement with his previous employer's plan to transfer (roll-over) the vested portion of his first employer's contributions.

Unfunded total liabilities — They represent the extent to which all future pension liabilities exceed a pension fund's assets.

Unfunded vested liabilities — These are the difference between a plan's assets and the vested portion of pensions.

funding would have required huge contributions and might have led employers to terminate plans to avoid bankruptcy.)

The act established complex reporting requirements (which, critics noted, could discourage companies from establishing pension plans), involving reports filed with the Labor Department and the Treasury (Internal Revenue Service) and information made available to plan participants and beneficiaries. A company must notify the IRS when a participating employee leaves; the IRS then sends that information to the Social Security Administration. Thus, when the worker retires and files for Social Security, he will also be informed of the vested benefit rights he has accumulated from various jobs.

In addition, ERISA laid out rules to be followed by pension fund trustees and managers. Those rules spelled out their fiduciary duties and were designed to guard against conflicts of interest, self-dealing and unwise investments. Pension plan fiduciaries were required to manage the fund assets "solely in the interests of the plan's participants and beneficiaries." They must invest the assets in such a way "as to minimize the risk of large losses, unless under the circumstances it is clearly prudent not to do so." No more than 10 percent of the assets were allowed to be in securities or real property of the employer.

Establishment of the PBGC

One of Congress' central concerns was to guarantee benefits of private pension plans. To accomplish this, a provision of ERISA set up a self-financing Pension Benefit Guaranty Corporation (PBGC) in the Labor Department to provide insurance for employees' benefits if their pension plans were terminated or inadequate to provide full benefits. Pension plans are required to pay a premium for pension termination insurance. The agency can attach up to 30 percent of a company's net worth to cover pension fund losses, and it also acts as a counselor to persons who wish to set up their own retirement savings plans. The agency is headed by a board of directors consisting of the secretaries of labor, Treasury and commerce. The labor secretary is permanent chairman. The board appoints the executive director.

PBGC insures only defined-benefit pension plans, that is, plans that promise a specific benefit determinable in advance and payable to plan participants when they retire. The plan may express the benefit either as a stated dollar amount, or through a formula used to calculate the benefit (age, salary and years of service are typical elements).

Information and Fraud Protection

Suppose a worker accepts a job with a company after listening to a union agent extol the virtues of the company-union pension plan. Later the worker finds out that the union agent "puffed up" key aspects of the plan. Does the worker have any legal recourse?

The answer is yes, no or maybe, depending upon who is talking. The Employment Retirement Income Security Act of 1974 (ERISA) does provide grounds for lawsuits if a plan participant or beneficiary believes the trustees have violated their responsibilities by making questionable investments or by misrepresenting important aspects of their pension plans.

But ERISA's protections apply only to participants in the pension plan and beneficiaries, not to potential workers. The law's safeguards also do not apply to representations by a non-fiduciary (often a union business agent or company personnel director) even if made to a participant or beneficiary.

Some members of Congress have supported legislation that would make it unlawful for any person knowingly to misrepresent the terms and conditions of a pension plan, its financial status, or the status under the plan of any employee, participant or beneficiary. The proposal would allow a worker or pensioner who claimed misrepresentation to file civil charges.

But critics have questioned the practicality of the proposal. Many union business agents, labor spokesmen argued, are not skilled in the ins and outs of pensions. Thus, they might easily wind up misrepresenting potential pension benefits unintentionally. "How do you distinguish between an honest mistake and a calculated lie, especially when it may be one person's word against another?" asked one pension specialist.

However, supporters of a fraud provision believe it is necessary in light of a 1979 Supreme Court ruling that an individual's interest in a compulsory pension plan to which he did not contribute was not a "security" like stocks or bonds, protected by the anti-fraud and disclosure requirements of federal securities laws. In ruling on the case (*International Brotherhood of Teamsters v. Daniel*), the court reversed an appeals court ruling that would have imposed a multitude of new regulations and information requirements on private pension plans.

The agency does not insure defined-contribution plans, or individual-account plans, which provide for each participant's benefits based solely on the amount contributed to his account. Other plans generally not covered by ERISA and the PBGC include those sponsored by professional service employees with fewer than 26 employees (such as physicians, attorneys, public accountants and performing artists), church groups and government employees.

Individual retirement accounts, known as IRAs, were a major innovation of ERISA. The act allows individuals to set aside for retirement money that is exempt from federal income taxes until it is drawn out during retirement. At that time the taxpayer presumably is in a lower tax bracket. In 1981 eligibility for establishing IRAs was expanded to cover almost all persons. *(Details, Chapter 6, IRAs and Keoghs.)*

New Requirements for Vesting Rights

A key section of the 1974 act established principles for determining how long an employee must work to qualify for at least some portion of a pension (called vesting). Before passage of the law, most private pension plans did provide a certain degree of vesting, but age and service requirements varied considerably. In 1974 only about 20 percent of private plans provided full vesting rights after 10 years of service.

"The largest number of complaints against private pensions came from individuals who had worked for as much as 30 years for a company but still had not qualified for a pension," Peter Henle and Raymond Schmitt wrote in their 1974 legislative history of the act. "The law attempts to remedy such conditions by setting forth specific standards for vesting, the non-forfeitable right to a pension. Once the individual becomes vested he is entitled to a pension at a retirement age based on his service, even though at that time he may no longer be working under the plan."

Under the 1974 law, employers may choose one of three vesting formulas:

● Gradual vesting in which a worker becomes entitled to 25 percent of his or her accrued pension rights after five years of service, another 5 percent each year during the next five years and an additional 10 percent each year during the following years. This means that the benefits must be fully vested after 15 years of recognized service.

● The "Rule of 45" whereby an employee whose age and number of service years total 45 is 50 percent vested after five years of service.

● Full vesting after 10 years of service. This is the simplest standard and calls for no degree of vesting short of 10 years of service. Most companies offering plans have opted for this formula.

In *The Fundamentals of Private Pensions,* Dan M. McGill pointed out that the graded vesting system (that is, provision of a certain percentage of accrued benefits when minimum requirements are met) "avoids anomalous treatment of employees terminating just before and just after meeting the requirements for full vesting and minimizes the danger that an employee will be discharged just before his pension benefits vest. . . . On the other hand, graded vesting is more difficult to explain to plan participants. . . . It is also more difficult to administer."

All three vesting options require that an employee be at least 50 percent vested after 10 years of service and 100 percent vested after 15 years of service. (A "year of service" is defined as a 12-month period during which the employee works at least 1,000 hours.) The law mandates that all employees with at least one year of service be eligible at age 25 to participate in company pension plans. (Prior to ERISA, it was not uncommon for a plan to require a minimum age of 30 or 35 for participation.)

The act also contains a general prohibition against the use of maximum age limits. However, defined-benefit plans are allowed to exclude from participation any employee who is within five years of normal retirement age when first employed. (The "normal retirement age" is the earliest age specified in a plan at which eligible participants are permitted to retire with full benefits. However, most plans permit retirement before the normal retirement age with partial benefits, usually subject to age and service restrictions, and many allow employees to defer retirement beyond normal retirement age.) Previous service with the same employer counts as service toward vesting, although breaks in service may affect the amount of benefits accrued or forfeited. Seasonal and maritime workers are covered by special regulations established by the Labor Department.

Employers may not discriminate in favor of corporate officers or other highly paid executives, and the government may impose strict standards if an employer shows a pattern of firing workers before they become vested. However, there were loopholes in the discrimination law that could allow employers to favor higher salaried workers. Congress tightened the law in 1982. *(See p. 135.)*

Once vested, benefits cannot be forfeited except if the participant dies before retirement (and if there is no provision for joint and survivor annuities).

Criticism and Confusion

During ERISA's first few years the new regulations caused considerable confusion among companies, pension plan managers, employees and retirees. Most pre-ERISA plans had to be modified, and others were terminated. Administrative costs, as well as those involved in vesting and amortizing unfunded liabilities, were high, but under ERISA many of the worst plans were weeded out.

Soon after the 1974 law's enactment, private industry began to complain of the paper work and administrative costs it generated and of government slowness in drawing up guidelines and regulations. "We're having a number of firms with pension plans come to us and ask to serve as trustees," Randy Mott, president of First Tennessee Investment Management Inc., said in 1976. "These executives no longer want the responsibility and liability connected with pension fund trustees." (Under ERISA provisions, fiduciaries can be sued for mishandling pension money.)

The promoters of pension regulation were disappointed that the act did not include a strong portability provision to permit workers to carry their accrued pension rights as they moved from one job to another. "While this legislation does remove some of the restrictions hampering full freedom of employment, it does not entirely free an employee from the need to stay at one place of employment for a certain length of time . . . in order to have his credits vested," Rep. Michael J. Harrington, D-Mass. (1969-79), complained at the time of the act's passage.

As mentioned, ERISA did not require employers to offer pension plans. Nor did it deal with the adequacy of pension benefits, particularly in the face of inflationary pressures. Its thrust was to require those employers who offered plans to meet specified minimum standards.

The act "by no means begins to solve our retirement income problem," said Karen Ferguson, director of the Pension Rights Center, a private Washington, D.C.-based operation. "Pension coverage is still only provided for one-half the private work force. The only realistic supplement called for is the IRA [Individual Retirement Account]." Noting that the law was designed to correct the "outrageous horror stories" of the past, Ferguson predicted that many expectations would not be fulfilled.

Divided Responsibilities

ERISA divided jurisdiction over pension regulation between the Treasury (through the IRS) and the Department of Labor. In addition, it established the Pension Benefit Guaranty Corporation (PBGC) to ensure payment of benefits if pension plans ended, lacking the money to handle all claims.

That structure, reflecting the compromise of a jurisdictional dispute among congressional committees, was criticized from the outset. By 1978 a House pension task force reported that "the task force's files and hearing record is replete with illustrations of the adverse effects of multiple administration — complexity, confusion, delay, duplication and waste, inefficiency, lack of a comprehensive and coordinated policy, etc."

Employers, pension plan managers, bankers, accountants, actuaries, consultants and others who make up the "pension industry" also continued to complain bitterly about ERISA's paperwork requirements.

"In simple terms, ERISA — probably as much or more than any other federal law — is virtually synonymous with bureaucratic confusion . . . unnecessary paperwork and understandable frustration," commented Rep. Frank Horton, R-N.Y. A March 1979 study sponsored by the Business Roundtable, an association of corporate chief executives, investigated a sample of 48 companies of varying size and found that compliance with ERISA requirements had cost them $61 million in incremental operating and administrative costs.

The Carter administration took some steps to remedy the situation, persuading Congress in 1978 to accept a reorganization plan designed to clarify the roles of the IRS and Labor Department and ending overlapping responsibilities. Proposing the reorganization, President Carter said ERISA's administrative provisions "have resulted in bureaucratic confusion and have been justifiably criticized by employer and unions alike." The "biggest problem," Carter said, was "overlapping jurisdictional authority." His plan transferred most of the administrative functions to the Treasury from the Labor Department.

Some members of Congress favored establishing a single agency to take over all of the ERISA-related duties of the Labor Department and PBGC and many of the duties of the IRS. In its final report, issued in February 1981, the President's Commission on Pension Policy also recommended that a single agency administer the ERISA regulations.

Congressional jurisdiction over retirement programs was equally fragmented. According to the General Accounting Office (GAO), 119 committees and subcommittees had policy-making, fiscal or oversight responsibilities for income security programs (including Social Security and public programs).

Impact of ERISA on Plan Terminations

During the debate over enacting ERISA, some opponents argued that federal regulation would discourage employers from forming pension plans. On the surface at least, statistics appeared to support those contentions.

In the decade before ERISA was enacted, from 13 to 16 new plans qualified for tax exemptions for every plan that terminated, according to IRS data. (For a pension plan to be covered by PBGC it must be qualified for favorable tax treatment under the Internal Revenue Code. Tax qualification does not mean a plan is actually operating, but it is considered one of the best measurements available of pension plan formation.)

But in 1975, the first year after passage of ERISA, the ratio of qualified new plans to terminated plans dropped substantially. Fewer than four new plans were established for each plan that ended. In 1976 the ratio decreased even more; only 1.6 plans were established for every plan that was terminated. The hard numbers broke down this way that year: 25,820 plans were begun, but 15,859 plans were ended.

Those statistics produced outcries from Capitol Hill. More than 100 members of Congress asked the GAO to study ERISA's effects on pension plans, especially those set up by small businesses. The agency's findings were a surprise. In an April 1979 report the GAO concluded that "economic and other factors played a more significant role [than ERISA] in decisions to terminate pension plans."

Arguing that the "adverse effect indicated by the number of terminations is misleading," the GAO concluded:

● Where plan sponsors called ERISA a major reason for termination, the plans generally did not meet the act's minimum participation and vesting requirements designed to make sure that employees would benefit from a pension plan without having to meet unreasonable age and years-worked requirements.

● Participants of terminated plans had received or were to receive almost all of their vested benefits under existing plan provisions.

● About 41 percent of the companies that terminated pension plans continued pension coverage for their employees through new or other existing plans. Other employees had an opportunity to continue pension coverage by starting IRAs.

The GAO found that ERISA in many cases had increased the costs of pension plan formation and operation. And it agreed that the law had caused unnecessary paperwork burdens. Essentially what ERISA did, the GAO report indicated, was to "prune away" those pension plans that would not have been able to deliver on their promises. "ERISA got rid of a lot of bad plans that led to the law in the first place," said Schmitt of the Library of Congress.

Following the GAO report, the ratio of newly qualified to terminated defined-benefit private plans increased almost back to pre-ERISA days. In 1979 40,664 new plans were established, while only 3,335 plans were terminated. However, in 1982 the PBGC received about 6,000 termination notices, while 28,189 plans received preliminary qualification by the IRS. As of the end of 1982, the PBGC had received about 47,000 plan-termination notices since the program began.

The Economics of Private Pension Funds

The growth of private pension funds in the three and a half decades since the end of World War II has been explosive. The Department of Labor has estimated that private pension assets will approach $3 trillion by 1995. As pension assets accumulate and become an increasingly major source of long-term capital, questions have arisen concerning the use and control of those assets. Corporations, labor and professional money managers have different answers to those questions, which have wide ramifications for economic and social policy.

ERISA's fiduciary code, which spells out rules and regulations to be followed in handling pension fund assets, has come under repeated criticism. Some think the code is too restrictive and has prohibited financial transactions that would benefit a pension fund's growth.

The 1974 act established a process by which exemptions could be obtained from the law's "prohibited transactions" section, which sets out what kinds of financial and business dealings were prohibited (primarily those involving parties-in-interest). But employers, labor unions and others, including some members of Congress, have complained that the exemption process takes too much time. As a result, proposals have been offered to revise some of the fiduciary rules to make it easier for pension plans to conduct business with others who have an interest in the pension plan.

Concentration of Control

The capital market in the United States is dominated by so-called "institutional investors," a large portion of them pension fund managers (fund trustees). Most pension money is in the hands of between 1,000 and 1,500 large corporate pension funds. Most of these funds give investment responsibility to outside professional asset managers, the majority of which are major banks. The existence of large stock holdings by pension funds, combined with the concentration of some holdings in particular companies, has raised questions about the impact of pension fund capital on the economy as a whole. Although the funds are by far the largest source of capital for American industry, there is growing concern that their management may be having a restrictive, rather than expansive, effect on the economy.

Under terms of the 1974 ERISA, fund managers must adhere to the so-called "prudent man" rule, requiring them to make solid and generally conservative investments, based on risk-return criteria "so as to minimize the risk of large losses." In the capital market this translates into investments based on past performance rather than future profit potential. Many observers believe such a practice favors investment in older (and sometimes troubled) industrial giants rather than in smaller, technologically innovative ventures.

Plan Management and Investment

The role of private pension plans as financial intermediaries was examined by Alicia H. Munnell, vice president of the Federal Reserve Bank of Boston and a senior staff member at Brookings Institution, in her book *The Economics of Private Pensions* (1982). Pension plans usually are funded either through a group annuity contract offered by a life insurance company, or through a trust established by the employer and administered by a bank or trust company (in 1980, 63 percent of pension assets were held in trusts). Trustees do not always have sole discretion over investments and may seek the advice of an investment counselor. Moreover, the employer himself may retain decision-making authority. Multi-employer plans are administered by a joint union-employer trusteeship.

According to government estimates, pension funds will own more than half the corporate stock in the United States by 1995. A study by the Federal Reserve Board and the American Council of Life Insurance showed that about 50 percent of non-insured pension trust funds in 1980 were held in stocks, 25 percent in corporate and other bonds, 11 percent in government securities and 1.6 percent in mortgages. In contrast, only 39.5 percent of pension funds held by life insurance companies was invested in corporate bonds; mortgage holdings amounted to 28 percent, stocks 11.2 percent and government securities 3.6 percent. Pension fund assets accounted for a rising share of life insurance companies' total reserves — 37.8 percent of total life insurance assets in 1980, compared with less than 7 percent of the total in 1946.

The average annual rate of return of pension investments during 1970-80 was 4.9 percent for pension trusts and 6.5 percent for insurance companies, according to statistics compiled by Munnell. However, that average did not indicate the wide swings in pension trusts' performance resulting from their large stock market investments. Variations on returns during that period ranged as low as -21.3 percent and as high as 24.4 percent. In contrast, life insurance investments registered consistently positive returns (life insurance companies generally have been more conservative than pension trusts in making investments, due partly to state laws and industry standards). "Because contributions considerably exceed benefits, pensions experience a net inflow of funds every year that provides a cushion to weather swings," Munnell noted. "Pension funds, therefore, have the unique opportunity to profit from the higher return on equities." However, as mentioned previously, ERISA regulations that require contributions to be adjusted to investment experience have dampened risk-taking.

In recent years, the issue of "social investment" has arisen with respect to private pension plans. Some observers have argued that pension managers should forgo some investment yield to further social objectives, such as investing in low-cost housing for retirees. By the same argument, pension managers should avoid "undesirable" investments, such as those in companies that violate government-established health or safety standards or firms conducting business in nations practicing racial discrimination. Moreover, since pension plan assets are deferred wages, participating employees should have a voice in determining investment decisions, it is argued. They might, for example, prefer an investment that brings construction activity to their locale to a higher-yield investment elsewhere. Union employees might object to investment in a non-unionized corporation.

However, ERISA regulations limit the discretion of pension managers, requiring that fiduciaries carry out their duties "solely in the interest of the participants and beneficiaries and ... for the exclusive purpose of providing benefits to participants and their beneficiaries; and defraying reasonable expenses of administering the plan."

Professional money managers argue that investment strategies based on something other than strictly financial decisions are risky. They have pointed to examples of corruption in union-managed pension funds and to instances of corporate executives using private pension funds to further company ends in illegal or quasi-legal ways. If the best return on the safest investment is not the paramount principle, the managers have said, there could be massive failures of thousands upon thousands of pension systems, with disastrous results for the country.

Addressing the social considerations of pension investments, Jeffrey Clayton, Labor Department administrator of pension and welfare benefit programs, testified in 1981, "ERISA already has a social purpose, that purpose is to assure that funds are available to pay the anticipated retirement and other benefits of plan participants and beneficiaries. . . . Our Nation's retirement system is too important and has too many financial problems of its own to expect it to subsidize special investments which cannot stand on their own merits. The pension fund is not for the use of the employer, nor is it for the use of the union [to further their own interests]."

In its September 1981 report on "Reforming Pension Plans," the Committee on Economic Development (CED) agreed with Clayton's observations. "We believe that the primary purpose of a pension plan investment is to provide the maximum return consistent with safety of principal for benefit of its participants. We do not believe that there should be any additional government mandate with regard to the social or political direction of pension investments," the CED concluded.

The issue of pension fund control is complex, and research and debate have barely begun in this area. The President's Commission on Pension Policy hinted at the struggle to come in its final report, declaring:

> The legal framework surrounding the determination of decision-making in this area is an issue for future debate. Specifically, it must be determined to what extent under present law the dictates of prudence allow fiduciaries to use non-traditional investment criteria. In addition, it must be determined who should have the right to determine investment decisions, or to vote the shares of corporations in which funds invest.

Funding Problems and the PBGC

Prior to enactment of ERISA, employers were not legally responsible for unfunded liabilities remaining after a plan had terminated, nor were they responsible for funding the so-called prior cost or past service liability. If a company terminated its plan, employees were guaranteed benefits only insofar as the assets in the pension fund were adequate. The passage of ERISA and the establishment of the Pension Benefit Guaranty Corporation led to substantial changes in pension plan funding.

The PBGC administers two pension protection programs (called "risk pools"):

● A plan-termination insurance program covering more than 28 million participants in about 110,000 single-employer, defined-benefit pension plans. (About 15 million others participate in defined-contribution or profit-sharing plans. Those plans are not covered by the PBGC because defined-contribution plans by definition are always fully funded.)

● A plan-insolvency insurance program covering about 8 million participants in about 2,000 multi-employer pension plans.

Under ERISA, companies must finance defined-benefit plans (the majority of plans) by paying "normal costs" each year and the amortization payment of so-called "supplemental costs" or past service benefit credits. In other words, those plans must pay annually for each year's current costs, but they may spread payments for past service credits and any benefit improvements over a 30-year period.

The PBGC will take over the payment of a participating plan's vested benefits, even if the plan terminates with insufficient assets. The agency can hold the employer liable for unfunded benefits up to an amount equal to 30 percent of the company's net worth.

Benefit Guarantees. The PBGC guarantees "basic benefits," including pension benefits beginning at normal retirement age, certain early retirement and disability benefits, and benefits for survivors of deceased plan participants. Not all benefits provided by a plan may be considered basic benefits. For example, health, welfare, severance or lay-off benefits are not covered by the PBGC.

Moreover, ERISA has established a maximum limit for PBGC guaranteed benefits, based on a formula contained in the act, adjusted periodically. For pension plans terminating in 1983, the maximum guaranteed amount for persons retiring at age 65 was $1,517.05 a month, or the average wage during an employee's highest five years of coverage, whichever was less. The guaranteed benefit is actuarially reduced for persons below age 65. If a plan has been amended within five years of termination to provide an increase in basic benefits, the increase may not be guaranteed in full.

Under the existing PBGC system, the well-funded plans essentially subsidize the underfunded plans or those that terminate. Some experts have advocated changes in the form of risk-related or variable premiums that would essentially "reward" companies for funding their plans and remove the inequities in the existing system. However, calculating risks is a complex undertaking and many experts have concluded that available data is insufficient to do this.

Termination Insurance. The plan-termination insurance program administered by the PBGC has itself suffered from lack of adequate funding. As of Sept. 30, 1982, the PBGC had a deficit of about $333 million, while its future obligations exceeded $3 billion. (The agency's assets include premiums collected from ongoing plans, investment income and assets acquired from terminated plans. The major portion of liabilities is the PBGC's reserve for guaranteed benefits, which is the current value of guaranteed benefits payable to participants of terminated plans.)

Benefit guarantees are financed by per capita assessments, taxes, or contributions on the individual plans. The per capita insurance premium for single employer plans was $2.60 in mid-1983, although the agency had requested that it be raised to $6.00. That still would be less than 1 percent of the annual cost to an employer of maintaining a pension plan. The premium for multi-employer plans was $1.40 per participant in 1983. Without the proposed premium increase, the agency estimated its deficit would amount to $448 million by 1986.

During its first 10 months of operation (in fiscal 1975), the PBGC was trustee of only three plans covering 400 participants. By fiscal 1981 it had taken over 659 plans covering 71,200 participants; another 126 potential plan trusteeships were pending. As trustee of plans with insufficient assets or terminated plans, the PBGC in fiscal 1981 made payments in the single-employer program to slightly more than 39,000 participants, for a total of $57 million. Payments were estimated to rise to $75 million in fiscal 1982. On the basis of experience, the agency expected that claims would increase at about $8 million a year in the future.

Bills that would raise the premiums on PBGC single-employer insurance and tighten regulations on terminating plans to prevent a company from passing on liabilities to a purchasing company or the

PBGC were introduced in 1981 and 1982 by Sen. Don Nickles, R-Okla., and Rep. John N. Erlenborn, R-Ill. Hearings were held on the legislation, but no action was taken during the 97th Congress. The bills were reintroduced in 1983, and sponsors predicted action would be forthcoming in view of the PBGC's growing financial troubles.

Adequacy of Pension Plan Funding

Despite enactment of ERISA, adequate funding of pension plans has remained a major cause of concern. According to a 1977 article in *Fortune* by A. F. Ehrbar, 10 of the top 100 companies in the list of the *Fortune* 500 had unfunded vested liabilities equal to one-third or more of their net worth. In seven of those cases, the liability was greater than the market value of the companies' shares.

In 1980, 86 of 6,000 publicly traded companies had unfunded liabilities in excess of 30 percent net worth, according to Standard & Poor's Compustat Services. If all of those corporations terminated their plans, the PBGC would have faced a liability of about $4 billion in 1980.

The financial well-being of pension funds depends in the last analysis on the state of the economy as a whole, of the stock market and of particular industries. The financially troubled Braniff International Airlines provides a concrete recent example of the relationship between pension funding and economic well-being. As a result of severe economic problems, the company's various pension plans (covering 9,500 employees) steadily deteriorated, beginning in 1980. The bankrupt airline owed $279 million in vested benefits in 1982 but had only $130 million in pension assets. The shortfall eventually will have to be assumed by the PBGC.

Even with a premium increase, funds available in the PBGC would not be sufficient to cover any large business failures or the record number of small- and medium-sized business shutdowns. (During the first three months of 1982, 36 businesses filed for bankruptcy every hour, for an annual rate of 75,000 businesses a year, according to reports by Dun & Bradstreet and *The Wall Street Journal*.)

Nonetheless, a number of analysts have concluded that in general the private pension system is well funded. A 1978 survey by Kenneth K. Keene and Sandra M. Kazinetz found that only 5.4 percent of 336 respondents had unfunded liabilities amounting to 30 percent or more of net worth. Almost 31 percent reported no unfunded liabilities, and 46 percent reported liabilities of less than 10 percent. A survey of 40 large companies in 10 major industries by BEA Associates Inc., an investment counseling firm, showed that the median company had vested benefits equal to 91.7 percent of pension assets, meaning that the typical company was fully funded on vested benefits at the end of 1980. And a 1981 survey by *Business Week* found that 100 large corporations had pension assets of $134 billion to offset liabilities of $123 billion.

A 1982 executive report by Johnson & Higgins concluded that pension plans were not a drain on company profits and generally were well funded. Nearly three-quarters of the 627 companies surveyed (among the largest firms) had completely funded plans.

The 1,000 largest pension funds increased their assets in 1982 by 20 percent, to $622 billion, according to *Pensions and Investment Age*. Employer contributions exceeded benefit payments by 30 percent. However, it is difficult to compare unfunded liabilities among companies because each plan uses its own actuarial statistics concerning future wage levels and the future earnings of the plan's investments.

The problems involved in funding private pensions have led a number of experts to conclude that a universal pension system should be established. Testifying before the House Select Committee on Aging June 7, 1982, Thomas Woodruff, former director of the President's Commission on Pension Policy, said, "We cannot raise the premium levels, we cannot improve the minimum funding standards, we cannot close the loopholes, because if we do that, companies will start terminating their plans.

"That is one of the dilemmas that we have with ERISA and the attempt to regulate a voluntary system. If you make the system work, people will stop funding them. They will terminate them. Then people will be left unprotected. So, we have to have a universal system."

"Whatever the case may be, some troublesome issues remain," Bruno Stein concluded in *Social Security and Pensions in Transition*. "Retirement systems, whether private or public, can only deliver from what the economy produces. There is no way in which the risk of economic fluctuations can be averted. The mechanisms that we have adopted can only shift the risks among different members of the community."

Private Pensions and Taxes

Finding ways to stimulate the formation of new private pension plans has the potential for prompting a major policy debate. Some critics, among them the Pension Rights Center, question the fairness of proposals that would give additional tax incentives subsidized by all taxpayers to a system that covers less than half the non-farm work force. Moreover, the tax-concession benefits from private plans accrue primarily to higher-paid workers in unionized industries.

Tax Advantages. Observers also have pointed out that private pension plans meeting the requirements set forth by ERISA and the Internal Revenue Code already enjoy considerable tax advantages; that is one reason many employers have been willing to establish plans. A company's contributions to pension plans generally are tax deductible. Earnings on business contributions held by pension trusts are not taxed, and employees do not pay taxes on their pension money until they receive the benefits at retirement, when they usually are in lower tax brackets.

Tax laws also have influenced the structure of the plans, encouraging the formation of plans financed almost entirely by employer contributions. To qualify for tax advantages, plans must meet certain coverage, vesting and participation criteria.

These advantages in turn have had an adverse impact on government revenues. According to Treasury estimates, the tax provisions for private pension plans amounted to a $14.7 billion revenue loss in 1981, an amount roughly 23 percent of estimated total private pension plan contributions for that year.

1982 Tax Law and Pensions. The Tax Equity and Fiscal Responsibility Act of 1982 (PL 97-248) made dramatic changes in the tax treatment of private pension plans. The act required many companies, particularly small businesses, to shift benefits from more highly paid employees to low- and moderate-income workers. "The idea is to make sure that more of the money that is being taken as tax deductions goes to more people," said Daniel Halperin, a professor at the Georgetown University Law Center and former assistant secretary of the Treasury under Carter.

Under existing law, if a company has a pension plan, the plan technically must include all employees. But because regulations allow employers to reduce their pension contributions to offset their contributions on earnings subject to the Social Security tax — wages up to $35,700 in 1983 — some companies make no pension contributions for their lower-paid employees.

The 1982 legislation established new regulations for "top heavy" companies, those where more than 60 percent of the accumulated benefits went to a limited number of top employees. In defined-benefit plans considered to be top-heavy, the company was required to make annual contributions for each employee so as to provide annual retirement benefits equal to at least 2 percent of the employee's salary multiplied by the number of years of employment. The amount does not have to exceed 20 percent of the employee's annual wages.

In defined-contribution plans that are considered top-heavy, the company must make annual contributions for each employee of not less than 3 percent of the employee's compensation, unless the contribution rate for key employees is lower than 3 percent. Other provisions of the 1982 act:

● Reduced the maximum employer annual contribution for each employee to a defined-contribution plan to $30,000 from $45,475, beginning in 1983. It retained an existing requirement that contributions not exceed 25 percent of an individual's compensation.

● Decreased the maximum limit on annual pension benefits for defined-benefit plans to $90,000 from $136,425, beginning in 1983.

● Froze those limits on benefits and contributions until 1986, at which point they would be adjusted for cost-of-living increases after 1984. (*For IRA and Keogh provisions of 1982 act, see Chapter 6.*)

Representatives of corporate pension plans objected strongly to the changes, arguing that they were costly (more than $2.5 billion, according to the American Society of Pension Actuaries) and would inhibit creation and expansion of pension plans, hurting all workers in the long run.

Some pension consultants predicted that owners of small companies might choose to close down their pension plans rather than increase the benefits. Those employees then would be more dependent on Social Security and their own savings when they retired.

"There were abuses, but the provisions in the [1982] bill are Draconian," said Jerry Facciani, president of the American Society of Pension Actuaries. "I see this bill chipping away at the private pension system. A lot of small companies will simply terminate their plans, and private pension coverage will shrink."

The tax advantages of a pension plan already were much less for small businesses than for larger corporations. Companies earning more than $100,000 enjoyed a tax rate of 46 percent. Hence for large firms in the 46 percent marginal tax bracket, every one dollar in pension fund contributions resulted in a 46-cent reduction in corporate tax payments. For small businesses the tax reduction was between 17 to 40 cents, depending on net earnings. (Another factor that discourages small businesses from offering private pension plans is that they frequently have small profit margins and operate in highly competitive economic conditions. The administrative costs involved in operating a plan are proportionately higher for them, while the smaller size of their plans' assets means that they cannot take advantage of many investments available to larger pension plans.)

Issues Affecting Plan Participants

By the late 1970s Congress was once again taking a closer look at the private pension plan system. Hailed as a legislative milestone when it was enacted, ERISA had fallen short of its sponsors' expectations.

Critics suggested that ERISA, with its complex array of reporting requirements and funding standards, had actually discouraged private employers from establishing new pension plans. "Seldom has a law on so dry and dull sounding a subject had more far-reaching effects, raised more serious points of law, or heated more emotions than ERISA," said Rep. J. J. Pickle, D-Texas, chairman of the House Ways and Means Social Security Subcommittee, expressing a view shared by many of his colleagues.

Even its most ardent supporters acknowledged that ERISA did not solve all of the ills of the private pension system. Some issues were ignored when ERISA was first debated. Others posed such difficult choices that they, too, were shunted aside until a later time. Implementation of the act also highlighted weaknesses that were not readily apparent in the late 1960s and early 1970s, most notably the financial hardships of some major multi-employer pension plans. (*Details, p. 147*)

Finally, few disagreed that the law itself created new problems that might require action by Congress.

A major issue confronting lawmakers, economists, pension plan managers and government officials in the 1980s was whether the plans provided adequate coverage and benefits. Other controversial questions concerned the relationship between Social Security and private pension plans, whether the plans encouraged early retirement and whether ERISA had adequately protected employees from losses of expected pension income due to inflation, job transfers, unexpected layoffs close to retirement and other factors.

Who Participates in Pension Plans?

"The most serious problem facing our retirement system today is the lack of pension coverage among private sector workers," concluded the President's Commission on Pension Policy. Only about 45 percent of the private work force participate in private pension plans, and only about half of those are vested.

Pension plan coverage varies widely by sex, age, race and industry. Workers who participate in private pension plans generally have higher incomes than those who do not: 73 percent of workers earning $25,000 or more are covered by pension plans, compared with 38 percent for those earning between $5,000 and $10,000 annually and 13 percent of workers earning less than $5,000. Non-participants tend to be concentrated in marginal industries. Approximately 79 percent of them work for companies that employ fewer than 100 workers, according to the President's Commission on Pension Policy. Those employers are in lower corporate tax brackets and therefore do not receive the same tax incentives for pension fund contributions as large employers. Nearly all (about 90 percent) of the non-covered workers do not belong to a union.

Persons under age 25 and over age 55 and part-time workers are less likely to be covered. (ERISA standards do not require participating pension plans to cover employees under age 25, workers within five years of normal retirement age, or men and women who are employed less than 1,000 hours a year.) Nonetheless, data compiled by the president's commission showed that 71 percent of the non-covered are "mainstream," full-time workers whose earnings place them in or near the middle of the U.S. income distribution. Fifty-nine percent of them are in the trade and service industries.

The likelihood that a worker will become vested depends in general on the same factors that influence whether he or she is covered in a pension plan. Transportation, mining and manufacturing are industries with high vesting rates. In those sectors, respectively, 51 percent, 48 percent and 43 percent of workers age 25-64 are vested. The self-employed and those in agriculture and the trade industry have the lowest proportion of workers with vested benefits (15 percent for each sector).

Minorities in particular face problems in accumulating pension benefits because of mobility, high unemployment rates and employment in jobs not covered by a pension plan.

Special Problems of Women

Women, who make up 43 percent of the total labor force, generally have lower rates of coverage than men because many are employed in

Private Pension Plan Coverage

Following is the percentage of all U.S. workers covered by a private pension plan by sex, age group and annual income as of 1979.

Sex and Age Group	Less than $5,000	$5,000-$10,000	$10,001-$15,000	$15,001-$25,000	$25,000 or More	Total
Male:						
Less than 20	4%	14%	17%	36%	47%	9%
20-24	12	25	40	57	44	34
25-34	16	39	56	70	68	58
35-44	21	37	59	73	74	63
45-54	26	41	61	72	74	64
55 or older	17	37	62	70	78	54
Subtotal	10%	33%	55%	70%	73%	53%
Female:						
Less than 20	2%	18%	31%	19%	NA	7%
20-24	9	31	49	57	49	29
25-34	13	44	66	69	76	46
35-44	19	45	71	73	84	48
45-54	21	50	71	84	93	52
55 or older	19	48	69	77	71	44
Subtotal	13%	41%	66%	69%	79%	46%
TOTAL	13%	38%	59%	71%	73%	48%

Source: President's Commission on Pension Policy/ICF, Inc., 1980. Analysis of U.S. Bureau of the Census, Current Population Survey, May 1979. These numbers include imputed values.

low-wage industries and in jobs with little or no employee pension coverage. The fact that many women have interrupted work patterns is also a factor in their low rate of pension coverage.

"Private pension plans are structured on the assumption of a continuous worker, in the same job for the whole of his or her adult life," said Anita Nelam, vice chairwoman of the National Women's Political Caucus in 1979. But she noted that women's work patterns frequently do not conform to that model. Even with the influx of women into the paid labor force, she said, female employees still are clustered in sales and service jobs, which traditionally do not offer pension plans. Women earn less than men, even in the same work, and promotions are more likely to go to men, so women are less able to save.

Moreover, she said, "Women are more likely than men to take time out for child rearing, to change jobs if their spouse is transferred and to work part-time or part-year because they still bear the major responsibilities for their families."

Not only is it often more difficult for women to participate in pension plans; their benefits also may be reduced because of their sex. That issue came before the Supreme Court in March 1983, when the justices heard arguments in the case of *Arizona Governing Committee for Tax Deferred Annuity and Deferred Compensation Plans v. Norris.* The case involved a public employer, but the outcome would have ramifications for some private pension plans as well. At issue was whether it was legal for insurance companies to pay smaller monthly annuities to retired women than to retired men simply because women as a group outlived men. Sex-differentiated annuities were a common feature of public pension plans and those of non-profit institutions such as universities and hospitals.

The suit against the plan was brought by Nathalie Norris, an employee of the Arizona Department of Economic Security. Norris was backed by the AFL-CIO, the Women's Rights Project of the American Civil Liberties Union and more than 20 other civil liberties and women's rights groups. The Reagan administration also supported the case. They argued that a ruling upholding differential payments would "perpetuate the second-class status of women workers by guaranteeing that, upon retirement, women will be relegated to a lower standard of living."

In arguing her case, Norris cited a 1978 Supreme Court decision (*City of Los Angeles v. Manhart*) in which the court ruled that an employer violated the ban on sex discrimination in Title VII of the 1964 Civil Rights by requiring women to pay more into a pension fund than men, just because women as a group lived longer and drew more out of the pension fund.

The same prohibition on unequal payments applied to unequal benefits, the Supreme Court ruled July 6, 1983, in a 5-4 decision in favor of Norris. Federal law requires employees to be treated as individuals rather than as members of a group, Justice Thurgood Marshall wrote for the court. "Even a true generalization about a class cannot justify class-based treatment" under the law, he said. The decision would allow the continued use of separate actuarial tables for men and women in establishing an overall group plan, but not for distributing individual benefits. Also, in a separate 5-4 ruling, the court said the decision would apply only to future contributions and benefits and would not be retroactive.

The decision was expected to give impetus to bills introduced in Congress that would bar insurers from adjusting premiums or payments on the basis of sex. The bills, part of a larger package known as the Economic Equity Act, would require companies to increase the benefits of current retirees if their contracts provided for lower benefits because of sex-based tables.

Despite intense opposition from insurers, the measures were expected to be approved at least by House and Senate committees in 1983 because of strong support on the panels. One of the insurance industry's objections to the bills was based on cost. The American Academy of Actuaries estimated that equalizing pension programs alone would cost about $2.5 billion a year (the Labor Department estimated the cost at $1.7 billion).

Another issue of concern to women in particular was the treatment of pensions in cases of divorce. Women's groups and other organizations supported a proposal (included in a bill sponsored by Senate Finance Committee Chairman Robert Dole, R-Kan.) that would make pensions a legitimate property right in divorce cases, with the courts empowered to split the proceeds between employee and spouse. Women gained a notable victory in 1981 when the New Jersey Supreme Court ruled that, based on the premise that rights acquired during a marriage should be included in the division of property, a pension could be divided between man and wife at the time of divorce even though benefits were not payable until later.

The court also ruled that other property equal to the wife's share in the pension could be handed over by her spouse. The President's Commission on Pension Policy in 1981 recommended that pensions be defined as property and thus divisible. In cases of divorce, the exact division of the pension benefits would be left up to the discretion of the courts.

A related issue concerned a provision of ERISA that protects against court assignment of pension benefits. The provision had come in conflict with state court rulings directing that pensions be used to provide for divorced women and their children. Legal affairs observers said several court decisions had made it clear a pensioner could not escape his obligations of support, but it was uncertain, they said, whether a pension plan itself could be required to redirect a pensioner's benefits to his or her spouse under ERISA.

Costs of Benefits: The Inflation Dilemma

Unlike Social Security and federal employee plans, private pensions rarely are fully indexed to make automatic adjustments for inflation, although a handful may provide indexing with a cap of 3 to 4 percent. Some employers periodically raised benefits for those already retired to help offset inflation, but that decision was exclusively in the hands of the employer. A Banker's Trust Company survey issued in 1980 found that only nine of 291 companies studied had automatic annual adjustments based on the consumer price index (CPI). The survey found that 70 percent of the plans of 325 large companies provided some cost-of-living adjustment to some or all of their beneficiaries. However, most did so only occasionally and the common amount was 2 or 3 percent.

Some pension plans subject to collective bargaining between unions and employers have included cost-of-living escalators, but that has been the exception rather than the rule.

Defined-contribution pension plans and IRAs are exposed to exceptional risks as the purchasing power of dollars contributed early in a plan is reduced. Since most defined-benefit plans are based in part on a participant's highest five-year average salary, those plans are more likely to compensate for inflation to some degree. Workers who change jobs frequently feel the cut of inflation even more sharply due to the lack of indexing benefits to compensate for the period between the time they stop working for a company and retirement.

In briefing papers, the staff of the President's Commission on Pension Policy outlined the dilemma inflation posed for the private pension system. Requiring private plan benefits to be adjusted for inflation would be costly at a time when the plans still were absorbing cost increases mandated by ERISA requirements, the commission briefing papers noted. The staff cited an estimate by one actuarial consulting firm that pension plan costs would be increased at least 50 percent if the plans provided post-retirement cost-of-living increases and inflation rose at an annual rate of 5 percent.

Such a cost increase, the staff said, without some offsetting relief might cause many employers to terminate plans or stop increasing benefits for active workers covered under the plans.

In its final report, the commission called on the Bureau of Labor Statistics to develop a separate cost-of-living index to be used in adjusting retirement income. The existing system, tied to the CPI, it has been argued, may overstate the expenses of the retired. The CPI, for example, includes a factor for mortgage payments. But many elderly people have either paid off their mortgages or have owned their homes so long that the interest rates are low. Retirees also probably spend less on household furnishing, food, clothing, transportation and other items included in the CPI. The commission recommended that participants at least be given the choice of taking reduced benefits initially on retirement in return for subsequent cost-of-living increases.

"The failure of private plans to provide meaningful benefits in an inflationary environment has created a vacuum," Munnell concluded. "Either private plans must improve their benefits or political pressure will develop for government action. This action may take the form of mandatory cost-of-living adjustments or, perhaps, an expansion of Social Security. Without indexing, the role of private pensions in the provision of retirement income can be expected to decline in the future."

Age and Retirement Benefits

A little more than one-half of all employed Americans work in jobs that require them to retire at a specified age. The typical retirement age for workers in private industry is 65 (for federal, state and local employees, it is about 70; the mandatory retirement age was abolished for many federal workers in 1978). Although surveys have indicated that about two-fifths of those who are within one year of retirement would rather continue working, the average age of retirement in the United States has been sharply decreasing. Statistics compiled by W. Kip Vicusi in *Welfare of the Elderly* provided evidence of this trend. In 1900, 68.3 percent of males aged 65 and over were employed; by 1960 the percentage had shrunk to 30.5 percent, and by 1980 it stood at 19.1 percent. Among the primary reasons cited for early retirement are poor health, lack of job opportunities and availability of retirement income.

The decline in the retirement age has continued despite congressional passage in 1978 of legislation making mandatory retirement illegal prior to age 70 (however, 65 still is generally accepted as normal retirement age). The impact of that act has been difficult to assess. However, one explosive issue has involved attempts to increase eligibility age for private pension and Social Security benefits. A number of observers have suggested a phase-in of changes in age eligibility for retirement benefits to protect persons close to retirement or already retired. Among them was the President's Commission on Pension Policy, which recommended that the age at which an employee would be able to collect full pension benefits be raised to 68. (At the same time, it did not propose any changes in the law barring mandatory retirement before age 70, although the Reagan administration wanted to eliminate mandatory retirement.) (*Increasing retirement age, see Chapter 2, p. 70.*)

Congressional passage in March 1983 of legislation gradually raising the retirement age for receiving full Social Security benefits from 65 to 67 by the year 2027 could lead private pension plans to do likewise. "For Social Security to move off that fixed figure of 65 is a tremendous catalyst," said Gary A. Pines, senior vice president of Meidinger Inc., a consulting company. "It may take a period of time for things to change in the private pension sector, but there is going to be a natural process of moving back the age."

The change in retirement age could have a two-pronged impact on businesses with private pension plans. On the one hand, it could raise a company's salary expenditures because businesses would have to retain higher-paid employees longer; but, on the other hand, it could reduce the amount of retirement benefits paid out.

The effect of the trend toward early retirement on pension benefits also varies. Under many pension plans, retirement benefits paid out before age 65 are actuarially reduced to offset the lengthened time of retirement. However, other plans, particularly government plans, do not reduce benefits for early retirement.

Under many plans, retirement age is linked to 10 years of service or participation in the plan, but some companies require a much longer service period if the minimum retirement age for receiving full benefits is under 65. For example, a plan may allow retirement at age 55, but the employee must have 30 years of service. Many plans have multiple "normal retirement ages," depending on the years of employment required and the age of the participant when he enters the plan. However, some plans allow early retirement only in the event of permanent and total disability.

A survey of 107 private pension plan sponsors by Connecticut General Life Insurance Co. found that 72 percent felt older workers should be encouraged to remain in their jobs; 69 percent already were providing incentives to do so by giving pension credit for employment after age 65. Nonetheless, statistics compiled by the House Select Committee on Aging showed that only 19 percent of males and 8 percent of females remained in the workforce after age 65 in 1982.

Survivor Benefits

Private pension plan benefit targets vary widely. Large companies typically have higher benefit objectives than do small companies. Benefits generally are higher in high-wage companies and in those that are organized by unions. Industries such as manufacturing provide higher benefit targets than programs in service industries.

In addition to the dollar amount of the benefits and the age of the beneficiary at the time the benefit becomes payable in full, an essential component of a pension plan is the form of the annuity under which the benefit is payable. A plan may express benefits in terms of a single life annuity (normal retirement benefit) or a joint and survivor annuity. Each type has a number of variations. The simplest form of life annuity provides periodic monthly income payments that continue as long as the beneficiary lives. This type of annuity usually provides the largest dollar amount of benefits.

The joint and survivor annuity is designed primarily to provide retirement income to husbands and wives. It provides payments as long as either spouse lives but may be reduced if either annuitant dies.

Prior to enactment of ERISA, many large companies provided for post-retirement death benefits, but smaller businesses were reluctant to offer them because of the cost. Under ERISA, defined-benefit plans must offer joint and survivor options to a participant when he or she reaches earliest retirement age. Defined-benefit plans must automatically provide 50 percent of benefits to a surviving spouse who has been married at least one year before the employee's retirement. However, the employee is free to waive this provision to receive a higher monthly benefit in his own lifetime.

Under existing law, employee pensions often are terminated upon the death of the worker. If a worker dies before the earliest retirement age, ERISA does not require the plan to give his or her pension to the survivor, even if the worker was vested. In many cases, the survivor is left high and dry. However, other forms of income, such as life insurance, often are available to surviving spouses. Survivor-protection gaps in pension plans affect women almost exclusively; 72 percent of the elderly poor are women.

Support has grown in Congress to expand pension benefits for spouses of deceased or divorced workers. A proposal introduced by Sen. Dole would require written notarized consent of both participant and spouse to waive the survivor annuity option. *(Divorce issue above, p. 141.)*

According to the Labor Department, most pension plans appear to be absorbing the cost of survivor benefits. But some analysts said the costs of extending the survivor benefit might be too much for plans to incur alone. Because women are assumed to live longer than men, pension plans often have taken this into consideration in calculating the monthly benefit for female survivors by lowering the benefit below what it would be if men lived as long as women. If the courts should rule that this is illegal sex discrimination, then the cost of providing the joint and survivor's option are likely to rise.

The President's Commission on Pension Policy recommended that survivor benefits be more fully protected, arguing that pensions, as deferred wages, should be considered a benefit earned jointly by both spouses. If an employee dies before age 55, the panel recommended survivor protection "either through the pension plan or through life insurance." The commission said that both spouses should be required to consent before forgoing the survivor annuity benefits option in favor of a normal retirement benefit. However, a number of groups, among them the Citizens' Commission on Pension Policy, recommended that survivors automatically receive a pension if a worker dies after earning one.

Private Pensions and Social Security

Almost all workers covered by private pension plans also are covered by Social Security, with its increasing benefit levels. The situation has led many observers to conclude that an integration of private pension plans and Social Security is urgent. Compounding that urgency is the fact that private coverage in large part extends to the more powerful and well-paid workers (usually unionized), while less organized and economically less powerful employees must rely primarily on Social Security for their retirement income. Moreover, private pension plans are heavily subsidized through favorable tax treatment. These factors have raised questions concerning the equity of the system.

ERISA allows plans to be integrated with Social Security if the targeted or defined benefit is composed of both pension and Social Security benefits. Thus, a rise in Social Security taxes can be offset by a reduction in private pension contributions. However, once they retire, beneficiaries are protected from a decrease in their pensions if Social Security benefits should rise.

President Ronald Reagan's 1981 proposal (later abandoned in the face of opposition) to reduce Social Security benefits would have forced many companies to increase their pension contributions. That was because most pension plans based the size of employees' benefits on the amount they received from Social Security. Under contractural arrangements, if Social Security benefits were reduced, the companies would have to make up for at least part of the difference through their own funds.

A 1980 Bankers Trust Co. study of 325 large corporations found that more than half had "offset integrated" pension plans that took Social Security benefits into account when pension payments were calculated. Donald Grubbs of George B. Buck Consulting Actuaries Inc. said the "overwhelming majority" of small pension plans were also of the "offset integrated" type.

"Those who retire on pensions plus Social Security constitute a retirement elite," wrote Bruno Stein in *Social Security and Pensions in Transition*. "Many of the rest retire on benefits that result in a serious decline in their previous standards of living. This is because individual savings rates, over a lifetime, would have to be impossibly high to enable this group to acquire the equivalent of pension benefits."

In light of that situation, many experts have suggested instituting a mandatory minimum private pension system, such as those in force in France, Britain, Switzerland and the Netherlands. "If it is a social goal that the workers without pension coverage should receive better retirement benefits, and if further expansion of Social Security is undesirable, then some form of minimum mandatory coverage may be indicated," wrote Stein. But, he cautioned, "it would, however, present economic problems to the industries involved, since they are predominantly in the low-wage, labor-intensive and competitive sectors."

The Special Problems of Multi-Employer Plans

About 2,000 multi-employer private pension plans provide retirement benefits to eight million Americans in industries such as trucking, coal mining, construction, food retailing and entertainment. Those plans confront many of the same problems and issues faced by single-employer plans. But multi-employer plans, negotiated in collective bargaining between unions and a number of companies in an industry, have other difficulties as well. First of all, their viability is dependent on the economic health of an entire industry, which, in turn, may be adversely affected by changing consumer habits and technology.

For example, permanent press clothing has caused hard times for dry cleaners. Technological advances have made certain printing trades obsolete. Preference for air, rather than water, transportation has almost eliminated passenger ships. For those and other industries faced with a shrinking active workforce and a large number of retirees, pension plans have been strapped to come up with the money to make good on benefits promised to workers years ago.

The structure of multi-employer plans compounds their problems: like most single-employer plans, they are defined-benefit plans in which employers promise levels of future benefits to workers but are not required to set aside money for the benefits on a dollar-for-dollar basis. Actuaries estimate how much money will be needed, and when, based on various assumptions about expected worker service with the company. But those assumptions do not include the prospect of the industry going into economic decline.

Coverage Under PBGC

Like single-employer defined-benefit plans, multi-employer plans are guaranteed by the Pension Benefit Guaranty Corporation and subject to its and ERISA's regulations. When Congress established the PBGC, it required most single-employer pension plans to be insured immediately. The legislators did not, however, make insurance mandatory for multi-employer plans, largely because it was thought that the plans would be able to cover their potential liabilities on their own because risks and costs were shared among large numbers of employers. Congress did give the PBGC discretionary authority to insure multi-employer plans in case of an emergency. The discretionary authority expired July 1, 1978, at which time insurance was to become mandatory.

But the assumptions made about multi-employer plans proved to be wrong. Whole industries, rather than single employers, increasingly were facing economic hardships.

Initially, many companies participating in multi-employer plans felt they would never be covered by the PBGC regulations because the insurance provisions applied only to defined-benefit plans. Traditionally, multi-employer plans had been considered to be defined-contribution plans because unions and management bargained only over the amount that the company was to give to the pension plan for each worker.

In 1978, however, the Supreme Court upheld a lower court ruling that multi-employer plans also were defined-benefit plans and thus subject to ERISA insurance provisions.

Plans Face Financial Collapse

At about the same time, the ERISA insurance provisions applying to multi-employer plans were scheduled to go into effect. Congress quickly realized, however, that application of the insurance provisions to those plans could lead to disaster. The 1974 law prohibited pension plans from reducing benefits to recipients even when the plans, or the participating employers, faced financial difficulties. A number of multi-employer plans were in weak financial condition, in part because they were in declining industries. As the funding base for the plans shrank, there was increased incentive for individual employers to get out of the plans. That left the remaining employers, and the PBGC, with responsibility for paying benefits. As a result, it was feared that most employers would abandon the plans, letting them go bankrupt. Then the PBGC would be stuck with providing benefits to their current and future retirees.

A September 1977 study by the PBGC showed that about 40 multi-employer plans, covering about 385,000 workers, were on the verge of financial collapse. The total unfunded liabilities — liabilities that the PBGC eventually could wind up assuming — amounted to some $350 million.

The study also found that another 200 plans covering nearly 1.2 million workers faced growing financial hardships. Officials estimated a potential liability of another $3.5 billion over the next decade.

Alarmed by the prospect of a massive bill for private pension benefits, Congress delayed mandatory insurance for multi-employer plans for one more year, until July 1, 1979, thereby preventing the plans from dumping their pension liabilities on the federal government. (The PBGC meanwhile used its discretionary authority to take over some small plans, such as those covering millinery workers.)

In April 1979 the PBGC sent an 18-page report to Congress, recommending a "tightening all around." The recommendations included reducing the level of benefits the agency would guarantee, providing insolvent pension plans with direct federal loans and raising employer contributions to PBGC's multi-employer fund.

"The nub of it is there are some big losses sitting out there and nobody knows how to pay for them," said Grubbs.

1980 Law: Revision of Coverage

By the end of the decade a consensus between business and labor had formed on the need for some long-term solution to the withdrawal problem. The result was passage, with virtually no opposition, of legislation intended to discourage companies from pulling out of multi-employer plans by making them responsible for their share of future benefits to enrolled workers. Withdrawing employers were made liable for the amount by which future benefits already promised to workers exceeded funds accumulated by the plan.

The new law (PL 96-364) established the following minimum level of benefits for terminated programs insured by the PBGC: 100 percent of the first $5 in monthly benefits earned by a participant for each year of service, and 75 percent of the next $15 in monthly benefits. The 75 percent guarantee level would be reduced to 65 percent for plans that did not meet certain funding requirements set by the PBGC. The PBGC was required to guarantee the full level of benefits for persons who already were receiving retirement benefits, or who would reach normal retirement age by July 29, 1983.

The bill established standards governing the merger or transfer of multi-employer plans; allowed financially troubled plans to reorganize; and required increased contributions from employer members of such a plan.

"We have learned since 1974 that because of economic and demographic pressures in certain industries, employers and active workers in some multi-employer plans are paying an intolerably high price to maintain the often meager benefits of growing numbers of retirees," said House Management and Labor Relations Subcommittee Chairman Frank Thompson Jr., D-N.J. (1955-81), during a May 22, 1980, debate on the legislation.

Employer Complaints

The purpose of the 1980 law was to crack down on employers who were trying to avoid their responsibilities to their employees' retirement. But critics charged it snared scores of innocent business owners in its net as well. Businesses that ceased employing union workers and making contributions to their pension funds — whether because of owner retirement, a shift to non-union workers or a decline in business — were saddled with big bills from the pension funds.

Groups such as the American Trucking Associations said the law made it nearly impossible for their members to sell, merge or move their companies, or even to borrow money, because of potential pension liabilities. In a number of cases, companies were faced with pension bills far greater than their net worth.

Examples brought out during March 1982 hearings by the Senate Labor Subcommittee included:

● Johnson Motor Lines, a North Carolina trucking company. Bought by another firm, Republic Industries Inc., for $16.8 million in 1979, Johnson ceased operations in 1980. Shortly after closing Johnson, Republic Industries received bills from five Teamster union pension funds totaling $19.7 million — far more than the company's net worth.

● Sierra Pacific Industries, a California lumber company. The company had paid into the Lumber Industry Pension Fund on behalf of workers represented by the Lumber and Sawmill Workers' Union. In 1980, however, the workers decided to decertify the union as their bargaining agent. That forced the company to withdraw from the pension fund, with an estimated liability of $748,000.

● T.I.M.E.-DC, a Texas trucking company. Hit by hard times, the company sought in 1981 to reduce its operating losses by merging with another firm, East Texas Motor Freight Lines. The merger, which would have allowed the combined company to make a profit, was all set until the question of pensions came up. The deal fell through when the companies realized they faced a potential withdrawal liability of $30 million.

The chief complaint of business critics of the 1980 law — and the main legal argument in the dozens of court cases challenging the law — was that it imposed a financial responsibility to which companies never agreed. After bargaining for years with unions over their pension plan contributions, the companies found that they were potentially liable for much more.

Multi-employer pension plans are controlled by trustees, half of whom are appointed by management and half by labor. In many instances, however, it is the union side that effectively controls the plan. In any case, one employer usually could do little to affect trustee decisions on benefits. So when pension trustees unwisely promise future benefits far in excess of the plan's resources, it is the employers who are liable for the bill.

Because of the 1980 law, employer trustees began to adopt a more militant stance toward benefit increases, according to Dan Knise of the Associated General Contractors. "It's the trustees who cause the problem. Labor historically has tried to increase benefits. Now employer trustees are fighting hard to make sure that plans are fully funded," he said.

Safeguards Against Plan Collapse

Groups representing truckers and contractors supported a bill sponsored by Senate Labor Committee Chairman Orrin G. Hatch, R-Utah, that would take virtually all multi-employer plans out of the ERISA insurance system. Employers no longer would have to pay withdrawal liabilities. Plans no longer would be insured against bankruptcy.

Critics of Hatch's bill — most notably Robert A. Georgine of the AFL-CIO-affiliated National Coordinating Committee for Multi-employer Plans — said that it would leave millions of workers without protection against the collapse of their pension plans. "Tragically, under this bill, the burden of risk is shifted so that it falls solely upon the participants and beneficiaries of multi-employer plans — and they are the parties who can least afford to bear the burden," Georgine said.

Most multi-employer plans were financially stable, argued AGC's Knise.

"It could be that most are in good shape," said Stephen Bruce of the Pension Rights Center. "But it only takes one plan to go under to produce a crisis."

The threat of a possible collapse bothered business groups, worried that a plan bankruptcy could lead to further federal involvement in pensions. "Many groups in the business community are apprehensive about what a plan failure would do to their efforts to reduce the ERISA regulatory system," said Michael Romig of the U.S. Chamber of Commerce.

Meanwhile, as of the end of 1982 more than 100 suits had been brought against provisions of the 1980 law that could force withdrawing companies to pay at least part of the future benefits to which their employees and other participants in the plan were entitled. Some pension funds contended the law made unionized companies reluctant to join the plans. Employers contended that, although they agreed to participate in a pension fund, they never bargained with unions over the responsibility to pay any specific retirement benefits. That responsibility belonged to the fund, they argued.

In a suit filed by trustees of Teamsters union Local 705's pension fund and some employer trade groups, a Chicago federal judge on May 17, 1982, upheld the constitutionality of the 1980 law. Conceding that "withdrawal liability can be harsh and onerous," Judge Susan Getzendanner nonetheless said there was no evidence "that the 'mere enactment' of [the law] was unconstitutional." She concluded that "Congress acted rationally in making its basic decision" to put employees' interests ahead of those of employers.

Major business organizations were sympathetic with the problems experienced by companies under the 1980 multi-employer law. But they were not prepared to go so far as the Hatch bill provisions that would remove all multi-employer plans from the insurance protections created by ERISA.

Proposals for Reform

Legislative changes in the landmark 1974 ERISA law, as it applied to single-employer pension plans, appeared to have a good chance of passage early in the 97th Congress. But the push in 1982 to weaken the multi-employer pension law complicated greatly the campaign by large corporations to loosen provisions of ERISA that applied to their own pension plans. They wanted to free the hands of plan managers to make a wider variety of investments with pension funds.

In contrast to the controversy surrounding the multi-employer issue, there was widespread congressional support for revisions of the law as applied to single employers. Among the relatively non-controversial changes were those that would remove some of the act's strict reporting and disclosure requirements. In addition, bills were introduced in the 97th Congress and again in 1983 that would crack down on companies attempting to avoid their responsibilities by turning their pension costs over to the PBGC.

ERISA's prohibition on certain business transactions by pension plans was the chief target of the coalition of large corporate plans that lobbied for reforms in ERISA as applied to the single-employer plans. One measure that was proposed in 1982 would have removed the existing prohibitions. Instead, it would have established a new standard that trustees make sure their investments provide an adequate return to the plan, regardless of whom the investments involved. The Reagan administration, however, opposed the proposal. Labor Secretary Raymond J. Donovan said it would hamper his department's efforts to prevent illegal transactions that hurt pension recipients.

The department instead in December 1982 proposed new regulations that would allow pension fund managers to invest in ventures in which their clients had an interest without requiring prior Labor Department approval. "There are literally thousands" of "harmless situations" that were prohibited by law unless a specific exemption was granted, said Clayton, administrator of the department's pension office. As an example, he cited the fact that a union pension fund could not invest in a shopping center that had a restaurant employing unionized workers unless it obtained Labor Department approval. "It takes three or four months to acquire an exemption and, particularly for real estate operations, they could lose a good investment opportunity," said Clayton.

Another key legislative proposal, this time supported by the Reagan administration, involved the termination of single-employer pension plans. Under existing law, a company terminating its pension plan must, if it lacks sufficient assets in its pension fund, turn over 30 percent of its net worth to the PBGC. The agency then assumes responsibility for any remaining shortfall.

Most single-employer plan terminations have been due to company bankruptcy. However, some firms discovered that they could use the law to pass off their pension responsibilities to the PBGC. For many companies, 30 percent of net worth was far less than their future pension liabilities. They could save money by terminating their plans, at relatively low cost, and thus free themselves from future pension debts.

The Reagan-supported proposal would block that strategy by allowing PBGC to pay benefits only when a plan was terminated as a result of liquidation of the plan sponsor.

The Effort to Expand Coverage

By the early 1980s it was evident that the rate of private pension growth had slowed significantly and that the rate of plan formation in proportion to the labor force had leveled off. Concluded the President's Commission on Pension Policy, "The low rate of increase [in private pension coverage] since 1960 raises doubts as to whether there will be substantial voluntary gains in the future without considerably more or different economic incentives or new retirement income policies."

In response, some members of Congress began to explore ways of enabling workers enrolled in company pension plans to supplement their potential benefits through tax deductions and tax exempt savings accounts. Others proposed additional ways to stimulate formation of private pension plans, including tax breaks for small employers and "special master plans" designed to reduce the administrative costs involved in operating pension plans. The special master plans would allow employers to join pension plans sponsored by banks, insurance companies and investment companies. For a fee, the financial institutions would manage the funds and assume the fiduciary responsibilities.

One controversial proposal was some form of national private pension coverage. The centerpiece of the final report of the President's Commission on Pension Policy was its call for legislation establishing a pension system that would require participation by all employees and employers. The minimum universal pension system (MUPS) would be financed by a 3 percent payroll contribution to be paid by employers, who would be able to take a tax credit of 46 percent for the contribution. Under the program, benefit payments from employee pension plans would increase by an estimated 75 percent.

All employees over the age of 25 with one year of service and 1,000 hours of employment with a company would be eligible to participate in the MUPS. Beneficiaries under the system would be vested immediately. Existing pension plans that fell below MUPS minimum requirements would be forced to rewrite their standards. MUPS would be a fully portable system: Employees could transfer their accumulated pension rights from job to job, and a recordkeeping clearinghouse would be established within the Social Security Administration. Pension funds could be deposited in any approved employee pension plan or with the Social Security Administration for investment in a central pension fund facility. The panel contended the new system would reduce record-keeping and administrative costs.

The commission further recommended that MUPS not be integrated with the Social Security system; income from MUPS would be in addition to Social Security payments. Moreover, employees would be encouraged to make additional contributions to their MUPS accounts and, as in the case of Keogh plans and IRAs, the voluntary contribution would receive favorable tax treatment.

Extending this principle, the commission said that all savings for retirement income should get tax breaks, including voluntary contributions to existing private pension plans. The commission also recommended that employers voluntarily shorten existing vesting schedules and write mandatory survivor benefits into their plans.

Reaction to MUPS Proposal

Although some provisions of the commission's proposal were

commended, they also were criticized as inadequate. Claude Pepper, D-Fla., at the time the chairman of the House Select Committee on Aging, said at a Feb. 26, 1981, hearing on the report that the commission failed to "address the abuses and forfeitures which still occur in the system, except to provide all workers a very modest pension. I believe that all employees must be entitled to all of the benefits they have worked for, not just a mere fraction."

In a response critical of the report, the Citizens' Commission on Pension Policy, a volunteer group, recommended the following changes in private pension plans: immediate vesting whereby workers receive a pension benefit for every year worked; protection of benefits against inflation; automatic provision of a pension to widows; provision of an equal share of pension benefits in case of divorce; and complete portability.

The group said the MUPS would provide an inadequate pension. The employer's 3 percent contribution would amount to $450 a year if the worker earns $15,000. By comparison, the average existing pension plan is based on contribution rates of about 9 percent of payroll, which amounts to an annual contribution of $1,350 on a salary of $15,000, the group noted.

After almost a decade of ERISA, the outlook for a coordinated pension system for American workers remained uncertain. Yet development of the means to coordinate private pensions with Social Security and public retirement plans was becoming increasingly urgent as the retirement age population continued to increase.

"Both Social Security and private pensions face severe economic constraints," concluded Munnell in *The Economics of Private Pensions*. "The ability of private plans to aim at full replacement of preretirement income is ... limited. Insofar as employer contributions to private pensions are actually paid by the employee through lower wages, higher pension benefits will result in reduced income for today's workers. Most people are already under some financial pressure from declining real wages in the face of accelerating inflation and would be reluctant to trade current consumption for future retirement income."

Perhaps, as the President's Commission on Pension Policy suggested, "the definition of 'retirement' itself may need changing. Today, retirement is thought of as the transition from full-time employment to full-time leisure. This abrupt change in life-style can dramatically affect individual retirees. In addition, sudden and complete removal from the labor force, particularly if it occurs below the normal retirement age, may create undesirable financial dependency on our retirement and income transfer programs. While affirming the right of every American to full retirement at a stipulated age, [the nation also should find] ways to encourage work opportunities for older Americans."

Government employees covered by their own Civil Service Retirement system protest the March 1983 bill including new federal workers in Social Security.

Chapter 5

PUBLIC PENSION PLANS

The federal government is the largest single provider of retirement income to American workers. Excluding Social Security and public welfare programs, there are 38 retirement systems encompassing 51 retirement programs available to those who have worked for the federal government. Twelve are retirement systems for employees in the armed forces and civil service, Foreign Service, Federal Reserve Board, Tennessee Valley Authority (TVA), the federal judiciary, the U.S. Tax Court and Central Intelligence Agency (CIA). Comptrollers general, members of Congress, congressional employees and U.S. presidents also are covered by federal retirement systems.

In 1983 the Civil Service Retirement system (CSRS) covered approximately nine out of 10 civilians working for the federal government. Participation was mandatory, except for members of Congress, congressional employees and workers covered by special systems, such as those operated by the Foreign Service or the CIA. An average of 92,500 employees retire each year under the CSRS. With its generous retirement payments, participation in the CSRS is the most important non-salary benefit available to federal civilian workers.

The CSRS was almost the only federal retirement plan that was entirely separate from Social Security and, therefore, owed nothing to it. However, after considerable controversy, and following the recommendations of a presidential commission, Congress in March 1983 cleared legislation that required future civil service employees to participate in Social Security, contributing to its funding through payroll taxes, beginning in January 1984. *(1983 legislation, see p. 169.)*

In addition to the federal government, about 85 percent of state and local government employees participate in more than 7,000 retirement plans. About 70 percent of those workers belong to plans that also provide Social Security coverage.

By the late 1970s and early 1980s critical scrutiny — which only a few years earlier had focused on mismanagement and misuses of pension plans in private industry — turned to the adequacy of financing for government-supported retirement programs.

In the federal government there were warnings that the ample pensions it provided for civilian and military employees were becoming so expensive that they would pose a severe financial burden on the nation and its taxpayers. Many state and municipal governments also became aware that they had not set aside enough money to pay for the pensions of those who would retire in the years ahead.

This situation developed largely due to the disproportionate growth of benefits over the years. State and municipal officials were under pressure from public employee unions to increase pension income. Many of the officials who supported the requests did not obtain tax raises to provide enough money to pay for the benefits they promised. Similar charges of overly generous benefits were made against the federal civil service and military retirement systems.

The Civil Service Retirement System

When the Social Security program was enacted in 1935, civil servants already were eligible for a dependable retirement income under their own program, so they were not covered by the Old Age and Survivors Insurance (OASI) trust fund. Since then, the CSRS has paralleled the growth of Social Security, with both programs adding new features such as survivors' benefits and both confronting the problems of funding, inflation and an aging population.

Among the federal government's civilian pension programs, the CSRS is by far the largest, in terms of assets (about $96 billion at the end of fiscal 1982) and numbers of workers covered (2.8 million). It is also one of the most generous. By 1983 the system was providing an estimated $21 billion in benefits to 1.8 million retired federal employees and their survivors and dependents. The lion's share of contributions (which amounted to about $20 billion in fiscal 1982) comes from the plan's employers, federal government agencies. By contrast to the Social Security system (under ordinary circumstances), the fund also can draw on substantial appropriations from the general Treasury to cover interest on unfunded liabilities, the difference between future obligations and expected contributions to the pension fund.

Civil Service Retirement annuities are based on a formula that considers a worker's length of service and his salary during his three highest years of earning. Although the plan favors workers with long government careers, analysts believe two factors have made the CSRS more attractive than many private industry pensions: a liberal early retirement policy and an annual cost-of-living adjustment (COLA), in which the government ties pensions to increases in the Consumer Price Index (CPI).

The cost of the CSRS has risen dramatically. Between 1970 and 1980 annual outlays grew from $2.7 billion to $14.7 billion. A large portion of that increase has been due to automatic COLAs. In 1980 each one-percentage-point COLA cost $161 million in annual outlays. A 1981 study by the Congressional Budget Office (CBO) projected the same COLA would cost $341 million by 1986.

Target of Criticism

To federal budget cutters, civil service pensions have long been viewed as an easy target. While most lawmakers recoil when cuts are proposed in Social Security benefits, they have been more compliant when the knife is pointed at federal pensions, which are easier to attack for a number of reasons. For one, there are fewer beneficiaries, and, therefore, fewer people to fight against cuts. Second, because federal retirement benefits are higher than Social Security and many private pensions, resentment has built up against government retirees.

In addition to many Americans' belief that federal employees are overpaid and underworked, an anti-bureaucracy attitude fostered by President Ronald Reagan and former President Jimmy Carter led both administrations to recommend slashing federal retirement benefits. Also, the Reagan administration and fiscally conservative lawmakers argued that controlling federal pensions and other entitlement programs was a key to controlling the budget.

Even though budget struggles in 1981-82 left federal retiree benefits basically intact, CSRS beneficiaries were significantly affected by a March 1983 bill (PL 98-21) to rescue the Social Security system. Beginning Jan. 1, 1984, all new federal employees, current and future members of Congress, the president, the vice president, sitting federal judges and top political appointees and civil servants would be required to participate in the Social Security system. Legislative branch workers who did not choose to go under the CSRS by Dec. 31, 1983, also would be covered.

The bill contained language assuring current and retired federal workers that their Civil Service Retirement benefits would not be reduced because of the bill.

Development of the CSRS

The modern civil service system was inaugurated in 1883 with passage of the Pendleton Act. The legislation sought to do away with the abuses of patronage by basing federal government service on merit (through competitive examinations), and providing continuity and political neutrality through security of tenure. The act did not, however, provide federal employees with retirement benefits. As the numbers of government workers grew, pressure built up to enact pension legislation. The product of a 20-year effort, the Civil Service Retirement system was established in 1920, when employment in the federal government stood at about 691,000. Employees were required to pay 2.5 percent of their salaries into the retirement fund and could receive the full amount of benefits due them after 15 years or more of service at age 70 (or 65 for mechanics and postal employees and 62 for railway postal clerks). Generally, retirement was mandatory at those ages, regardless of the length of service.

The act contained no provisions for optional retirement, no survivors' benefits, and no protections for employees who were involuntarily separated from their jobs through no fault of their own.

During the early years, according to an April 1983 Congressional Research Service report on the CSRS, employee contributions more than covered pension payments because benefits were small and eligibility requirements were strict (only about 330,000 federal employees were covered in 1920).

Benefits and Eligibility in 1983

The existing CSRS is considerably changed from the original program established by the 1920 act. Basically, it is much more generous. As it applies to current federal employees, only five years of service are required before an employee becomes vested, that is, entitled to receive benefits upon retirement. Vested employees who leave the government may receive either a lump-sum refund equal to their contributions to the system or a deferred retirement annuity payable when they reach 62 years of age. Employees who leave government service before becoming vested receive only the amount of their contribution, plus 3 percent interest.

Over the years, the "normal retirement age" at which an employee receives full benefits has been revised: federal workers now may retire at age 55 with 30 years of service, age 60 with 20 years of service, or age 62 with five years of service.

Benefits in general are determined by a formula taking a percentage of average salary during the highest three consecutive years of earnings, multiplied by years of service (1.5 percent times the first five years of service, 1.75 percent times the next five years of service and 2 percent times the remaining years). The total is the basic annuity. The maximum benefit is 80 percent of the retiree's "high-3" average annual pay (the maximum would be reached with 41 years and 11 months of service). Added to this are periodic COLAs. *(See below, p. 166)*

Employees affected by reductions in force (RIF) situations are allowed to elect voluntary retirement, with reduced benefits, after 20 years of service and at age 50, or after 25 years at any age.

The system provides disability payments to employees who have five years of service and whose disease or injury prevents performance of their jobs. The CSRS also provides benefits for survivors of employees with at least 18 months of federal service (the spouse receives 55 percent of the

Civil Service Retirement System Beneficiaries
(As of Sept. 30, 1982)

Age	Nondisability		Disability		Survivors	
	Number (thousands)	Average monthly annuity	Number (thousands)	Average monthly annuity	Number (thousands)	Average monthly annuity
Under 45	[1]	$ 935	15	$672	63	$239
45 to 55	13	1,236	45	772	28	462
55 to 65	325	1,230	153	885	95	525
65 to 75	432	1,110	103	827	128	538
75+	240	916	33	621	157	455
Total	1,010	$1,116	349	$819	471	$463

[1] Less than 100. Those annuitants who are under age 45 are employees who were voluntarily separated, but who could elect retirement at any age with at least 25 years of service.

Source: Office of Personnel Management, *Federal Fringe Benefits Facts*, 1982; Congressional Research Service, *Background on the Civil Service Retirement System* (Washington, D.C.: Government Printing Office, 1983).

employee's earned benefit at the time of death) as well as for survivors of retired workers receiving civil service pensions. At the time of retirement, an employee may choose to receive either a full pension without a survivor provision or a reduced annuity with a survivor option. The CSRS provides children's benefits that are based on a formula separate from the annuity payment.

Adequacy of CSRS Funding

Like Social Security (and unlike private pension plans), the Civil Service Retirement system operates on a "pay-as-you-go" basis, with the current contributions of employees and general revenues paying for current beneficiaries.

Originally, the system was designed to be virtually self-sufficient, relying on employee and agency contributions. But several factors, including increased benefits and the government's failure to ante up its share during certain years, placed the system on shaky footing by the late 1960s. The CSRS's unfunded liability rose from $31.1 billion in 1960 to $61.1 billion in 1969.

After years of ignoring the growing gap between benefits owed and contributions taken in, Congress in 1969 decided to shore up the system. The major purpose of the 1969 act (PL 91-93) was to stabilize the unfunded liability. To accomplish this, the bill increased payroll contributions by employees and government agencies. It also authorized direct appropriations to the fund by Congress to cover certain types of costs and financial deficits, including new or liberalized benefits (excluding COLAs), extensions of coverage to previously uncovered employees and increases in salaries on which benefits were computed. Finally, the bill provided permanent appropriations (automatic transfers from the Treasury to the fund) to make up the sums lost in interest because the system was underfinanced and to cover benefits for military service.

The amount contributed by the Treasury started at $231 million in fiscal 1970 and by 1980 totaled about $11.2 billion a year, according to the CBO. Appropriations from the Treasury amounted to 46.5 percent of the system's revenue in 1980. Other income came from payroll withholdings (14.9 percent of total trust fund income in fiscal 1980); matching agency contributions to Civil Service Retirement and Disability Trust Fund (17.8 percent); and interest earned on investments in U.S. government securities (20.7 percent). The balance, 6.2 percent, came from off-budget agencies such as the U.S. Postal Service.

The system's annual cost to the government, calculated as the difference between CSRS outlays and receipts from employees and agencies not included in the federal budget (off-budget agencies), continued to rise sharply. Estimated by CBO at $9.5 billion in 1980, the cost was projected to reach $20.2 billion annually by the year 2030 (not taking into consideration the inclusion of new employees in Social Security.) In 1983 the difference between the benefit rights earned by workers (35 percent of payroll) and payroll taxes credited to them (14 percent of payroll) amounted to 21 percent.

Positive Balance vs. Unfunded Liabilities

From one point of view, the CSRS as a pay-as-you-go plan was in good financial shape, at least compared with the Social Security system. According to an April 1983 study by the Congressional Research Service, the CSRS at the end of fiscal 1982 had a positive balance of about $96 billion. Those reserves could increase to $280 billion by the early 1990s. At the same time, expenditures (mainly for benefit payments) were projected to total $325.6 billion over the same period.

If viewed against the same accounting criteria applied to private pension funding, where the *full* cost of future commitments must be accounted for, the CSRS was in trouble. Despite a positive balance, the CSRS's unfunded liability continued to grow. Estimates varied according to whether the amount was computed using "static costs" (excluding consideration of future increases in benefit and salary levels caused by COLAs and inflation-related salary hikes) or "dynamic costs" that include assumptions about wage increases, inflation and interest rates. The Congressional Research Service has put the system's unfunded liability at about $200 billion in "static costs" and more than $500 billion in "dynamic costs."

More important than the actual amount of unfunded liability, according to the Congressional Budget Office, was the fact that "because [CSRS] is backed by a permanent institution — the federal government — the system does not need full funding as a safeguard against bankruptcy or insolvency, prospects that cannot be overlooked in private pension plans. The taxing power of the federal government provides the ultimate assurance that federal retirement benefits can be paid."

Moreover, as Robert W. Hartman noted in his 1983 book, *Pay and Pensions for Federal Workers,* the only "clear" input into the system is the 7 percent payroll tax paid by employees. (New federal workers covered by Social Security also would pay a 7 percent payroll tax.) Noting the problems created by this situation, Hartman wrote:

> In 1980 about 80 percent of the receipts of the CSRS fund were simply internal transactions of the government. While they raised the income (and the surplus) of the CSRS fund, they raised outlays (and the deficit) on other government accounts. . . . The net effect of CSRS on the federal budget is far from comforting; the annual deficit attributable to CSRS rose from $1 billion in 1970 to nearly $10 billion in 1980 and is projected to more than double to $22 billion in 1986. These are the amounts that taxpayers must contribute (concurrently or in the future) to fulfill the government's retirement commitments to its employees. This burden, although only about 1.5 percent of total federal spending in 1980, is significant, especially in contrast to the surplus that arises when the CSRS fund is viewed inclusive of intragovernmental transfers.

Curbing Costs Through COLA Changes

Several times since the late 1970s, Congress has tinkered with inflation factors in the CSRS (as well as other government-sponsored retirement plans) without radically changing the system.

In 1976 Congress eliminated the 1 percent bonus, or "kicker," given to retirees based on increases in the cost of living. Whenever the CPI rose by 3 percent over the preceding period, they became eligible for the bonus. In its place, legislators approved the COLA system adjusting pensions according to inflation every six months.

As part of the 1981 budget reconciliation act, Congress replaced the twice-yearly COLAs for federal retirees with an annual adjustment made each March 1. Reagan supported the move, despite campaign promises to preserve two COLAs a year.

The 1982 assault on federal pensions occurred when Congress placed a lid on annual COLAs for former federal workers without doing the same to Social Security beneficiaries. Led by Budget Committee Chairman Pete V. Domenici, R-N.M., the Senate in May canceled the 1983 COLA for federal pensioners and placed a 4 percent cap on their March 1984 COLA, while giving Social Security retirees a full inflation adjustment in 1983 and 1984 (Social Security COLAs for July 1983 were deferred until January 1984 by the Social Security rescue bill that cleared Congress in March 1983).

Congress finally cleared a compromise (contained in a budget reconciliation conference agreement) that rejected the across-the-board cap and instead cut COLAs for younger retirees in half. The measure also ended the practice of awarding COLAs each March; they would be granted in April 1983, May 1984 and June 1985. Civil service, military, intelligence and foreign service retirees were affected by the changes. *(Impact on military, p. 178)*

By reducing benefits for pensioners below age 62, the compromise attempted to focus cuts on individuals who left military or civil service work at an early age but who still might hold other jobs. All survivors, disabled retirees and retirees above age 62 would get a full COLA in spring 1983, equal to the increase in the CPI. Retirees under 62 would receive only 50 percent of the COLA.

If the CPI were higher than assumed, pensioners under 62 would receive the 50 percent COLA, plus the difference between the projected and the annual CPI.

The bill also adjusted the way military service was counted toward Civil Service Retirement benefits, to resolve a problem of dual coverage by the military and civil service systems.

One change stated that employees hired after the bill's enactment would not receive military service credit toward a civil service pension unless the employees deposited to the Civil Service Retirement Fund an amount equal to the calculated contributions for their military service.

Early Retirement and 'Double Dipping'

Complicating the system's money problems, according to a 1982 study by the Congressional Research Service, was the program's promise of a full annuity for employees who retired at age 55 with 30 years of service, combined with the guaranteed annual COLA. "During periods of high inflation, federal pay increases tend to lag behind increases in consumer prices, and many employees find it to their advantage to retire early because their pension checks are fully indexed while their salaries are not," the Library of Congress researchers said.

Still another abuse critics found in the system was the practice known as "double dipping." This occurred when a federal employee worked in a job outside government long enough to qualify for Social Security benefits, so that upon retirement he could collect Social Security on top of his federal pension. The option of early retirement further added to the potential for double dipping.

Data compiled by the Office of Research and Statistics (ORS) of the Social Security Administration showed that 73 percent of civil service retirees aged 62 or over received Social Security payments. About half of all civil service annuitants under 62 would be eligible to receive Social Security benefits when they reached age 62.

However, according to the ORS, the average monthly benefit for civil service retirees who received no Social Security payments actually was larger than the average total monthly benefit amount for retired federal workers who received benefits under both programs ($845 and $959, respectively, in 1979 for beneficiaries age 62 or older). Much of the reason for the difference is that the CSRS annuity formula is designed to reward the long-term government worker.

Advantages of Non-Federal Work

Even though their total income from pensions might be smaller than if they had remained in government service, many civil service employees opt to retire at the minimum age and work in non-federal jobs. This gives them several years to increase their total retirement income base through additional non-federal earnings plus their annuities. (Their non-federal salaries do not affect either eligibility for or amount of a CSRS pension.)

A 1982 study of double dipping by Gary Burtless of the Brookings

CSRS Annuitants Who Took Optional Retirement
(on retirement rolls Sept. 30, 1982)[1]

Conditions of optional retirement	Number (in thousands)	Percent of total	Average age in September 1982	Average service (in years)	Average monthly benefit
30 yrs. or more age 55 to 59	268	35.6	63.8	33.7	$1,466
30 yrs. or more age 60	174	23.1	72.0	35.5	1,517
20 to 29 yrs., age 60 to 61	74	9.8	67.6	25.4	958
12 to 29 yrs., age 62	210	27.9	73.9	21.4	747
5 to 12 yrs., age 62	27	3.6	74.2	9.1	253
Total	753	100.0	69.3	29.0	$1,184

[1] Excludes survivor annuitants.

Source: Office of Personnel Management. Federal Fringe Benefit Facts, 1982.

Institution and Jerry Hausman of the Massachusetts Institute of Technology in the *Journal of Public Economics* pointed out that because of the redistributive tilt in the Social Security benefit formula "that favors wage earners who have made only modest contributions to the system, there may be a substantial payoff in Social Security retirement benefits for federal employees who leave federal employment to work only a few years in the Social-Security-covered sector." Nonetheless, Burtless and Hausman concluded that their analysis "did not reveal any massive shift of federal workers into Social-Security-covered employment in order to benefit from the 'tilt.'. . ."

The authors also noted that the rate of anticipated salary increases "significantly affects individual decisions to remain in federal employment" because pension benefits are a function of the high-3 average salary. "The more rapid the wage rise, the larger the gain in ultimate pension benefits from remaining in federal service."

In *Pay and Pensions for Federal Workers*, Hartman pointed out that it would be advantageous for a federal worker to continue working for the government beyond full vesting only if he or she could substantially increase the high-3 salary, if private sector employment was unavailable or if inflation was so low that he would not benefit from the COLAs if he retired at that point.

Integration with Social Security

Even before Congress enacted Social Security reform, full integration of the CSRS with Social Security was one of the most widely discussed and most popular — except with federal employees — proposals to reform the civil service system.

According to Hartman in *Pay and Pensions for Federal Workers*:

> The case for coverage [under Social Security] is impressive: elimination of windfall benefits to dual beneficiaries, elimination of the unjust sheltering of high-paid federal employees from taxes used in a redistributive manner [as performed by Social Security], better protection for lower-paid employees, and the gain in public confidence in government from knowing that federal employees are in the same retirement boat as everyone else.

Although the March 1983 CSRS-Social Security merger affected future federal employees only, the revision met with immediate opposition from leaders of 25 federal employee groups representing six million active and retired employees. They formed a coalition called the Fund for

Assuring an Independent Retirement (FAIR) and Jan. 20 launched a $6 million fight against the proposal, which had been recommended five days earlier by President Reagan's National Commission on Social Security Reform. The groups feared the existing civil service pension plan could collapse without support from new workers.

It was not the first time Social Security coverage for federal workers had been seriously considered. Congress in 1977 rejected such a plan.

Reasons for Opposition

Although the National Commission said the proposal would not adversely affect financing of benefits for existing federal employees, AFL-CIO President Lane Kirkland, a member of the commission, offered a dissenting view. "The commission cannot know in advance whether the pension rights of present and future employees will be adequately protected if Congress enacts mandatory coverage," he said.

Vincent Sombrotto, president of the National Association of Letter Carriers, warned that the Civil Service Retirement Fund would run out of money in about 20 years if new workers were pulled out. To cover the fund's existing liability at that point, Sombrotto said, it would cost the government at least $185 billion from the general Treasury. "Extending Social Security coverage to new federal and postal employees will bankrupt the present Civil Service Retirement system and cost the taxpayers billions more," he said.

Opponents of the proposed merger also contended that universal coverage would cost taxpayers more because the government, as the employer of federal workers, would have to contribute to both Social Security and a supplemental pension plan to bring federal retirement benefits up to their existing level.

Moreover, because a lucrative pension program was one of the principal attractions of federal service, the government might have trouble recruiting and retaining good workers if the plan were changed, they argued. Employee morale would be hurt if one set of workers was covered by the traditional civil service pension plan and another was covered by Social Security and a new supplemental plan. "You can't have a very effective work force if you have people working side by side who are receiving different benefits," said Steve Skardon, a lobbyist for the National Association of Retired Federal Employees.

However, according to the CBO in 1981:

Recruitment and retention of qualified federal employees might be enhanced if a deferred fringe benefit such as retirement were decreased somewhat to permit higher salaries. Many professionals and younger employees, who do not foresee long government careers, or who have a choice between federal and non-federal work, may attach greater importance to salaries than to retirement benefits.

Congressional Reaction

While congressional leaders embraced the broad Social Security reform package, members who represented large pockets of federal workers criticized the portion affecting their constituents.

"It's being very penny-wise and pound-foolish," said Rep. Mary Rose Oakar, D-Ohio, chairman of the House Post Office and Civil Service Subcommittee on Compensation and Employee Benefits. "In the short term, injecting new employees helps the Social Security system. But it hurts the Civil Service Retirement system."

"I can't see using federal employee contributions to solve the short-term solvency problems of Social Security unless we're willing to look at the long-term problems of the civil service system," said Senate Majority Whip Ted Stevens, R-Alaska, chairman of the Governmental Affairs Subcommittee on Civil Service.

Final congressional action on the Social Security rescue plan came only after the Senate approved an amendment offered by Russell B. Long, D-La., to defer Social Security coverage of federal employees until a supplemental retirement system — comparable to private pension plans — was in place to provide them with an additional retirement income.

Stevens argued against Long's amendment, charging that it would only give federal employees the opportunity to fend off Social Security coverage indefinitely. But Long objected to including federal employees under the ailing Social Security system without a specific guarantee of supplemental benefits.

Voting to place civil servants under Social Security was uncomfortable for many in Congress, particularly liberals, union supporters and others who generally sympathized with federal workers but who represented only small numbers of such workers. Heavy lobbying, especially by anxious postal clerks and unhappy federal office workers from across the country, made those members even more uncomfortable.

"You have to choose between civil service and Social Security recipients. How do you pick from two strongly organized special interest groups?" said one congressional aide.

The CSRS Compared With...

It is somewhat difficult to compare the Civil Service Retirement system (CSRS) with private pension plans, since the civil service is a unified system and there are many varieties of private pension plans. However, the CSRS and most private plans base benefits on salary and length of service. This feature distinguishes both systems from Social Security, where workers with lower incomes tend to receive proportionately larger benefits (this is often referred to as the "redistributive effect" of Social Security).

Coverage. The CSRS covered more than 2.8 million civilian workers and paid benefits to approximately 1.8 million retirees and survivors at the end of 1982. About 116 million workers participated in Social Security, and 36 million individuals drew benefits. In the private sector, between 36 million and 43 million persons participated in employer pension plans, and more than nine million received benefits.

Contributions. Federal employees must contribute 7 percent of their basic pay through payroll deductions to the Civil Service Retirement Fund, compared to a 6.7 percent payroll deduction for Social Security participants. Federal agencies must put in a matching amount for each employee, just as private employers match their workers' Social Security contributions. The U.S. Treasury also contributes to the civil service fund from general revenues to help cover unfunded future liabilities caused by an anticipated gap between contributions received and benefits owed. The majority of workers covered by private pensions do not contribute to their companies' retirement funds.

Lobbying Criticized

However, most members of Congress believed allowing any amendments to the Social Security bill could eventually unravel the fragile compromise recommended by the president's bipartisan commission.

"It's not that they [the unions] fought it," said Stevens after the vote. "It's how they fought it. . . . There is just very poor communication right now between employee organizations and the Congress, and it is going to hurt very much in the latter part of the year if they don't get

... Social Security and Private Pensions

Benefits. The average monthly civil service benefit is $1,047, according to the Office of Personnel Management, compared to more than $400 a month for Social Security. Many Social Security recipients supplement their retirement income with private pension benefits. Civil service, private pension and Social Security benefits are all taxable (prior to 1983, Social Security payments were tax-free). CSRS and Social Security beneficiaries receive inflation-related cost-of-living-adjustments (COLAs); the majority of private pensions do not have COLAs.

In contrast to the private pension system, where only 34 percent of workers between the ages of 25 and 64 are vested (that is, they have acquired some right to a pension benefit), 77 percent of federal employees are vested.

Retirement Age. A federal worker can collect a full pension if he retires at age 55 with 30 years of service, age 60 with 20 years, or age 62 with five years in government. Under Social Security, a worker can retire at age 62 with partial benefits and age 65 with full benefits. The retirement age is scheduled to gradually increase from 65 to 67 by the year 2027. Private pension benefits usually are based on retirement at age 65.

Approximately 80 percent of male retirements under private plans occur at age 62 or later, compared with 36 percent of male civil servants, according to figures compiled by the Congressional Budget Office (CBO). Nearly half of all male civil service retirements occur before age 60, compared with less than 10 percent of the male work force covered by a company pension and Social Security.

some of those bridges rebuilt."

Many, including Stevens, believed that the unions should have concentrated on drafting a supplemental civil service retirement plan rather than fighting to keep their members out of the Social Security system. "The basic mistake that was made was in not seeing what was going to happen — not recognizing that the momentum was there to carry new members under Social Security and using that as a wedge to create a better system," Stevens said.

"The ability to achieve that system now — after the new employees were already covered under Social Security — is lessened," he added.

Reagan Reform Proposal

Reagan's fiscal 1984 budget submitted in January 1983 contained a number of wide-ranging recommendations to change the CSRS, which the budget described as "one of the most generous pension plans available in the United States."

Under Reagan's plan, employees would be forced to increase their payroll contribution to 9 percent, from 7 percent, in fiscal 1984 (6.7 percent of their salary toward Social Security and another 2.3 percent toward the federal retirement plan, rising to a total of 11 percent in 1985). Employer contributions also would increase to match the higher employee deductions.

The administration's plan would require federal employees to work until age 65 to receive full pension benefits. The benefit formula also would be changed so that annuities would be calculated on the average of a retiree's highest five years of earnings, instead of the high-3.

Federal employee and retiree groups attacked the president's proposals and pledged a vigorous fight against them. "I have never seen such a direct, all-out attack on a group of employees like this is," said Jane McMichael, legislative director for the American Federation of Government Employees. McMichael said if Congress approved the proposal to delay full retirement benefits to age 65, "you are going to see an exodus [from the government] like you've never seen before of the most senior level employees. It will be a terrible blow to many agencies."

Both the House and Senate Budget committees also were cool to the recommendations. During consideration of the fiscal 1984 budget resolution, both panels rejected the president's plan to raise employee contributions.

Following the Social Security debate, congressional and union interest in dealing with the problem facing new federal employees appeared to wane. Union lobbyists and their congressional supporters feared that any revisions in the civil service retirement system plan before the 1984 elections could subject the system to unfair election-year cutbacks that would make representatives look good back home but further erode the federal workers' retirement system.

"It's almost impossible to deal with something like the retirement system in an election year," said Stevens.

In the House, William D. Ford, D-Mich., chairman of the House Post Office and Civil Service Committee, was expected eventually to play a leading role in revising the civil service pension system. Stevens and

Ford planned to commission a study in 1983 on the existing system and alternatives that would serve as a basis for any reforms.

Military Retirement: System of Diverse Goals

As with the Civil Service Retirement system, there is growing concern over fast-rising pension costs of the military retirement program, which covers members of the Army, Navy, Air Force, Marine Corps, Coast Guard and the commissioned officers corps of the Public Health Service and the National Oceanic and Atmospheric Administration. Like the Civil Service Retirement system, it is an extremely generous plan. It also is underfunded.

The rationale for the liberal military retirement system was set forth by the Advisory Commission on Service Pay in 1948. Not only would a generous pension benefit plan attract "the right kind of men to the services" and "meet the government's broad social obligations with respect to its employees," but it also was "essential as an aid in administration, that is, that without such a plan, undesirable men and those who cannot advance in grade cannot be separated from the services." The major reason for the program, in the commission's opinion, was "to meet the superannuation problem.... [A] sound retirement plan with a proper compulsory retirement age will permit youth and brains to rise to the top in time to be effective."

The military retirement system is unique in that those who benefit do not contribute to a retirement fund. The federal government pays the entire bill through annual congressional appropriations. The system allows retirement with full immediate benefits at any age after 20 years of service. However, those who leave before completing 20 years of service have no pension rights. The average age of non-disability retirement from the military in 1978 was 42.

Retirement benefits are based on 2.5 percent of final basic pay multiplied by years of service; there is no additional retirement benefit beyond 30 years of service. Survivors receive 55 percent of the participant's retirement benefit. The survivor benefit also is available to military personnel with 20 years or more of service who still are on active duty at the time of death. The survivor benefit must be elected, and a retiree's benefits are reduced according to his selection of options for spouse and children. Concurrent payments to both a surviving spouse and surviving children are not allowed. (In contrast, the Civil Service Retirement system

175

pays children's benefits, calculated under a separate formula, regardless of whether the retiree elected survivorship coverage for a spouse.)

Participants in the military retirement system have been fully covered under Social Security since 1956. As of 1982, each person contributed 6.7 percent of the first $32,400 of annual basic pay; the government matches the amount. There is no reduction in military retired pay when Social Security is received on retirement. Widows and dependents of military personnal who die in active duty or from service-connected disability receive monthly survivors' benefits both from the military and Social Security.

Military personnel also are eligible for Veterans Administration (VA) benefits, which are deducted from benefits payable from the military retirement system. Federal civilian service is not credited in military retirement, but military service is credited in the federal civilian systems.

The military pension program has been the fastest-growing part of the defense budget. The budget outlays for military retirement for fiscal 1964, $1.2 billion, had soared to $15 billion by 1982.

History of Military Retirement Laws

The first service-connected disability compensation benefit for veterans was enacted during the Revolutionary War and the first non-service-connected pension was established in 1818. Prior to the Civil War, pensions (in fact, compensation for service-connected injuries or death) were the same for both regular and temporary (civilian volunteer) members of the armed forces.

The first Officer Retirement Act for Regular Army officers was enacted in 1861. The act was intended to retire officers with 45 years of service who had reached the age of 62 and were unfit to serve because of age or ill health. The new law, which applied to all branches of the armed forces, was not intended for the benefit of the individual but was meant to weed out unfit officers, according to Prof. Michael S. March of the University of Colorado in his December 1981 study of the history of U.S. retirement programs for the House Select Committee on Aging.

In 1862 a "General Law" was enacted providing compensation for war veterans for disabilities suffered as a direct consequence of military service. The act also provided for survivors' benefits for women and children of servicemen who died in the course of military service. The amount of benefits was scaled according to rank. That system remained in force until it was replaced by the War Risk Insurance Act of 1917 providing disability and death compensation benefits as well as life insurance.

Laws enacted in 1870 and 1873 authorized retirement pay of 75 percent for Army, Marine and Navy officers. An act passed in 1870 allowed Army and Marine Corps officers to retire voluntarily after 30 years of service, at the discretion of the president. Non-disability retirement for officers in all branches of the services at age 64 was made mandatory in 1882. The act also allowed officers to retire at their own volition after 40 years of service.

In 1885 Congress passed the first non-disability retirement law covering enlisted personnel. Army and Marine Corps servicemen were allowed to retire voluntarily after 30 years of service, with the approval of the secretary of war. The act was extended to Navy personnel in 1899 and consolidated for enlisted personnel in all services in 1907.

In 1916 a "promotion up or retirement out" system was established whereby an individual who was not promoted to a certain rank by a given age would be retired. That feature was designed to open the ranks of promotion to younger personnel.

Making the System More Generous

By 1935 the military retirement system "had the most liberal benefits at the earliest ages of any substantial public retirement program for which records are known," wrote March. Benefits applied to both officers and enlisted men and length of service required to qualify was relatively short.

Most of those general features were retained in subsequent laws. Navy and Marine officers in 1946 were allowed optional 20-year retirement if they had 10 years of commissioned service. The Officer Personnel Act of 1947 provided the framework for officer promotion and involuntary retirement systems for all service branches. It was based on length of service, time in rank, age and retirement after 20 years if passed over twice for promotion in the four lowest officer grades. In 1948 a plan was established for career reservists who could retire at age 60 after completing 20 years of service.

A law enacted in 1953 allowed military personnel to elect reduced retired pay to provide benefits after their death to dependents. The plan was liberalized somewhat in 1961 and again in 1972.

In 1965 retired military personnel were authorized to receive periodic pay adjustments based on increases of 3 percent of the

Consumer Price Index (CPI). (Various other methods of adjusting retirement pay had been enacted in previous years.)

Rising Costs of Military Retirement

It is difficult to calculate the total costs of the military retirement system, because many of the expenditures are borne by the Veterans Administration, Social Security and other programs.

Defense Department outlays for military retirement were only about $51 million in 1935, as compared with $52 million for the CSRS and $509 million for veterans' pensions, compensation and insurance. By 1950 military retirement outlays had climbed to $304 million.

In an attempt to curb the system's costs, the Defense Manpower Commission advised in April 1976 that the number of service years required for retirement of non-combat personnel be increased to 30, from 20. Citing indications that the military retirement system "motivates early retirement," the commission, in its final report to the president and Congress, noted that few served beyond age 55.

In 1977 President Carter appointed a nine-member Commission on Military Compensation to study the retirement system, among other issues. The existing system, the commission found, "can no longer be justified." The commission recommended a new type of non-contributory retirement for the armed forces that would provide deferred annuities and benefits instead of allowing the retiree to begin collecting immediately upon retirement. Addressing the controversial issue of double dipping, the panel recommended that no pension annuities be paid to former military members while they were employed by the government. A deferred-compensation plan was suggested instead.

Curbs on Double Dipping, Reduced COLAs

Despite the commission's recommendation and endorsement by the Senate Appropriations Committee, the full chamber in July 1977 rejected a ban on double dipping that had also been recommended by its Appropriations Committee. Speaking in favor of the ban, Sen. Thomas F. Eagleton, D-Mo., said, "We are getting to the point where with respect to the defense budget, we will have to talk about guns or pensions." But Alaska's Sen. Ted Stevens, R, in defense of dual compensation, said those who collected salaries while drawing retirement benefits were "receiving compensation for a job currently being performed and they are receiving retirement for a job they have honorably completed." He argued it was in the nation's interest to encourage early retirement of military personnel so that the armed forces would remain young and vigorous.

Nonetheless, Congress in 1982 enacted legislation intended to curb double dipping by reducing an individual's civilian pay by the amount of his military retiree COLA. It was estimated the measure would save about $143 million over a three-year period.

To cut down on rising military retirement expenditures, both the House and Senate Budget committees in 1980 had recommended a once-a-year COLA for military retirees in place of the twice-yearly adjustment. The cut was contingent upon a similar change in pensions for civil service retirees. But because Congress failed to clear that measure, the COLA adjustment for military retirees also was shelved that year.

However, in 1982 Congress enacted legislation reducing COLAs for younger retirees in the civil and military service. By reducing benefits for pensioners below age 62, the measure attempted to focus cuts on individuals who left the military at an early age but who still might hold other jobs. *(See also p. 166.)*

Several senators protested that the compromise shifted the burden to military annuitants because early military retirees greatly outnumbered civil service pensioners under 62. Senate aides said there were about 980,000 military retirees under 62, compared with 150,000 civil service retirees below that age.

The Special Status of Railroad Retirement

Established in 1937, the Railroad Retirement system (RRS) enjoys a unique place in the federal pension lineup: it is the only *private* pension plan that is managed by the government. But, like other plans — both public and private — the RRS found itself in difficult financial straits by the late 1970s. Congress enacted a major overhaul of the system in 1981 (PL 97-35), with the hope that some one million railroad retirees, their survivors and dependents would be assured full pensions for at least a decade, if not longer.

When the revisions were approved, Congress assumed that rail employment would level off at approximately 500,000 workers for years to come. But with the deep economic recession, the numbers dropped dramatically — from 510,000 in August 1981 to 388,000 in January 1983.

As a result of the decline, Congress was faced with the question of

179

whether to bail out a system that had an income of $5.6 billion in fiscal 1982, but expenditures of approximately $700 million more. With the taxes of each worker supporting almost three retirees, the RRS had few reserves from which to draw. *(Compare with Social Security dependency ratio, p. 37.)*

Aggravating the retirement fund's financial plight was the railroad unemployment system (separate from state and federal unemployment programs), which borrowed almost $500 million from the retirement fund between 1981 and early 1983 to pay benefits to jobless rail workers. The administration estimated additional borrowing for jobless benefits of $1.8 billion by 1988, further draining the pension fund.

Projections by the Railroad Retirement Board indicated that the retirement fund could be in the red $548 million by fiscal 1984 and $13 billion by 1992. If nothing was done soon, certain railroad retirement benefits would be slashed by 40 percent Oct. 1, 1983, and by an additional 40 percent the following year, the board warned in a report issued Feb. 18, 1983.

Few members of Congress relished, or even understood, the task of bailing out the RRS. In previous years, prearranged agreements between labor and management often set the congressional agenda on railroad retirement. After being burned by past "rescue" plans, such congressional acquiescence was less likely to occur again.

"This is a very complex and a very serious matter and I don't see any easy answers," said J. J. Pickle, D-Texas, chairman of the House Ways and Means Subcommittee on Social Security, which has partial jurisdiction over the fund. "I hope we can reach some consensus between the House, the Senate and the administration."

Financial Status of the Railroad Pension

The Railroad Retirement system was established during the Depression in response to failing railroad pension plans and to encourage older workers to retire so there would be more jobs for younger workers. The system excluded rail workers from Social Security but guaranteed them parallel, and somewhat more generous, benefits.

RRS is basically financed the same way as Social Security, with an equal payroll tax paid by both employee and employer, although its payments are set apart and known as Tier I benefits, provided through an interchange system between the RRS and Social Security.

The interchange is a system of funds transfer that is designed to put the Social Security system in the same financial position it would be had railroad employment been covered directly under Social Security. Under the system, Social Security is reimbursed for the additional taxes it would have collected from railroad employers and employees (that is, the Tier I tax). Social Security in turn pays to Railroad Retirement the additional benefits it would have paid to railroad retirees.

The net result is a positive annual transfer of about $1.6 billion to the RRS. The rail industry has complained, however, that the time lag between RRA payments to Social Security and Social Security's payments to the RRA cause financial strain for the Railroad Retirement system.

In addition to Tier I, rail workers receive so-called Tier II benefits that parallel those they would have received under a private pension plan. These, also, are funded by rail labor and industry taxes.

A quirk in the retirement law before 1974 also allowed workers who had been employed in both railroad- and Social Security-covered jobs to earn generous dual, or "windfall," benefits under each program. These payments drained the system over the years, leading to a major overhaul in 1974. As part of that reorganization, Congress agreed that the Treasury would assume the cost of those payments.

Despite the 1974 changes, the RRS trust fund, like many large pension systems, continued to face financial troubles. Outlays increased from $1.6 billion in 1970 to $5.3 billion in 1981, with projections put at about $7 billion by 1987. Receipts did not keep up with those increases, and trust fund reserves dropped from $2.7 billion to $1.9 billion in 1981.

To avert a funding shortfall, Congress, the administration and rail labor and management agreed in 1981 to increase employer-employee taxes to keep the system solvent for another 10 years. Other changes included a more generous benefit formula, authority for short-term borrowing from the Treasury and restricted windfall benefits. But even with that stopgap agreement, lower-than-expected railroad employment threatened to drain the system further.

At the end of 1981, 477,000 workers were covered by the RRS and an equal number were receiving benefits of $3.1 billion. In addition, nearly $2.3 billion was paid to about 559,000 dependents and survivors. According to the Railroad Retirement Board, the average monthly pension check was about $630. Approximately two-thirds of that amount was made up of Tier I benefits.

Generous Benefits

A December 1981 Congressional Budget Office (CBO) study of the

RRS found that railroad workers received unusually high benefits, in part because payments were exempt from federal tax. For example, a married rail worker who retired at age 62 after 36 years of service, with a final salary of $30,000, would receive a pension equal to 105 percent of his take-home pay. Some could receive as much as 129 percent of their highest take-home pay. Railroad workers also could retire as early as age 60 without a cut in benefits.

Industry representatives pointed out that rail employers and employees paid dearly for those benefits — a 13.75 percent payroll tax for Tier II benefits, on top of 10.8 percent for Tier I, by itself equal to the total paid by employers and employees for Social Security retirement and disability benefits in 1981. "The federal government pays nothing, absolutely nothing [for railroad retirement benefits]," Ole M. Berge of the Railway Labor Executives' Association (RLEA) said during March 1982 congressional hearings.

Reagan Proposal: End Federal Involvement

Hidden in President Ronald Reagan's fiscal 1983 budget was what was to become a controversial, and ultimately unsuccessful, proposal to revamp the RRS. The administration's plan would have essentially severed all federal ties with the "private" (Tier II) portion of the $5.3 billion plan; the rest (Tier I) would be assimilated into Social Security, with the Social Security Administration paying the monthly benefits.

Tier II benefits would be turned over to a private corporation to be run jointly by rail management and labor. The $3.6 billion in existing railroad retirement assets would be transferred to the new corporation. The government would continue to fund dual benefits, but only at the existing level of $350 million a year, even though the benefits were expected to cost $440 million in 1982. The shortfall would be made up by benefit cuts for individual recipients.

The Office of Management and Budget (OMB) justified the proposed revisions by labeling government involvement in railroad retirement as "an inappropriate federal function." The existing system was "an accident of history, an accident we're trying to correct," said OMB spokesman Edwin L. Dale Jr.

OMB argued there was no reason why the federal government should be burdened with the financial problems of the rail workers' retirement system. Moreover, even though Congress had to put its seal of approval on the pension agreements negotiated by labor and management over the years, "an unavoidable political cast" led to a generous benefit program not enjoyed by most workers, according to Dale.

Opposition Shelves Plan

Labor representatives charged that the proposed new arrangements could leave the rail system extremely vulnerable to financial mismanagement. "We prefer to have the federal government involved," said James Snyder, legislative director for the United Transportation Union. "Look at our track record. There's been no abuse of funds, no racketeering. It's one of the most highly respected pensions."

In addition, Snyder argued, negotiations between the 20 unions representing labor and the 400 or so rail companies for which they worked would be "unmanageable" without congressional oversight. "Many small railroads may not wish to remain in the system . . . thereby rendering the revenue base of the system too small to support it," said Berge.

Several resolutions opposing the administration's proposal were introduced in the House and Senate, including one by James J. Florio, D-N.J., chairman of the House Energy and Commerce Subcommittee on Commerce, Transportation and Tourism, which oversees the system.

Perhaps the major objection on Capitol Hill was that the Reagan plan stirred up an unnecessary tempest for a Congress that had more than its share of budget battles to fight. "The main problem is that it solves a problem that members of Congress don't think exists," said one House Ways and Means Committee aide.

While the transfer would lower the federal deficit $2.2 billion for fiscal 1983-87, it would not really cut federal spending. Since the RRS was a trust fund, deficits were not made up by general Treasury revenues but could only be reduced with benefit cuts or tax increases.

In addition, members of the Ways and Means Committee warned that the proposal would present cash-flow difficulties for the financially troubled Social Security system and reduce its trust funds by more than $1 billion between fiscal 1982 and fiscal 1987.

With little economic justification for the plan, only the more philosophical issue remained: Should a private pension system be run by the federal government? That esoteric question was eventually obscured by the intense lobbying effort of rail workers and retirees who felt their pensions would be threatened by the Reagan proposal.

Emergency Bailout

Alarmed by the prospects of RRS insolvency, rail labor and management — with some congressional prodding — worked out an emergency bailout plan, most of which was adopted by the Energy and Commerce Committee in a bill (HR 1646) reported March 3, 1983. An amended version was approved June 23 by the House Ways and Means Committee. The full House was expected to take up the bills in July.

"We're convinced that the package if enacted intact would keep the system solvent through the coming decade, and probably indefinitely," said Charles Hopkins, chairman of the National Railway Labor Conference (NRLC), the negotiating arm of rail management.

For the most part, the plan dealt with Tier II benefits. The Energy and Commerce Committee's bill would require tax increases of close to $1.9 billion over five years for both rail workers and rail employers and benefit reductions of about $2.2 billion. The existing 11.25 percent employer payroll tax would be increased to 12.75 percent in 1984 and 13.75 percent in 1985. An additional tax hike of 1.5 percentage points would go into effect in 1986, if necessary. (The Ways and Means version proposed increases of 12.25 and 13.25 percent, respectively.)

The 2 percent tax employees already paid would be increased .75 percentage point in 1984, .75 percentage point in 1985, and another .75 percentage point in 1986, if necessary.

The bill also would reduce benefits for rail workers who retired before age 62 and reduce Tier II benefits by a portion of the Tier I COLA rail retirees received.

In addition, under both the Energy and Commerce and Ways and Means bills, Tier II benefits would be subject to income taxes for the first time, raising an additional $647 million for the system over a five-year period.

The Reagan administration applauded most of those changes as "moves in the right direction" for restoring solvency to the fund. But it had objections to other features of the bill, including a provision for complete funding of windfall benefits some retirees received for having worked under both Railroad Retirement and Social Security.

OMB Director David A. Stockman called instead for more "structural" changes, warning that without them, "the rail industry pension funding crisis will return in a few years." But the rail industry countered that it already had imposed a large burden upon itself in the rescue plan and that the administration should bear some of the cost.

"The railroads have stretched themselves to the limit and we do not see how anyone can doubt that they will have done their share towards preserving the financial integrity of the Railroad Retirement system," NRLC's Hopkins said in a joint statement with William H. Dempsey, president of the Association of American Railroads, before Florio's subcommittee.

Administration Counterproposal

Meanwhile, the administration was formulating a counterproposal that called for higher taxes on the industry, more benefit cuts and less federal government involvement. While rail labor and management opposed parts of the plan, industry representatives noted that the proposal was a far cry from the administration's 1982 call for virtual dismantlement of the RRS.

The administration plan would increase employer and employee taxes by 1 percentage point on July 1, 1983, in addition to the taxes proposed in the rail labor-management plan. It also would increase the taxable wage base for employers and employees and reduce Tier II benefits by the amount of the Tier I COLA.

The Energy and Commerce Committee estimated the change would impose an additional $3.4 billion in taxes on the industry over a six-year period. It argued that such a massive tax increase would lead to further unemployment, exacerbating the retirement system's financial problems.

OMB also proposed that, instead of requiring the Treasury to pay for past windfall benefits, the benefits become an entitlement program that would require full funding by Congress every year. The OMB plan did not, however, address the question of past underfunding. In effect, increased industry taxes and benefit cuts would cover the portion of the system's deficit that the rail labor-management plan would have wiped out with the almost $2 billion general fund transfer. The OMB counterproposal would also dismantle the railroad unemployment system and require that railroad workers be covered under the state-federal unemployment system to which other workers belonged.

Outlook

Until the spring of 1983, the plight of the Railroad Retirement system had taken the caboose to the financial troubles of Social Security. However, with Social Security legislation out of the way and major railroad benefit cuts set to go into effect Oct. 1, the pressure on Congress to shore up the retirement fund was expected to increase. "It is very important that this be dealt with very, very quickly," said Florio.

This sense of urgency was accompanied by a skepticism in Congress that the plan would work any better than the last one did. "The 1981 bill was supposed to do the trick," remarked Norman F. Lent, R-N.Y., ranking minority member on the Transportation subcommittee, "but here we are two years later back trying to bail out and salvage the Railroad Retirement system again."

State and Local Employee Pension Plans

State and local government pension programs provide retirement benefits for persons in a wide range of professions: teachers and school employees, police officers, firefighters, elected officials, judges and other salaried public employees. Nearly 14 million Americans participated in non-federal government-sponsored retirement plans in 1981. Those programs paid out about $13.8 billion to an estimated 2.4 million retired workers, their survivors and dependents. The Census Bureau estimated that state and local retirement plans had more than $209 billion in their coffers in 1981. During that year, employers and employees contributed $27.3 billion, with employers — the governments — picking up 73.3 percent of the tab.

Altogether, there are several thousand state and local retirement plans. Although 80 percent of them cover fewer than 100 active members, 6 percent (or about 400 plans) have more than 1,000 participants and cover more than 95 percent of all state and local government employees.

Data compiled by *Pensions and Investment Age* showed that six public employee plans were among the 10 largest retirement programs in the nation. These included New York state, with assets of $17 billion; New York City, $16 billion; California, $13.5 billion; New York State Teachers, $10 billion; Texas State Teachers, $7 billion; and California State Teachers, $7.3 billion. The four largest private funds included American Telephone & Telegraph, with assets of $45.8 billion; General Motors, $15.8 billion; General Electric, $9.4 billion; and IBM, $7 billion.

'Financial Time Bombs'

But for all their financial clout, many pension experts in the early 1980s believed the public plans could be in trouble. They cited the fact that the plans were not subject to federal regulations and funding standards similar to those established for private plans under the 1974 Employee Retirement Income Security Act (ERISA). On the other hand, antiquated state regulations could prevent fund managers from investing in profitable ventures. Finally, experts suspected that participants themselves were not receiving adequate information about their retirement benefits.

"Unlike private pensions, which are the subject of many books, the important area of state and local pensions historically has received little attention through the years," wrote Prof. March in his 1981 report for the House Select Committee on Aging. "Yet the area presents one of the sig-

State and Local Government Retirement Plans
(Thousands of persons and millions of dollars)

| Year | Coverage | | Contributions | | Benefits Paid | Total Assets |
	Contrib-utors	Benefi-ciaries	Employ-ers	Employ-ees		
1950	2,600	294	$ 510	$ 395	$ 300	$ 5,154
1960	4,500	660	1,725	1,170	1,015	19,600
1970	7,300	1,291	4,920	2,975	3,120	50,200
1971	7,700	1,379	5,495	3,280	3,620	64,800
1972	8,100	1,463	6,050	3,570	4,335	73,400
1973	8,300	1,550	6,649	4,166	5,075	82,700
1974	9,000	1,635	7,821	4,207	5,835	92,400
1975	9,500	1,730	9,116	4,488	6,725	103,700
1976	10,450	1,840	10,502	4,808	7,700	117,300
1977	10,951	2,173	12,369	5,233	8,455	130,800
1978	11,300*	2,240*	13,621	5,688	9,550	142,600
1979	11,400*	2,300*	15,336	6,069	10,770	161,650
1980	11,550*	2,350*	17,532	6,466	12,210	185,226
1981	11,500*	2,400*	20,020	7,289	13,830	209,444

Note: Beneficiaries are as of June 30. Financial data is on a calendar year basis prior to 1977, and on a June 30 fiscal year basis thereafter.
* Estimated.

Source: U.S. Bureau of the Census and U.S. Department of Commerce; American Council of Life Insurance, *Pension Facts,* 1982.

nificant financial time bombs in the pension field because liberal benefits have been promised by many jurisdictions without adequate funding and proper actuarial methods."

In a May 8, 1981, statement on public pension problems, House Republican John N. Erlenborn, Ill., an expert on pensions, summarized what he considered to be the plight of state and local retirement programs by quoting a state representative from Michigan, who said:

> Right now we have what amounts to a pork-barrel and piecemeal approach to pension modification. We modify one system without regard to fiscal consequences and then other systems want the same. This takes place in a totally political atmosphere without regard to how the bill will be paid, by whom, and when. There is a total absence of logical structure. Employees had better get concerned that there is enough cash on hand to meet retirement needs and taxpayers had better get concerned with these massive and increasing debt obligations. We simply cannot continue in this helter-skelter fashion.

Growth of State and Local Plans

Although the first public pension plan was established in 1857 by New York City for its policemen, it was not until the 1920s that state and local plans proliferated, according to William C. Greenough and Francis P. King in their 1976 study, *Pension Plans and Public Policy*.

By 1966 five million employees, or about 75 percent of those working for state and local governments, were covered by retirement plans, according to the Department of Health, Education and Welfare (now Health and Human Services). The majority of plans provided retirement income equivalent to about 50 percent of the high five-year average wage after 30 years of service.

Amendments to the Social Security Act in 1951 allowed state and local workers not covered by a retirement plan to elect Social Security coverage. In 1954 this was broadened to allow voluntary coverage by Social Security for workers also participating in a public retirement program. By 1973 more than half of the state and local employees covered by public pension plans participated in Social Security as well. Nearly all were covered by one, or both, programs.

A principal result of the dual coverage has been a windfall for those public service retirees entitled to both benefits. A 1978 report by a House Education and Labor Committee pension task force found that half of all employees with 30 or more years of public service would receive higher combined Social Security and public pension net income — after taxes and contributions — than their pay before they retired. However, state and local governments began to chafe at the expense of contributing both to Social Security and their own plans. Many of them began to withdraw from Social Security.

Coordination With Social Security

"The most significant policy question for the public [pension] systems is how they are to be coordinated with Social Security," wrote Robert Tilove in his 1975 study, *Public Employee Pension Funds.* "If a state does not somehow coordinate its system with Social Security it will have no control over its employee retirement benefits."

Initially, when state and local governments were given the option of joining Social Security in 1954, many of the public plans were integrated with Social Security by scaling benefits according to the Social Security wage base. But over the years, most integration efforts were abandoned, and Social Security benefits came to be considered as expensive supplements to public plans, with state and local governments paying in to both funds (as do most private employers with company pension plans).

Because many public pensions by themselves provide generous benefits, there has been a tendency for state and local government plans to withdraw from Social Security and stop paying taxes into the system, thereby contributing to Social Security's financial plight.

Indeed, prior to enactment of the Social Security rescue bill in March 1983, the system had been plagued by a rush of withdrawals by state and local governments, many of which faced their own fiscal problems and hoped to save some money by dropping out of the system. In 1982 a record 76,000 state and local government employees were dropped from the Social Security rolls. Another 104,500 were threatening to leave by the end of 1983.

To avert that possibility, Congress adopted the recommendation of the National Commission on Social Security Reform and included a provision in the rescue bill that prohibited public employers already participating in Social Security from leaving. However, the bill would give those state and local governments that had withdrawn the option of returning to the Social Security fold.

High Costs, Inadequate Funding

State and local plans are not regulated by federal funding laws, such as ERISA for private plans. As a result, financing levels vary considerably among public plans. The Education and Labor task force found that about 17 percent of public plans operated on a "pay-as-you-go" approach, funding benefits only as they became due. About one-fourth had never even had an actuarial evaluation (that is, an estimate of how much should be contributed to cover future retirement payments). These factors, combined with generous annuities, created substantial unfunded liabilities.

Liberal requirements for vesting — the point at which an employee becomes entitled to pension benefits — have added to the cost of public programs. Many state and local plans have relatively low "normal retirement ages" at which full benefits are available (60 or 62 is common, compared with 65 for Social Security and most private plans). Like the military retirement system, plans covering workers in hazardous duty occupations such as firefighting allow retirement with full benefits at very early ages, ranging from the early 40s to the early 60s, usually after 20 years of service.

Moreover, many plans provide inflation adjustments for retirement benefits. Both factors make early retirement more attractive, thereby substantially increasing the cost of the plans. Indeed, the costs associated with early retirement were identified by the President's Commission on Pension Policy, in its February 1981 report on "The Future of Retirement Programs," as "the biggest issue facing public employee pensions."

Investments and Plan Management

The investment performance of some public plans has been a subject of growing concern. According to a study by A. G. Becker Inc., the annual median return on investment by public plans surveyed was only 3.3 percent in 1981.

Unlike ERISA, which has established broad standards within which private plan managers are free to make investment decisions, state laws in many cases have mandated what some experts consider excessive restrictions on how their retirement funds' assets can be invested. For example, South Carolina prohibits fund managers from investing in stocks, allowing investments only in bonds or mortgages. (However, some states, such as Pennsylvania, have eased the restrictions in recent years.) Critics have also said that political interference may have hampered some plans' investment performance.

Some public plans have emphasized so-called "social investments" in real estate, home mortgages and industries that would benefit local interests, although the return on those investments often may be low. This issue has become one of the most fundamental problems confronting public retirement plans. Should managers seek out investments in local programs that will generate economic growth and tax revenues, or should their primary concern be to maximize the plans' revenues? The two considerations often may be in conflict. *(Details, "social investment" issue, see Chapter 4, p. 111.)*

Lack of experienced plan management has been another problem for public pension programs. But observers have pointed to improvements in this area. For example, with the Minnesota pension fund showing a low average annual return of 4.9 percent over the period 1973-80 under the management of the state's Board of Investment, a Minneapolis public employee fund pulled out of the system and turned over its assets to private management firms. According to Daniel Hertzberg in the June 16, 1983, *Wall Street Journal,* "The idea of hiring outside firms to help manage pension investments is taking hold in a number of states as they seek to improve the pension funds' performance." Nonetheless, he concluded, "The public-fund operations generally lag well behind the private-sector funds." Low salaries for public fund managers and high turnover also have contributed to management problems, Hertzberg reported.

Congressional Interest in Regulation

These concerns have not gone unnoticed by the nation's lawmakers. For more than a decade Congress has debated whether federal law should regulate state and local plans. Dan McGill, a pension plan expert at the University of Pennsylvania, urged as far back as 1972 that Congress enact legislation governing public plans. "There is a general consensus among knowledgeable persons that retirement systems for public employees are much more in need of regulation than the plans of private employers," McGill testified before the Senate Labor Subcommittee during hearings that year on the proposed regulation of private plans. "As a group, public employee retirement systems are inadequately funded, poorly designed and subject to unsound political manipulation."

However, state and local officials lobbied heavily against regulation and urged Congress to hold off until further studies had been made. As

State and Local vs. Private Pensions

In his book, *Social Security and Pensions in Transition*, Bruno Stein summarized the general features of non-federal public retirement systems. Income for public plans is generated by both employer and employee contributions as well as state and local taxes and, like the Civil Service Retirement system and Social Security, funding often is on a "pay-as-you-go" basis. In contrast, the majority of private plans are funded entirely by employers, who must contribute funds to cover anticipated future benefit costs (this is called "advanced funding").

Like private pension funds, state and local funds invest their assets primarily in private sector securities. However, their investments are (usually by law) more conservative than those of private plans. Compared to private plans, public plans invest more heavily in bonds rather than stocks and in local enterprises, real estate and mortgages. *(Discussion of private pension investment, p. 128)*

While most private pension plans determine vesting (the point at which a participant is entitled to benefits) by a formula that includes some combination of age, length of service and salary, most state and local plans have established vesting criteria on the basis of length of service, usually 10 years.

Unlike single-employer private pension plan participants, public employees generally are able to transfer their benefit rights from one employer to another within a pension system (a feature called portability). But they may lose some benefits if they move from one system to another. "This is of particular importance to teachers, who are probably more mobile than other civil servants," noted Stein.

Benefits provided by public systems generally are higher than those available from private plans. According to Stein, public plans that are combined with Social Security (about 70 percent of plans) have benefit levels approximately twice those in private plans. Those without Social Security pay about one-third more than private plans.

Unlike most private plans, public retirement programs usually provide adjustments for inflation. But such adjustments frequently are not made on a regular basis, as they are for the Social Security and Civil Service Retirement systems.

part of the 1974 ERISA legislation, Congress mandated further research into the public pension sector.

In its interim report issued March 31, 1976, the House pension task force criticized the management of state and local pension plans. "The absence of any external independent review [of public employee plans] has perpetuated a level of employer control and attendant potential for abuse unknown in the private sector," the report said. It accused public pension administrators of using poor accounting methods, investing funds for purposes other than to benefit the employees and failing to fulfill reporting and fiduciary responsibilities.

House Pension Task Force Report

The interim task force report was also highly critical of New York City for using public pension funds to help offset the city's huge deficit. Congress earlier in March of that year had given final approval to legislation allowing five New York City employees' pension plans to buy $2.5 billion in city bonds through mid-1978 without losing tax advantages. Under federal law, a pension plan qualifies for special tax treatment only if it is run for the exclusive benefit of its employees and their beneficiaries.

"As a matter of general policy we are convinced that such transfers from retirement programs to finance local governmental operations unduly impair the stability of the plans, substantially increase the cost of providing retirement benefits to the sponsoring employers, and reflect an absence of budgetary discipline on the part of these employers," the task force said. The panel noted it had discovered "numerous instances" of governments using pension plan assets to finance municipal operations.

Concern was heightened by the final report of the task force, issued in 1978. The panel found that lack of an overall pension policy and financial standards had led in many instances to favoritism and abuse. Because of the lack of uniform standards guiding plan trustees, "conflicts of interest in many instances have been permitted to ripen into clear examples of fiduciary abuse, with resultant losses of pension plan assets and income," the task force said.

The report also found that information provided about the plans, both to participants and outside experts, was inadequate in many cases. Only 40 percent of large state and local plans were audited annually by an external, independent auditor, and one-third were not audited on an annual basis at all. Moreover, 40 percent of public plans did not regularly

193

furnish participants with material describing how their plans operated, and participants in 18 percent of the plans were unable to obtain plan descriptions even on request.

Other studies substantiated the task force's findings. A 1979 survey by the accounting firm of Coopers and Lybrand found that 76 percent of the annual reports of public plans did not disclose the actuarially computed value of unfunded vested pension liabilities and 35 percent did not disclose their funding policies.

House, Senate PERISA Bills

One result of the criticism was introduction in 1976 of a bill by Erlenborn and John Dent, D-Pa., to regulate public employee pension plans. The measure, known as the "Public Employee Retirement Income Security Act of 1976" (PERISA), would establish reporting, disclosure and fiduciary relationship standards for all state and local employee pension systems. Although no action was taken on the bill, interest in public pension regulation persisted.

Erlenborn reintroduced his bill (HR 4929) in 1982; a similar measure (S 2106) was introduced in the Senate by John H. Chafee, R-R.I., chairman of the Finance Committee's Pension Subcommittee. Hearings were held in the Senate, and the House Education and Labor Committee reported the bill in July, but no further action was taken in the 97th Congress. Sponsors of the measure (a bipartisan coalition) planned to reintroduce the legislation in the 98th Congress.

Unlike ERISA, the bills would not set funding and vesting standards for public pension plans. They would focus on only two areas — reporting and disclosure requirements, and fiduciary standards for pension trustees, including prohibited transaction rules similar to those under ERISA (involving dealing in self-interest). The bills would impose on public pension plan trustees the ERISA "prudent man" test — that they make decisions based exclusively on the best interests of plan participants. These guidelines were intended in part to avoid the temptation to invest in high-risk and/or low-return ventures to promote social policies.

Supporting the legislation were the American Federation of State, County and Municipal Employees (AFSCME), the AFL-CIO, the National Education Association, the National Retired Teachers Association and the American Association of Retired Persons.

Although the measures would establish public employee pension standards that were much narrower in scope than those imposed on private pensions by ERISA, state and local government groups, including the National Conference of State Legislatures, opposed the bills as a usurpation of states' rights. A coalition of employee associations in Ohio, Colorado and Nevada formed OPPOSE (Organization for the Preservation of the Public Employment Retirement Industry and Opposition to Social Security Expansion to such industry) to fight the proposed PERISA legislation as an "unconstitutional intrusion on the right of the individual states to determine and regulate their relationships with their own employees."

The National Association of Counties and the National League of Cities also lobbied against the legislation. State and local governments already had begun to correct their pension problems, bill opponents said, and did not need a federal mandate. HR 4929 contained an exemption from its reporting and disclosure provisions for state and local plans that had their own equivalent standards.

"The states are more united in their opposition to PERISA legislation than on any other matter which has come before us in many years," testified Maryland state Sen. James Clark, during March 29, 1982, Senate committee hearings on the bills.

State Efforts to Improve Systems

In the absence of federally mandated standards, a number of public employee plans initiated their own reform measures. Oregon adopted a strong reporting and disclosure statute, Nevada developed an information program for plan members and California tightened its reporting requirements for local governments. Florida enacted legislation requiring local governments to prepare actuarial valuations every three years and to submit them to the state for review.

Moreover, some studies have indicated that public pension plans may not be in as much financial difficulty as critics have suggested. A 1981 study for the Department of Housing and Urban Development by the Urban Institute forecast funding conditions for state and local systems over a 50-year period. Based on actuarial calculations at the end of each year during the 50-year period from 1977 to 2027, employer contribution rates, as a percent of payroll, were projected to fall from 12.7 percent in 1980 to 8.6 percent in 2024. The ratio of unfunded liability to payroll was projected to decrease as well.

"On the whole, the benefits paid by the public systems have been a

Savings and loan institutions are major repositories for Individual Retirement Account (IRA) investments.

Chapter 6

INDIVIDUAL RETIREMENT SECURITY

IRAs and Keoghs — investment tools to stir the imagination of the ants among us, as opposed to the grasshoppers — are initiated by individuals for financial security in their retirement years. They are fostered by government tax policy and applauded by advocates of a greater reliance on private retirement income and a greater U.S. savings repository.

Billions of dollars are going into these investment programs, providing funds for American investment and, perhaps more important, building up value against the time when today's toiling Americans lay down their tools of labor and retire to a life of greater calm and leisure. The question is: Will they be financially comfortable in those so-called golden years of retirement? Or will they find economic hardship after relinquishing their steady paychecks?

IRAs and Keoghs represent an opportunity for Americans to ensure comfort in those retirement years, to provide a flow of dollars that could be the difference between a life of austerity and a life of plenty. They will not make retirees wealthy, but they are the government's way of injecting some powerful pertinence into Ben Franklin's old suggestion that a penny saved is a penny earned.

Individual Retirement Accounts

An IRA is precisely what the words "individual retirement account" imply. It is an individual's own personal pension plan, a system of providing for retirement by saving a portion of one's earnings every year. To encourage persons to do that, the government provides certain tax advantages. First of all, the money put away every year — up to $2,000 — is tax deductible. That means that if the maximum amount is deposited into an IRA, an individual will not have to pay any tax on that $2,000.

That amount can be put away every year for decades and not a cent of tax will have to be paid on it until the worker retires. In addition, the income generated by this IRA money is subject to the same tax advantage. No taxes are paid on an IRA account's income growth until the money is taken out at retirement.

Besides the obvious advantages of deferred taxes, most IRA holders also will benefit from favorable tax-rate differentials. Let us say Mr. Jones has an IRA. During much of the time he is putting money into his account, he is at the height of his earning power, and hence at his highest tax bracket. The higher his tax bracket, the greater his advantage in avoiding taxes on a portion of his earnings. Later, when he reaches retirement age, and his mortgage is paid off and his children gone, Mr. Jones can live quite comfortably on much less income. One result, of course, is that he slips down the tax-bracket ladder. And at this point, when Mr. Jones is at a lower tax bracket, he begins tapping into his IRA retirement pool. Thus, he has been able to avoid taxes when his tax rates were highest and now pays taxes when his rates are considerably lower.

Even if Mr. Jones does not benefit from his tax-bracket differential — even if his tax rate stays the same after retirement as before — he still reaps considerable financial benefits from his IRA. The essence of this advantage is tax postponement or deferral. Financial experts note that tax deferral is one of the two key features of "tax shelters," the other being conversion of ordinary income into capital gains. To defer taxation is to reduce taxation. This is especially true during times of high interest rates. Suppose 12 percent can be earned, a reasonable expectation in recent times. A $100 tax bill deferred for a year really costs only $89. That is because the individual can invest the $89 today and a year later have the full $100 that the investor owed the government. A five-year deferral of the same $100 tax bill drops its actual cost to $57. Thus, the inherent advantage in deferring taxation on retirement savings is obvious, and tax deferral is at the heart of any IRA plan.

The basic advantage of an IRA investment, then, is that it receives a full market rate of interest while deferring all taxes until it is cashed in at retirement. (This is the same advantage for Keoghs, which essentially are jumbo IRAs for self-employed persons.) *(Keogh details, see p. 214.)* Of course, the relative value of all this may depend on one's tax bracket as well as on the rate of interest available. And some investors — especially those in the lower tax brackets — should be sure they will not need the money before they reach the age of 59 and a half because withdrawing

IRA savings before that age carries with it a substantial penalty. But for most IRA investors, especially those in higher tax brackets, IRA investments make sense even if they plan to make early withdrawals from their IRA accounts. Penalties are more than offset by the monetary value of the tax breaks.

For a married couple with $20,000 a year in taxable income after all deductions and exemptions, an IRA would have reduced their tax bill by $440 in 1982. If each spouse had an IRA, the tax break would have been worth $880. With a taxable income of $40,000, the couple could reduce their taxes by $780 with an IRA and by $1,560 with two IRAs. Because single persons are taxed at higher rates than couples living on the same income, they get even larger tax breaks from an IRA. A single person with taxable income of $20,000 saves $613. With $40,000, he saves $880. That money ordinarily would go to the federal government; an IRA channels it into a person's savings. Justifiably, IRAs have been called tax shelters for the little guy.

In fact, for those who find themselves at tax-return time without the $2,000 to invest in an IRA, a good plan might be to borrow the money. The $2,000 can be repaid over the next year, and the tax benefits stemming from the IRA would be greater than the interest paid on the loan. Besides, the interest itself is tax-deductible.

It is important to note that it is possible to establish an IRA in addition to a work-place retirement plan. That was not always the case. When Congress in 1974 first created tax deferrals for IRA contributions, it restricted access to those who did not have employment-based retirement plans. The idea was to provide special benefits for those persons who did not have any retirement plan where they worked.

Popularity of IRA Plans

That first IRA legislation was modest. It was part of a comprehensive pension-reform measure — called the Employee Retirement Income Security Act (ERISA) — that cleared Congress that year. It allowed an individual not covered by a pension plan, a government plan or certain types of annuity plans to establish an IRA. Contributions were limited to the lesser of 15 percent of earned income or $1,500. Early withdrawals were subject to a tax penalty. Two years later, a higher "spousal" contribution limit was set at $1,750, meaning a person with a nonworking spouse could contribute that much to a "spousal" IRA.

By 1981, in the wake of the Republican Party's big gains in

Congress and growing pressure by members for tax reductions, the debate had shifted. Now it was portrayed as unfair to give IRA tax breaks to persons without retirement plans while denying them to others. "It should be clear that all employees should be allowed to deduct, within limits, amounts contributed to provide funds for retirement," declared Sen. Robert Dole, R-Kan., the new chairman of the Senate Finance Committee. "Discrimination between employees based upon the mere existence of an employer-sponsored plan is neither reasonable nor good policy."

Beyond that, concerns were growing in Congress over America's declining savings rate. Sen. John Chafee, a Republican from Rhode Island, pointed out that personal savings as a percentage of personal income had fallen to as low as 3.5 percent by 1980, down from just under 6 percent during the last half of the 1970s and more than 8 percent in the first half. Other industrial nations, meanwhile, had significantly higher rates of saving: Japan — about 20 percent; France — 12 to 13 percent; Germany — 13 to 14 percent; the United Kingdom — 7.1 to 8.4 percent. As Sen. Harrison Schmitt, R-N.M. (1977-83), put it at the time, "Recent studies have shown a close correlation between rates of growth and rates of savings and investment. It is, therefore, no coincidence that the United States, with the lowest rate of savings among the major industrialized nations, is also affected with stagnating economic growth."

Thus, when Congress enacted the Economic Recovery Tax Act of 1981, it opened up IRA eligibility to just about everyone. Today, an IRA is available as a supplement to an individual's Social Security retirement payments and any other retirement income plan.

The result has been startling. An estimated 10 million Americans put money into IRAs and claimed IRA deductions on 1982 tax returns. That was triple the number during the previous year, when IRA deductions were limited to persons without employment-based pension plans. The Internal Revenue Service announced that 18 percent of 1040 income tax returns contained the deductions. Federal Reserve Board data in early 1983 showed that IRA and Keogh accounts in commercial and savings banks, savings and loan associations and money market mutual funds totaled $59.5 billion, nearly double the total on Jan. 1, 1982, when the expanded eligibility began.

Government data also showed that the popularity of IRAs increased with income. While 18 percent of all tax returns contained IRA deductions, the figure was 25 percent for returns of taxpayers earning

$25,000 or more. By contrast, in 1981 only 10 percent of eligible workers took IRA tax deductions, according to a Washington, D.C.-based, public policy research organization called the Employee Benefit Research Institute. The institute's studies, based on IRS data, indicated that IRA popularity always has depended on income. In 1977, the organization said, fully 52 percent of eligible persons earning more than $50,000 had IRAs. For those earning between $20,000 and $50,000, the proportion was 21.7 percent. For those earning between $15,000 and $20,000, eligible workers availing themselves of the benefit totaled only 5.5 percent. Below $15,000, the percentages were negligible.

That differential among various income groups is expected to continue as more and more Americans take IRA deductions. The Treasury Department estimates that IRA deductions totaled about $229 million in reduced federal revenues in 1982. It projects the value of those tax breaks to reach $1.34 billion in 1983, $1.85 billion in 1984, $2.33 billion in 1985 and $2.58 billion in 1986. Though the numbers of persons opening IRAs has been surprisingly high, the Treasury Department says it does not anticipate a revision of those revenue estimates.

IRA Investment Options

A major factor in the establishment of an IRA is the particular despository chosen for the money. There are a number of possibilities: a bank, savings and loan, credit union, mutual fund, stockbroker, insurance company. The differences among these institutions generally hinge on what they do with the IRA funds, for which they serve as trustees. They may put the money in any number of investments, although the law specifically forbids investments in collectibles, such as art, furs, rugs and antiques.

Some institutions take a broader approach than others in terms of where they invest IRA money. Stockbrokers, for example, may channel IRA money into stocks, corporate bonds, even real estate. Banks and savings and loan associations are more cautious. The question is not unlike that posed by any number of investments: try to earn the highest possible return but at a greater risk of losing some of the invested principal? Or come down on the side of greater security, but at the possible cost of a smaller return?

Banks/Savings and Loans. A survey by the Life Insurance Marketing and Research Association during the first months that IRAs generally became available found that most investors opted for IRAs held by banks and savings and loan associations. Fully 57 percent of new IRAs in the first three months were held by these institutions. Next came stockbrokers, 11 percent; insurance companies, 10 percent; mutual fund companies, 9 percent; and credit unions, 8 percent.

In addition to the risk factor, there are other considerations to be made before establishing an individual retirement account, including interest rates, fee requirements, whether to have professional management and whether the IRA account should be insured by the U.S. government. IRAs at banks, thrift institutions and credit unions can offer this federal insurance up to $100,000. Banks, savings and loan associations and credit unions also offer convenience as well as the lowest fees available. It is easy to see why they are popular.

The options at these institutions include passbook savings accounts, which generally are not a good IRA vehicle because of their low interest rate, and certificates of deposit with a choice of maturities. Either fixed or variable accounts may be selected. A new instrument, available only for IRAs and Keoghs, is the 18-month "wild card" certificate of deposit (CD), which can carry any interest rate a financial institution chooses to pay. Generally, these are premium rates. But penalties for early withdrawal can be hefty, often twice as large as for IRAs at other institutions. This is because the only insured high-interest savings accounts that banks can offer are time deposits in which savers agree to tie up their money for specified periods of time — 18 months, for example, or even 30 months. These early withdrawal penalties are in addition to certain IRS tax penalties designed to discourage early withdrawals; thus it is highly undesirable to switch funds out of these IRAs prematurely.

There are wide disparities in interest rates offered by banks and other financial institutions. And it is not always easy to determine just how generous a particular financial institution plan is. Different institutions employ different methods of compounding interest. Some compound annually, others as frequently as daily. The difference can be significant. A 14.375 percent interest rate that is not compounded may yield the same income as a 13.25 percent rate compounded daily. The best way to make a determination is to translate each institution's interest rate into its effective annual yield. The yield reveals just how much an account will earn in the course of a year.

Other Vehicles. Money-market funds, the special mutual funds that invest in low-risk, short-term corporate notes, government securities and big bank certificates of deposit, are another option. Convenience is a factor, since money-market funds allow deposits and withdrawals by mail. Their fees for administering an IRA are low — generally less than $10 a year — and they are considered safe, although they are not federally insured.

The big brokerage firms offer the greatest variety of investments, although they generally charge higher fees and of course their IRAs are not federally insured. An interesting option offered by most brokerage houses is the self-directed IRA, which allows the individual to buy and sell stocks and bonds on his own and to manage investments in such things as real estate, oil and gas operations or equipment leasing. Fees hover in the $25 to $35 range for opening an account and about the same amount annually in maintenance charges. Brokerage commissions also are added. Costs are lower for professionally managed mutual-fund packages at brokerage houses. Such packages typically include a money-market fund and a variety of stock and bond funds. Nominal fees are charged for switching from fund to fund.

Then there are the no-load mutual fund families — those that do not charge brokerage fees. These are offered by such firms as Fidelity Group, the Dreyfus Service Corp., and the Vanguard Corp. With these, investors have a choice of several professionally managed funds without sales charges. There may be a small annual management fee — generally about $10 — but no charge for setting up the account or for switching from fund to fund.

Insurance companies offer an IRA called an individual retirement annuity. Annuities are contracts promising to pay income for a specific period of time, usually the rest of the investor's life. Most insurance companies offer both fixed-rate and variable-rate annuities.

Some insurers also provide switching privileges, for persons who want to help guide investment decisions, such as the offerings of some mutual fund companies. In this way, the IRA account can be divided among stocks, bonds and money-market securities. Fees generally are higher than at banks or through mutual fund companies. This is partly a result of the long-term risks insurance companies take on the investor's life expectancy. The company determines income payments based in part on anticipated growth in the funds invested, usually understated to lessen the risk, and in the IRA holder's anticipated life span. If the IRA holder's life span is longer than projected, the insurer ends up paying more than expected.

Insurance IRAs may be front-loaded or back-loaded. A typical front-loaded annuity likely will carry a sales charge of between 8 percent and 9 percent, which comes off the top of each $1,000 put in over the years. However, there is no penalty for withdrawing part of one's funds. A back-loaded annuity probably will not contain any sales charges but will carry a penalty for withdrawals. The penalty likely will be severe in the first year, 7 percent or so, then decline each year for a decade. In other words, a front-loaded plan takes the money off the top, then lets the IRA holder do whatever he wants with his funds. A back-loaded plan eliminates this front-end assessment but imposes withdrawal penalties as an incentive to keep the investor's money in over a substantial period of time. Both front-loaded and back-loaded plans normally carry a small maintenance fee, either an annual charge or a small assessment on payments.

Diversification/Flexibility. An individual may have more than one among the numerous types of IRAs. The $2,000 annual contribution may be split among several IRAs; alternatively, an individual may contribute to a different IRA each year. Either way, the IRA portfolio is diversified.

IRAs can be transferred from one trustee to another. If the IRA holder takes possession of the funds, they must be reinvested within 60 days, and this option cannot be used more than once a year. But there are no limits on trustee-to-trustee transfers in which the IRA holder does not actually take possession of the funds. However, some trustees impose certain fees and restrictions on such "rollovers." They may charge a fee to close an account or for handling an IRA transfer. Often, such fees are imposed only during the first four or five years, so the flexibility to make IRA rollovers may increase over time.

There is considerable value for the IRA holder in this flexibility. He may want to shift funds to a different type of account because of economic circumstances. In periods of high interest rates, for example, the IRA investor would be drawn to fixed-rate accounts. If interest rates decline markedly and the stock market takes off, variable-rate accounts may appear to be more attractive.

An individual's inclinations also may change as he gets closer to retirement age. When young, he may be willing to accept greater risks in quest of higher yields. Later, especially if this strategy has proved successful, he may become more cautious, more inclined to get his funds into investments with lower yields but also less risk of losing part of the fund's principal.

Eligibility, Other Requirements

Although the laws governing IRAs really are quite simple, there are a number of eligibility and procedural requirements that should be understood. IRA contributions are allowed during any year in which an individual earns compensation, defined generally as earned income — wages, bonuses, self-employment income, commissions, tips. Unearned income, for example, from property or securities investments, may not be used. An individual may contribute up to $2,000 to an IRA if he earns that much.

Anyone meeting the compensation requirements may contribute to an IRA. Thus, a husband and wife, if both work, may each contribute $2,000, making the total family contribution $4,000. The law also allows a contribution for what is called a "spousal" IRA. If one spouse earns no compensation while the other earns at least $2,250, then this married couple may contribute $2,250. They may divide this contribution into two IRA accounts in whatever way they wish so long as neither account receives more than $2,000 a year. The spousal IRA is allowed only if one spouse earns no compensation; any reportable compensation whatever eliminates a person's eligibility for a spousal IRA.

Interestingly, the IRA investor need not make his IRA contribution in the tax year for which he wants the deduction. The law allows the contribution to be made at any time before the investor files his income-tax return for a given year. That means, if he mails his tax return on April 15 of the subsequent year, he can contribute to his IRA at any time prior to that date. And if he gets an extension for filing his income-tax return, he also gets an automatic extension on his IRA-contribution deadline.

But it is not wise to wait. While the time of the IRA contribution does not make any difference as far as that $2,000 deduction is concerned, it makes a big difference as to the size of the interest on that $2,000. That money should be working, generating tax-deferred interest, as soon as possible. If an individual is in, say, the 35 percent tax bracket and contributes the maximum $2,000 every year for 30 years and earns an average of 10 percent on that investment over that time, he can accumulate 4 percent more (or $15,200) by making his IRA contributions at the beginning of each year rather than at the deadline.

Employer IRA Plans

An employer may get involved in his employee's IRA planning in a number of ways. The employer may establish a payroll-deduction plan for regular payments into an IRA. This may make IRA contributions more convenient but could limit the employee's flexibility. The employer plan may not include the full range of IRA options, for example. The employee may want to keep his IRA with a stockbroker, but that may not be possible under the employer plan.

Employees also may make voluntary contributions to an employment pension program. This is permissible regardless of the type of employment plan — profit-sharing, defined-benefit (guaranteeing certain pension levels, usually defined as a percentage of income) or defined-contribution (requiring certain contribution levels and proportionate benefits) — so long as it is a "qualified" pension plan, meaning it meets certain federal requirements for qualification for certain tax benefits. *(Pension Terminology in the Private Sector, see box, pp. 118-119.)*

Under these arrangements, up to $2,000 is funneled into the employer's retirement plan instead of into an outside IRA. But the contributions must be voluntary; they cannot be a condition of employment, nor can the employer contribute to the fund. In this way, the employee can build up his employment pension fund by an amount that otherwise could go into an IRA.

In addition, the law permits tax benefits for employer contributions to what is called a simplified employee pension (or SEP) plan. In an SEP, the employer makes a contribution for the employee. The employer takes the deduction, but the employee gets the benefit of having the income growth on the employer's contributions exempt from taxation until the money is taken out. Contributions may be as high as the lesser of $15,000 or 15 percent of an employee's income. In 1984 that goes up to the lesser of $30,000 or 25 percent of income. Having an IRA under the SEP program does not preclude an individual from creating his own IRA and taking tax deductions on contributions up to the standard $2,000 limit.

If an employee leaves his job or the employer pension fund is terminated, the employee's pension funds may be funneled into an IRA. Such "rollovers" allow an individual to keep deferring taxes on that money as well as on its future earnings. Also, he later may transfer these funds back into another qualified employer pension plan if he takes a new job that has a plan that allows such contributions.

Penalties for Early Withdrawal

By virtue of an IRA, an individual's taxable income can be reduced by $2,000 every year and his retirement fund can grow steadily by tax-deferred increments. Yet a question remains: What should persons do who are likely to need some of their money before they reach the magic age of 59 and a half? The short answer: They pay a penalty. Money distributed from an IRA is taxable as ordinary income, whether it is withdrawn before age 59 and a half or after. But if it is withdrawn before then, an additional 10 percent penalty tax must be paid on the amount withdrawn. The 10 percent penalty tax is waived if an individual is permanently disabled or if he dies before reaching that age and his survivors tap into the fund. Otherwise, the U.S. Treasury gets its 10 percent; that applies even if a person seeks to use his IRA fund to back up a loan. To use it as collateral, as far as the IRS is concerned, is the equivalent of a withdrawal.

The penalty payment requirement, however, does not necessarily mean that an individual should avoid that tax at all cost. Depending on the person's tax bracket and the rate of return on his money, he may find that his IRA investment has paid off even after accounting for the 10 percent penalty. That is because the tax deferral has the effect of increasing the size of his overall investment. As this investment accumulates compounded earnings, those earnings may overtake the 10 percent penalty. Ralph Bristol of the U.S. Treasury Department's Office of Tax Analysis calculates that "except for people in low tax brackets and/or people needing cash within the next few years, it is better to invest in an IRA today and, if necessary, cash it in and pay the penalty. You still come out ahead."

Writing in *Tax Notes*, a weekly publication produced by Tax Analysts of Arlington, Va., Bristol used the example of a person earning $29,900 (and thus in the 33 percent tax bracket). If he invested $2,000 in an IRA promising a return of 12 percent, he would do better with his IRA after four years, even with the 10 percent penalty tax, than with an after-tax investment of $2,000, according to Bristol. With a 16 percent return, the break-even point would be three years; at 8 percent, six years. Investors in lower tax brackets would have to hold their IRAs longer to overtake the penalty tax. At the 16 percent tax bracket, a person with an IRA paying 8 percent would not hit the break-even point until after 10 years, Bristol noted.

IRA Withdrawals for Retirement

As far as the federal government is concerned, IRAs are designed as a method of saving for retirement. However, the government does not penalize early retirement; withdrawals from an IRA become penalty-free at age 59 and a half. After that, taxes are paid at the regular rate on any money taken out of an IRA. And for 11 years thereafter, the retiree can take out as much money or as little as he wishes. Also, during those 11 years, he can continue contributing to his IRA. Thus, an IRA is probably the best investment for that period in an individual's life.

All these advantages end at age 70 and a half, however. At that point, all IRA contributions must stop, and the IRA investor must begin withdrawing his funds. One option would be to take all the money out at once. But the retiree probably would not want to do that because of the tax consequences; the whole sum would be taxable at ordinary tax rates, and that could be a tax jolt. For example, a married person has an IRA worth $85,600 after 1983 (when the final installment of President Reagan's individual income tax cuts is in place). If he were to withdraw his entire IRA sum in the first year of retirement, he would owe the government $25,920 in taxes. Thus his $85,600 would shrink to $59,680. And that assumes he had no other income for the year; otherwise, he likely would find himself in an even higher tax bracket. A single person with an IRA worth $81,200 would be left with only $48,165 if he withdrew his entire IRA sum and took the tax consequences. Also, once an individual closes out an IRA, his tax deferrals on interest accumulations cease.

Retirees with IRAs, therefore, should prepare a withdrawal schedule that meets their needs and reduces their tax burdens. They may want to make withdrawals on a monthly, quarterly or yearly basis. But any IRA withdrawal schedule must meet certain federal requirements.

The government expects a holder of an IRA to withdraw his money after age 70 and a half according to some minimum time limits. But determining a reasonable withdrawal timetable is complicated by the fact that nobody knows how long the individual will live. Likewise, nobody knows how much longer the retiree's spouse will live. The retiree probably established his IRA for his spouse's later years as well as his own. So the government allows four basic options for IRA withdrawals.

First, he may establish a timetable that extends IRA withdrawals for as long as he lives. Second, he may extend withdrawals over the combined lives of his spouse and himself. Third, he may make withdrawals over the period of his life expectancy at age 70 and a half, as determined by IRS tables. Fourth, he may establish a schedule based on the combined life expectancy of his spouse and himself, according to the IRS, at the time the IRA holder reaches age 70 and a half.

Under the first two options, the retiree transfers his IRA to an insurance company, which then provides an annuity contract for life, or, if he is married, for the combined lives of the couple. There is a certain gamble here on the part of both the retiree and the insurance company. The retiree with the IRA could die within a year, in which case payments cease (unless, of course, the contract includes a spouse). If the retiree's lifespan is shorter than anticipated, the insurance company comes out ahead. On the other hand, if he lives far beyond what he and the insurance company anticipated at the time the contract was sealed, the retiree reaps the extra benefits. An annuity contract covering an IRA holder and his spouse need not extend over the actual combined lives of both. The contract could cover a "time certain" period following the IRA holder's death, for 10 years, for example. But the specified period cannot exceed the combined life expectancy at the time the annuity contract is established.

Alternatively, the IRA holder may have his money distributed to himself over a period of time that matches his life expectancy at age 70 and a half. Based on IRS tables calculating the retiree's life expectancy, the IRA trustee distributes funds in yearly installments designed to exhaust the fund at the end of the retiree's expected life. Suppose one's life expectancy at age 70 and a half is 10 years, the IRA will provide a 10th of the money in the fund the first year, a ninth of the remainder the next year, and an eighth of what's left in the third year, and so on, as indicated in the following table:

Age	Remaining Years Of Life Expectancy	IRA Balance (10 Percent Annual Growth)	Annual Payment
70	10	$100,000	$10,000
71	9	99,000	11,000
72	8	96,800	12,100
73	7	93,170	13,310
74	6	87,846	14,641
75	5	80,525.50	16,105.10
76	4	70,862.44	17,715.61
77	3	58,461.51	19,487.17
78	2	42,871.77	21,435.88
79	1	23,579.46	23,579.46
80	0	0	0

The annual distributions will vary greatly, and actually will grow considerably throughout the 10-year distribution period. That is because the retiree takes a larger percentage each year and also because the fund continues to earn interest during the entire distribution period.

Suppose an individual has $100,000 in his IRA when he reaches age 70 and a half. His life expectancy is 10 years. He receives $10,000 — 10 percent of the $100,000 — in the first year. The next year he gets one ninth of the remainder. Meanwhile, his IRA fund has continued to earn interest at, for example, 10 percent annually. By the start of the second year, even though he has withdrawn $10,000, his fund has grown back up to $99,000 — the remaining $90,000 plus $9,000 in interest. That makes his yield for that year one ninth of $99,000 or $11,000. The third year he receives $12,100, or an eighth of $96,800, which is what his fund has grown to after that year's distributions and interest.

As seen from the table on page 211, the retiree's yearly distributions expand each year and his remaining IRA fund continues to earn interest. If an individual's life expectancy were higher and a retiree was allowed to make smaller withdrawals in the early years, his interest growth actually would expand his IRA pool in the early years of distribution. This is because the interest earned on his IRA fund would be greater than the amount paid out to him. For example, suppose the retiree's life expectancy were 20 years instead of 10 years. In that event, he could take out only $5,000 the first year, leaving $95,000 in his fund. But his interest growth — using the 10 percent figure — would swell his IRA pool that first year to $104,500 — $95,000 plus $9,500 in interest. That growth in the IRA balance would continue for a number of years before it started to decline because of ever larger withdrawals.

In fact, if the interest rate stayed at two percentage points above inflation, the payments to the retiree at the end of the distribution period, even in constant dollars, would be significantly larger than at the beginning.

It also is important to note that the institutional trustee of an IRA may impose certain withdrawal requirements, usually to prevent the holder from withdrawing his money more rapidly than the trustee desires.

Long-term Value of IRAs

An important variable in IRA planning is the account's value after years of contributions and income growth. That depends on how many years a person contributes to his IRA and the interest rate prevailing on it during his working years. At 8 percent, 10 years of contributions would produce $29,000; 40 years of contributions, $518,000. At 10 percent, by contrast, annual IRA contributions would produce $32,000 over 10 years and $885,000 over 40 years. Forty years of contributions at 12 percent would produce a whopping $1.534 million; at 14 percent, the IRA would be worth $2.684 million at the end of 40 years.

But those gargantuan figures can be misleading. An IRA holder is not very likely to receive a 14 percent return on his money unless interest rates are very high. That in turn would reflect persistent high inflation, and inflation would eat away at the buying power of the IRA savings. Thus, it should be noted that, whatever the financial institutions say in their advertising entreaties, IRAs will not produce retirement years of great wealth and ease. The most they can accomplish is to help people maintain the level of comfort they experienced in earlier years.

An IRA should be viewed as a supplement to Social Security and private pension plans, with those three income sources together designed to produce comfortable retirement years. It should be noted that Social Security generally replaces about 28 percent of the income of a single person earning about $30,000 during his last year of work. For a married couple earning the same amount, the Social Security replacement rate comes closer to 40 percent. Since a comfortable retirement income, according to experts in retirement matters, generally requires that about 75 percent of a person's last year of compensation be replaced by pension income, it can be seen that IRAs provide merely supplementary income.

It takes a substantial amount of personal savings to get one's retirement income up to that 75 percent level. Besides the inflation factor, which can reduce substantially the buying power of an IRA savings fund, it should be remembered that IRAs are taxed as funds are withdrawn. While these withdrawals may be subject to lower tax rates than those experienced during an individual's working years, they nevertheless are significant.

The Center for the Study of Services, a Washington, D.C.-based consumer-advocacy organization, has attempted to put this in perspective. It studied the outcome of 25 years of full IRA contributions to a fund paying 10 percent interest. It assumed an inflation rate of 8 percent over that 25 years and a 35 percent tax rate on the retiree's withdrawals. The value of the IRA after 25 years, before taxes and before adjusting for inflation, would be $216,364, the group noted. After taxes, the value dropped to $140,636. After adjusting for inflation, the IRA's value dropped to only $20,535. That does not negate the value of IRAs, it merely describes accurately what they can accomplish.

To point out what taxes and inflation do to an IRA savings pool is not an argument against IRAs. Certainly, building up a savings pool worth $216,364 at retirement will add financial comfort in those years, even with 8 percent inflation. And, alternatively, if an individual invested that $2,000 after taxes every year at the same interest rate, the investment would be worth only $81,530 after 25 years; adjust that for inflation and the non-IRA investment's value drops to $11,905. Clearly, the IRA investment is a better buy, but it cannot be considered some kind of financial coup de grace. It is merely a prudent method of helping to ease the financial burdens during retirement.

Keogh Plans

Keogh plans essentially are jumbo IRA programs for the self-employed. Like IRAs, they allow tax deductions for annual contributions and generate income growth that is tax-deferred. Like IRA savings, Keogh savings build up to age 70 and a half, at which time the distribution process must begin. Like the IRA law, the Keogh law allows withdrawals after age 59 and a half without penalty. Distributions from Keogh funds, like IRA distributions, are taxed at ordinary rates.

But unlike IRAs, Keoghs generally are available only to self-employed persons who are subject to the self-employment tax. Also, the contribution limits for Keogh plans are much higher. Annual tax-deferred contributions after 1983 can run as high as 20 percent of earnings, up to a maximum of $30,000. (For 1983, the limit was 15 percent of self-employment income, up to $15,000.) This may sound generous, and it is. But Keogh plans also carry certain requirements that may lessen their desirability for some self-employed persons. Also, persons with Keogh plans are not precluded from opening IRAs.

The Employment Benefit Research Institute notes that the last year for which comprehensive information is available on the utilization of Keoghs is 1977. At that time there were 649,456 plans in operation with 907,403 participants. At the end of that year, according to IRS data, these plans held $6.5 billion in assets.

Forging a Congressional Consensus

The Keogh plan is named for former Rep. Eugene Keogh, D-N.Y. (1937-67), who was the main proponent of the the Keogh law in

Congress. It took a lot of persistence. The idea of permitting tax deferrals for individual retirement programs was not warmly received in Congress when first introduced. Though such bills had been introduced since the early 1950s, the concept was not seriously considered until 1957, when Rep. Keogh introduced his version and received the backing of a new organization specifically formed to push the idea. Called the American Thrift Assembly, it consisted of a federation of 72 business and professional organizations representing small businesses, savings institutions and self-employed persons.

Although proponents of the idea began gaining strength after that, the measure still was vigorously opposed. Liberal members of Congress saw it as a tax giveaway for wealthy doctors and lawyers who did not need federal help to provide for their retirement. The Treasury Department during both the Eisenhower and Kennedy administrations opposed the measure because of the anticipated revenue losses. Generally, the idea of using the tax system to help individuals prepare for retirement was slow to gain political support. But in 1958 the bill was passed by the House. It died in the Senate. In the next Congress, the same thing happened.

In 1960 the Treasury Department offered some changes it said would make the measure more palatable. This enhanced its legislative stature and led eventually to passage by Congress two years later. Tax deferral was permitted only on earned income, not on unearned (investment) income. And anyone taking advantage of the tax deferrals also had to set up a retirement plan for his employees.

With these changes made, the legislation was approved by the Senate Finance Committee in 1960, but it still could not get through the Senate. Then the Kennedy administration came to office in 1961, and the government again opposed the legislation. But after some legislative maneuvering on the bill by Sen. Everett Dirksen (1951-69), it finally was passed by the Senate, and cleared by Congress, in 1962. That became possible only after another major amendment was adopted that diluted the measure. That amendment stipulated that a self-employed person could defer taxes on only half the income set aside in a Keogh. That reduced the Treasury's revenue loss, and the Kennedy administration then withdrew its opposition.

The result was that Congress accepted a concept that formed the basis for the present-day Keoghs and IRAs. Pressures to expand the concept continue to surface in Congress from time to time. Some lawmakers say tax deferrals should be allowed for savings pools used for other things besides retirement, such as buying a home or meeting college tuition costs. Such provisions are not likely to win congressional approval soon, but the support for them can be traced back to those seemingly endless debates over Keogh plans in the 1950s and 1960s.

1962 Law Provisions. The initial Keogh law permitted annual tax deferrals on the lesser of $1,250 or 50 percent of any amounts set aside in a retirement fund. Only earned income would apply, and self-employed persons setting up such plans were required to provide a similar plan for any employees with at least three years of service. Withdrawals were not permitted without penalty until age 59 and a half. In 1966 the one-half tax deferral limit was eliminated, and Keogh holders beginning in 1968 were permitted to defer taxes on all contributions up to $2,500.

1974 Revisions. In 1974, when Congress enacted the Employee Retirement Income Security Act (ERISA), it expanded the deductible limits further: to the lesser of $7,500 or 15 percent of annual earnings up to $100,000. (That 1974 law also created the IRA funds for persons not covered by employment-based pension programs.) The 1981 tax act expanded the limits even further to the lesser of $15,000 or 15 percent of the first $200,000 of income. It also contained provisions to ensure that contributions for employees could not be diminished as a proportion of an employer's contributions as the employer's contribution increased.

1982 Expansion. Then came the 1982 Tax Equity and Fiscal Responsibility act, which expanded Keogh contributions still further, beginning in 1984, to the lesser of $30,000 or 20 percent of income. That bill contained other important changes. One concerned the requirement that Keogh holders create retirement plans for employees. Any employee plan had to meet certain minimum contribution standards based on the employer's own Keogh contributions. The 1982 law allowed the employer, beginning in 1984, to calculate his employees' Social Security benefits into the formula, which had the effect of reducing the minimum contribution levels of employee-plan contributions. In addition, the employer was allowed to serve as the trustee of these plans instead of having to pay a bank or brokerage firm to monitor the investments. The cost savings could be significant, but there were dangers. Plan trustees were subject to strict fiduciary accountability, and employers could be sued by Keogh members for imprudent investment decisions.

Under the 1982 legislation, employers with Keoghs could put up to

10 percent of their own income into their Keogh plans without increasing their contributions for employees. Previously, these voluntary employer contributions were limited to $2,500 annually. Of course, such voluntary contributions are after-tax contributions; they are not tax-deductible. But the savings can generate income along with other Keogh funds, and taxes on these earnings are deferred until the money is withdrawn.

Keoghs and Corporate Pensions

But the 1982 law's most dramatic impact on Keoghs was wrought by a provision eliminating nearly all distinctions between Keoghs and corporate pension plans. Previously, limits on tax-deferred contributions for corporate pension plans were considerably higher than those for Keoghs. Corporate pension contribution limits were indexed to inflation, so they rose every year automatically. Keogh plan contribution limits were not indexed. And the law permitted holders of corporate plans to borrow generously from their plans. The result of all this was that many wealthy self-employed persons — notably doctors, lawyers, accountants, entertainers, athletes — incorporated in order to be eligible for those generous benefits.

Many law firms and accounting firms gave up partnership status to begin practicing in corporate form. Although many traditionalist professionals resisted the idea on the ground that standard partnership arrangements were the proper way for professionals to do business, the economic incentives to incorporate were tremendous. Compared with the flashy corporate plans, Keoghs looked pallid. And the number of self-employed professionals taking the corporate route mushroomed after 1969, when court rules and changes in Internal Revenue Service regulations eased procedures for professional incorporation. In 1971, 50,000 medical and dental practices filed corporate tax returns with the IRS. Eight years later, the number jumped to 105,000.

Changes in 'Top-heavy' Plans. All that changed with the 1982 measure. That act marked a major turning point for corporate retirement plans — and for Keoghs. Harold Dankner, a partner in Coopers & Lybrand, a major accounting firm, called the changes "the most significant development in rules governing retirement planning" since the 1974 ERISA law. Previously, Dankner notes, the big question in determining benefit and contribution restrictions was whether the employer was a corporate or non-corporate entity. With that distinction essentially eliminated, the big question became whether a plan was "top heavy." Top-heavy plans are subject to special rules affecting vesting, contributions and benefits. These rules are designed to protect employees from discriminatory plans in which the bosses give themselves disproportionately large pension benefits at the expense of employees. The top-heavy provisions apply to Keogh and corporate plans alike.

The top-heavy provisions apply to both defined-benefit plans and defined-contribution plans. Under the 1982 law, a defined-benefit plan is top-heavy if the current value of accrued benefits of "key employees" exceeds 60 percent of the current value for all plan participants. Key employees are defined as officers, 50 percent owners, 1 percent owners earning more than $150,000 annually, and employees owning the 10 largest interests in the company. For defined-contribution plans, the top-heavy designation applies if 60 percent of the account balances have been accumulated on behalf of the key employees.

The vesting provisions relating to top-heavy plans require 100 percent vesting after three years of service, with a participation requirement not exceeding three years or a six-year graded vesting schedule (20 percent after two years of service and 20 percent for each subsequent year) with a participation requirement not exceeding one year. *(Vesting and participation requirements in private pension plans, see p. 137.)*

The act also requires minimum benefits for middle- and lower-level employees: for defined-benefit plans, 2 percent of average annual compensation per year of service not to exceed 20 percent; for defined-contribution plans, a contribution of 3 percent of compensation for each year in which a key employee receives a 3 percent allocation of his annual compensation.

Curbing Corporate Advantage. Congress imposed these stringent top-heavy provisions because of what many legislators considered abuses by many holders of corporate pension plans. A doctor, say, would incorporate, funnel huge amounts of tax-free money into a pension plan from which he could borrow generously, and then provide little or nothing for his employees. But under the 1982 act, Keogh plans fell under the same provision because one of Congress' methods of curing such corporate-plan problems was to eliminate the special incentives for self-employed persons to adopt corporate plans instead of Keoghs. In eliminating that distinction, Congress also eliminated the disparity in contribution limits. Limits for corporate-plan contributions decline in 1984 to $30,000 from $45,000. Meanwhile, for defined-benefit corporate plans — those that allow contributions necessary to produce a specified benefit level at retirement — the maximum benefit falls to $90,000 a year from $136,425. This was designed to correspond generally to the $30,000 figure on contributions.

To curb the generosity of corporate plans further, Congress placed a two-year hold on the automatic inflation adjustments in corporate-plan contribution limits, beginning in 1984. Those adjustments resume in 1986, but then they will also apply to Keogh plans. Thus, another Keogh-corporate plan disparity is eliminated, and Keogh holders are given protection against inflation.

The law also clamps down on the generous borrowing privileges once accorded holders of corporate pension plans. In doing so, it increased the generosity of borrowing allowed Keogh holders. The maximum that can be borrowed from either type of plan is 50 percent of vested benefits up to $50,000. But holders will be permitted to borrow up to $10,000 even if that is more than half of their vested benefits. Any loan must be repaid within five years unless it is used to buy or improve a principal residence. Loans that are not repaid within five years would be treated as plan distributions, thus losing their preferential tax status. Personal loans for purchase or improvements of a principal residence would be accorded a more liberal repayment schedule; they must meet a test of being "reasonable."

Impact of 1982 Act

The question posed by all these changes is whether there remains any incentive to move to corporate plans rather than staying with Keoghs. Most experts feel that the elimination of the disparities between the two approaches also eliminates much of the value in choosing corporate plans. Dallas Salisbury of the Employee Benefit Research Institute tells of a large San Francisco law firm that had begun moving toward incorporation of its lawyers, 40 at a time, based on seniority. The junior partners had to wait for corporate status while their more senior colleagues enjoyed the more generous pension-plan provisions accorded the incorporated lawyers. Then came the 1982 act, and the senior partners suddenly were "behind the times," Salisbury noted.

A published analysis by Coopers and Lybrand suggests the new law essentially places noncorporate plans on a par with corporate plans. "Only minor differences remain," the firm says. "As a result, in the future there will be no incentive for professionals to incorporate their practices in order to obtain greater retirement benefits. Beginning in 1984, unincorporated professionals will be able to significantly increase their deductible contributions." For one thing, according to Salisbury, "it's very expensive to incorporate." Corporate papers must be filed and careful records kept; and there are legal fees to be paid as well as contributions to Social Security and unemployment taxes; finally, stock-holder meetings have to be held. Such requirements can cost several thousand dollars a year even for a small medical or dental office. On the other hand, there may not be much incentive to abandon corporate plans either because just changing status costs substantial amounts of money.

But some experts are of the opinion that the 1982 law will wipe out many corporate plans. James Conahan, a pension lawyer, suggests that the contribution restrictions on corporate plans will lead to plan termina-tions. "I'm convinced," he says, "that tens of thousands of plans will sim-ply shut down." Those now classified as key employees will channel their money into other retirement options, he maintains. The cost of compliance alone — hiring the expertise for making necessary changes — will cost between $2,000 and $4,000 for most small companies, he adds.

Other experts doubt there will be a rush to abandon corporate plans even if the rush into them ceases. Even Coopers & Lybrand suggests that "the benefits for key employees will still be substantial in most situations." Other considerations also come into play. For example, a corporation has the advantage of lower tax rates, which can be a plus for doctors, dentists and other professionals who must invest in expensive equipment.

Clearly, decisions on whether to continue with corporate plans will depend on why they were initiated in the first place. Some are for pension-plan benefits. Some are for overall tax planning. Some are for es-tate planning. And some are for cash-flow advantages. In the past, for ex-ample, many corporate plan participants took advantage of the liberal borrowing allowances to borrow for corporate purposes. It was a great cash-flow mechanism that now will be eliminated. That, of course, is an-other disincentive to move to the corporate option.

Thus, Keogh plans are sure to receive renewed attention as interest in corporate plans diminishes for self-employed persons. But the changes in the 1982 tax bill will not be universally beneficial. The dramatic increase in the contribution limit will not help the self-employed person without much money to sock away. Given the requirements for setting up employee plans, such persons may want to consider an IRA rather than a Keogh. And self-employed persons running small but growing businesses that are taking on new employees rapidly may find that they cannot save enough in taxes to make up for the cost of employee plans. Incorporation for such persons may be a wise course because it creates other pension-planning and tax-deduction options.

But Keoghs have grown tremendously in generosity since that first modest bill squeaked through Congress back in 1962. And many experts now feel that most persons will find the new Keoghs significantly better than the old, even with the top-heavy requirements. As Coopers & Lybrand puts it, "Although the top heavy rules will generally result in somewhat higher costs, top heavy plans will continue to provide substantial benefits for key employes."

Key Dates in the Development of U.S. Pensions

1798. Congress establishes a health-insurance program for the Merchant Marine. Sailors are required to contribute a few cents a month to pay for hospital care provided by a marine hospital.

1859. New York City policemen obtain a pension fund, the first created for state or local government workers.

1875. American Express Co. sponsors first pension plan in U.S. private industry. It is financed solely by employer contributions.

1880. Baltimore & Ohio Railroad Co. establishes first formal plan supported by both employer and employee contributions.

1892. Columbia University establishes first private college retirement program for professors at age 65 with a minimum of 15 years' service.

1893. Nation's first pension fund for public-school teachers is established in Chicago.

1901. Carnegie Steel Co. establishes first lasting plan for a manufacturing company. The pension plan subsequently is taken over by the United States Steel Co. in 1911.

1905. Granite Cutters union sponsors a pension fund, the first by organized labor that is destined to last.

1907. The International Typographical Union adopts a formal pension plan, the first of the large international unions to do so.

1920. Federal Civil Service Retirement and Disability Fund is created.

1921. The first group annuity contract for pension funds in the United States is issued by Metropolitan Life Insurance Co.

The Revenue Act of 1921 exempts from taxes employer contributions to profit-sharing trusts. Provisions are extended to pension trusts in 1926.

1935. Congress approves legislation to set up the Social Security system providing old age benefits to workers in commerce and industry. Benefits are to be based on cumulative wages and to be payable beginning in 1942 to qualified workers age 65 and older. A payroll tax of 1 percent on employer and employees, each imposed on a wage base of $3,000, will to be collected as of January 1937; the combined tax is scheduled to rise to 3 percent by 1949.

The Railroad Retirement system is established and amended in 1937 to create a unified system for the industry.

1939. The starting date for Social Security benefits is advanced to 1940. Benefits for dependents of retired workers and for surviving dependents in case of a worker's death are authorized.

1949. The Supreme Court rules that employers are required to include pensions in collective bargaining.

The Steel Industry Fact-Finding Board holds that employers are required to provide workers with pensions and other welfare benefits.

1952. The College Retirement Equities Fund (CREF) is established as the first variable annuity fund.

Social Security benefits are increased by 12.5 percent.

1954. The Social Security wage base is increased to $4,200, and benefits are increased by 13 percent. Coverage is almost universal except for federal government employees.

1956. Disability Insurance (DI) benefits are added to Social Security, payable at age 50. Women are permitted to retire at age 62 with actuarially reduced benefits.

1958. The Federal Welfare and Pension Plans Disclosure Act becomes law, requiring periodic reports on the operation and administration of welfare and pension plans. (The law is repealed by ERISA in 1974.)

Benefits are added for dependents of Social Security Disability Insurance recipients, and the DI eligibility standard is liberalized.

1959. The Life Insurance Company Income Tax Act is passed, excluding from taxation investment income attributable to insured pension reserves.

1960. The age 50 limitation for DI eligibility is eliminated.

1961. Social Security is revised to allow men to retire at age 62 with an actuarial reduction in benefits.

1962. The Self-Employed Individuals Retirement Act (HR 10, or Keogh Act) opens pension planning to the self-employed, unincorporated small businesses, farmers, professional people and their employees.

1965. Hospital Insurance (Medicare) is added to Social Security, providing health care payments for persons age 65 and older.

Social Security cash benefits are increased by 7 percent.

The President's Committee on Corporate Pension Funds and Other Private Retirement and Welfare Programs issues its report, a precursor of

ERISA.

1968. Social Security cash benefits are increased by 13 percent. The tax rate is now 4.4 percent and the wage base $7,800.

1969. Social Security cash benefits are increased by 15 percent.

1972. Legislation is enacted to provide a new program of benefits — supplemental security income (SSI) — to persons 65 or older, blind, disabled, with little or no income. The SSI replaces the original Old Age Assistance program.

Social Security cash benefit increases, which previously had been made in an ad hoc fashion by Congress, are made automatic, as is the increase in the wage base.

1974. The Employee Retirement Income Security Act (ERISA) is signed into law. The act provides protection to participants in private pension plans for plan terminations, establishes funding and fiduciary standards for private plans and provides individual pension incentives to those whose employers have no pension plans through individual Retirement Accounts (IRAs).

1977. Congress enacts a major overhaul of the Social Security system to correct a technical error in computing the starting benefit levels of future retirees. The revision is designed to reduce deficits caused by inflation. The deficit necessitates the largest increase in scheduled tax rates in the system's history to date, culminating at 7.65 percent on employees and employers in 1990.

1978. Congress passes the Age Discrimination in Employment Act Amendments, raising the mandatory retirement age from 65 to 70 for most private sector and state and local government employees and eliminating it for federal employees.

1980. Congress completes action on legislation tightening funding requirements and reducing government liability for multi-employer pension plans covering 8 million workers.

1981. The Economic Recovery Tax Act of 1981 raises contribution limits on Individual Retirement Accounts and Keogh plans and extends IRA eligibility to persons covered by employer pension plans.

The President's Commission on Pension Policy, established in 1978, issues its final report recommending a minimum universal pension system (MUPS), separate from Social Security, financed by employer contributions.

1982. The Tax Equity and Fiscal Responsibility Act of 1982 reduces the benefit and contribution limits for qualified private plans, raises the age at which defined plan participants may receive the maximum benefit without actuarial reductions and decreases the aggregate dollar limit for individuals participating in defined benefit and defined contribution plans.

1983. Following the recommendations of a National Commission on Social Security Reform, Congress in March enacts a comprehensive Social Security rescue package. The legislation increases employer and employee payroll taxes; gradually increases the retirement age; extends coverage to all new federal civilian employees; makes cuts and adjustments in the cost-of-living adjustments; and revises certain accounting procedures.

SELECTED BIBLIOGRAPHY

Chapter 1 - Social Security: The Funding Crisis

Articles

Burkhauser, Richard V., and Smeeding, Timothy M. "The Net Impact of the Social Security System on the Poor." *Public Policy*, Spring 1981, pp. 159-178.

Capra, James R., et al."Social Security: An Analysis of its Problems." *Federal Reserve Bank of New York Quarterly Review*, Autumn 1982, pp. 1-17.

Chen, Yung-Ping. "The Growth of Fringe Benefits: Implications for Social Security." *Monthly Labor Review*, November 1981, pp. 3-10.

Ehrbar, A. F. "Social Security: Heading for the Wrong Solution." *Fortune*, Dec. 13, 1982.

Gwirtzman, Milton. "What the Social Security Commission Must Confront." *Journal for the Institute of Socioeconomic Studies*, Autumn 1982, pp. 25-33.

Morrison, Peter A. "Demographic Links to Social Security: An Aging Population, More Women Workers, and Longer Life Expectancy are Some of the Demographic Factors that will Shape the Future of Social Security Financing." *Challenge*, January-February 1982, pp. 44-49.

Munnell, Alicia H. "A Calmer Look at Social Security." *The New York Review of Books*, March 17, 1983.

Pepper, Claude. "The Social Security System." *National Forum*, Fall 1982, pp. 12-14.

Peterson, Peter G. "Social Security: The Coming Crisis." *The New York Review of Books*, Dec. 2, 1982.

——. "The Salvation of Social Security." *The New York Review of Books*, Dec. 16, 1982.

Pitts, Joyce M. "Economic Well-Being of the Elderly: Recommendations from the White House Conference on Aging." *Family Economics Review*, October 1982, pp. 23-27.

Books

Burkhauser, Richard V., and Holden, Karen C., eds. *A Challenge to Social Security: the Changing Roles of Women and Men in American Society.* New York: Academic Press, 1982.

Campbell, Colin. *Financing Social Security.* Washington, D.C.: American Enterprise Institute for Public Policy Research, 1979.

Crystal, Stephen. *America's Old Age Crisis: Public Policy and the Two Worlds of Aging.* New York: Basic Books, 1982.

Derthick, Martha. *Policymaking for Social Security.* Washington, D.C.: The Brookings Institution, 1979.

Gordus, Jeanne Prial. *Leaving Early: Perspectives and Problems in Current Retirement Practice and Policy.* Kalamazoo, Mich.: Upjohn Institute for Employment Research, 1980.

Kutza, Elizabeth Ann. *The Benefits of Old Age: Social Welfare Policy for the Elderly.* Chicago, Ill.: University of Chicago Press, 1981.

Lammers, William W. *Public Policy and the Aging.* Washington, D.C.: CQ Press, 1983.

Olson, Laura Katz. *The Political Economy of Aging: the State, Private Power and Social Welfare.* New York: Columbia University Press, 1982.

Robertson, A. Haeworth. *The Coming Revolution in Social Security.* Reston, Va.: Reston Publishing Co., 1981.

Vicusi, W. Kip. *Welfare of the Elderly.* New York: John Wiley & Sons, 1979.

Government Publications

National Commission on Social Security. *Social Security in America's Future.* Washington, D.C.: Government Printing Office, 1981.

U.S. Congress. House. Committee on Ways and Means. Subcommittee on Social Security. *Administration of the Social Security Program. Hearing, Dec. 11, 1981.* Washington, D.C.: Government Printing Office, 1982.

———. *Summary of Testimony on President Reagan's Social Security Financing Package. Committee Print, 1981.* Washington, D.C.: Government Printing Office, 1981.

U.S. Congress. House. Select Committee on Aging. *An Analysis of the Development and Rationales of the United States Income Security System, 1776-1980. Committee Print, 1981.* Washington, D.C.: Government Printing Office, 1981.

———. *Retirement: The Broken Promise. Committee Print, December 1980.* Washington, D.C.: Government Printing Office, 1981.

Chapter 2 - Rescuing Social Security

Articles

Hsiao, William C. "An Optional Indexing Method for Social Security." In *Financing Social Security.* Campbell, Colin D., ed. Washington, D.C.: American Enterprise Institute for Public Policy Research, 1979.

Salisbury, Dallas L. "Toward a National Retirement Income Policy: Priorities for the '80's." *Pension World,* May 1981. pp. 52-56.

Books

Levy, Mickey D. *Achieving Financial Solvency in Social Security.* Washington, D.C.: American Enterprise Institute for Public Policy Research, 1981.

McGluskey, Neil G., and Borgatta Edgar F., eds., *Aging and Retirement: Prospects, Planning and Policy.* Beverly Hills, Calif.: Sage Publications, 1981.

Stein, Bruno. *Social Security and Pensions in Transition.* New York: The Free Press, 1980.

Government Publications

National Commission on Social Security Reform. *Report of the National Commission on Social Security Reform.* January 1983. Washington, D.C.: Government Printing Office, 1983.

U.S. Congress. Congressional Budget Office. *Financing Social Security: Issues and Options for the Long Run.* Washington, D.C.: Government Printing Office, 1982.

U.S. Congress. House. Select Committee on Aging. *Impact of Administration's Social Security Proposals on Present and Future Beneficiaries. Committee Print, July, 1981.* Washington, D.C.: Government Printing Office, 1981.

———. Subcommittee on Retirement Income and Employment. *Social Security Financing and Options for the Future. New York, Hearing, Oct. 26, 1981.* Washington, D.C.: Government Printing Office, 1982.

U.S. Congress. Senate. Committee on Finance. Subcommittee on Social Security and Income Maintenance Programs. *Social Security Financing and Options for the Future. Hearings, July 7-10, 1981.* Washington, D.C.: Government Printing Office, 1981.

U.S. Department of Health and Human Services. Social Security Administration. *Social Security Bulletin.* Selected issues. Washington, D.C.: Government Printing Office.

Chapter 3 - Health Care: Medicare and Medicaid

Articles

Baucus, Max. "The Federal Response to Medicare Supplementary Insurance." *Journal of the Institute of Socioeconomic Studies*, Autumn 1980, pp. 65-73.

Demkovich, Linda E. "Reagan Takes on the Elderly Again as He Seeks to Slow Medicare's Growth." *National Journal*, Sept. 12, 1981, pp. 1616-1620.

Fallows, James. "Entitlements." *Atlantic*, November 1982, pp. 51-59.

Freelander, Mark S., and Schendler, Carol Ellen. "National Health Expenditure Growth in the 1980s." *Health Care Financing Review*, March 1983.

Gibson, Robert M., and Waldo, Daniel R. "National Health Expenditures, 1981." *Health Care Financing Review*, September 1982.

"Hospital Case Mix Reimbursement: The New Jersey Diagnostic Related Groups Experiment." *State Health Notes*, September 1980. Intergovernmental Health Policy Project, George Washington University, Washington, D.C.

Link, Charles R. et al. "Cost Sharing, Supplementary Insurance and Health Services Utilization Among the Medicare Elderly." *Health Care Financing Review*, Fall 1980, pp. 25-31.

McNerney, Walter J. "Control of Health Care Costs in the 1980s." *New England Journal of Medicine*, Nov. 6, 1980, pp. 1088-1095.

"Recent and Proposed Changes in State Medicaid Programs: A Fifty State Survey." Intergovernmental Health Policy Project, George Washington University, Washington, D.C., April 1983.

Russell, Louise B. "Medical Care." In *Setting National Priorities, the 1984 Budget*. Pechman, Joseph A., ed. Washington, D.C.: The Brookings Institution, 1983.

"When Medicare Doesn't Pay Enough." *Business Week*, Aug. 30, 1982, p. 91.

Books

Davidson, Stephen M. *Medicaid Decisions: A Systematic Analysis of the Cost Problem*. Cambridge, Mass.: Ballinger Publishing Co., 1980.

Feder, Judith, Holahan, John, and Marmor, Theodore. *National Health Insurance: Conflicting Goals and Policy Choices*. Washington, D.C.: Urban Institute, 1980.

Harrington, Geri. *The Medicare Answer Book*. New York: Harper & Row, 1982.

Muse, Donald N., and Sawyer, Darwin. *The Medicare and Medicaid Data Book, 1981*. Baltimore, Md.: Department of Health and Human Services, Health Care Financing Administration, Office of Research and Demonstrations, 1982.

Numbers, Ronald L., ed., *Compulsory Health Insurance: the Continuing American Debate*. Westport, Conn.: Greenwood Press, 1982.

Spitz, Bruce. *State Guide to Medicaid Cost Containment*. Intergovernmental Health Policy Project, George Washington University, Washington, D.C., 1981.

Government Publications

U.S. Congress. Congressional Budget Office. Human Resources and Community Development Division. *Prospects for Medicare's Hospital Insurance Trust Fund*. Washington, D.C.: Government Printing Office, 1983.

U.S. Congress. House. Select Committee on Aging. *Medicare After 15 Years: Has It Become a Broken Promise to the Elderly? Committee Print, Nov. 17, 1980*. Washington, D.C.: Government Printing Office, 1981.

U.S. Congress. Senate. Special Committee on Aging. *Health Care Expenditures for the Elderly: How Much Protection Does Medicare Provide? Committee Print, 1982*, Washington, D.C.: Government Printing Office, 1982.

U.S. Department of Health and Human Services. *Your Medicare Handbook*. Baltimore, Md.: Health Care Financing Administration, 1982.

Chapter 4 - Private Pension Plans

Articles

American Council of Life Insurance. "Pension Facts." Washington, D.C.: American Council of Life Insurance, 1982.

Committee on Economic Development. "Reforming Retirement Policies." New York: CED, September 1981.

Curtis, John E. "Multi-employer Plan Amendments of 1980: Panacea or Poison?" *Journal of Pension Planning and Compliance*, November 1980, pp. 419-442.

Ehrbar, A. F. "Those Pension Plans are Even Weaker Than You Think." *Fortune*, November 1977, pp. 104-114.

Gill, James F., and O'Toole, Michael F. "Review of the Multi-employer Pension Plan Amendments Act of 1980." *Pension World*, August 1981, pp. 31-35.

Gropper, Diane Hal. "Can the PBGC Be Saved? Congress Has A Plan to Keep the Pension Benefit Guaranty Corp. from Going Broke." *Institutional Investor.* September 1982, pp. 123-124.

"Pension Coverage and Expected Retirement Benefits." Final report prepared for the American Council of Life Insurance by ICF Inc. Washington, D.C., October 1982.

Books

Allen, Everett T., Melone, Joseph J., and Rosenbloom, Jerry S. *Pension Planning: Pensions, Profit Sharing and Other Deferred Compensation Plans.* Fourth ed. Homewood, Ill.: Richard D. Irwin Inc., 1981.

Bureau of National Affairs. *Pensions and Other Retirement Benefit Plans.* Washington, D.C.: Bureau of National Affairs, 1982.

Clark, Robert. *The Role of Private Pensions in Maintaining Living Standards in Retirement.* Washington, D.C.: National Planning Association, October 1977.

Guide Book to Pension Planning. Chicago: Commerce Clearing House Inc., 1981.

McGill, Dan M., ed. *Social Security and Private Pension Plans: Competitive or Complimentary?* Homewood, Ill.: Richard D. Irwin, Inc., 1977.

Munnell, Alicia H. *The Economics of Private Pensions.* Washington, D.C.: The Brookings Institution, 1982.

Government Publications

President's Commission on Pension Policy. *Final Report.* Washington, D.C.: Government Printing Office, 1981.

U.S. Congress. House. Select Committee on Aging. *The End of Mandatory Retirement. Hearing, July 16, 1982.* Washington, D.C.: Government Printing Office, 1982.

———. *Fraud and Abuse in Pensions and Related Employee Benefit Plans. Hearing, Nov. 4, 1981.* Washington, D.C.: Government Printing Office, 1981.

———. *The Future of Retirement Programs. Hearing Feb. 26, 1981.* Washington, D.C.: Government Printing Office, 1981.

———. *Pension Funding Problems. Hearing, June 7, 1982.* Washington, D.C.: Government Printing Office, 1982.

U.S. Congress. Senate. Committee on Labor and Human Resources.

Subcommitee on Labor. *Multi-employer Pension Plan Stabilization Act of 1981. Hearings, March 11-12, 1982.* Washington, D.C.: Government Printing Office, 1982.

U.S. Department of Justice. Task Force on Discrimination, Civil Rights Division. *The Pension Game: American Pension System from the Viewpoint of the Average Woman.* Washington, D.C.: Government Printing Office, 1979.

U.S. Department of Labor. *Patterns of Worker Coverage by Private Pension Plans.* Washington, D.C.: Government Printing Office, 1980.

Chapter 5 - Public Pension Plans

Articles

Burtless, Gary, and Hauseman, Jerry. "Double Dipping: The Combined Effects of Social Security and Civil Service Pensions on Employee Retirement." *Journal of Public Economics,* July 1982, pp. 139-159.

Schulz, James H. "Public Policy and the Future Roles of Public and Private Pensions." In *Income Support Policies for the Aged.* Tolley, G.S., and Burkhauser, Richard V., eds. Cambridge, Mass.: Ballinger Publishing Co., 1977, pp. 11-36.

"State Retirement Systems: Ninth Annual Survey." *Pension World,* August 1982, pp. 35-47.

Books

Greenough, William C., and King, Francis P. *Pension Plans and Public Policy.* New York: Columbia University Press, 1976.

Hartman, Robert. *Pay and Pensions for Federal Workers.* Washington, D.C.: The Brookings Institution, 1983.

McGill, Dan M. *Financing the Civil Service Retirement System.* Homewood, Ill.: Richard D. Irwin, Inc., 1979.

Tilove, Robert. *Public Employee Pension Funds.* New York: Columbia University Press, 1976.

Winkleross, Howard E., and McGill, Dan M. *Public Pension Plans: Standards of Design, Funding and Reporting.* Homewood, Ill.: Dow Jones-Irwin, 1979.

Government Publications

U.S. Congress. Congressional Budget Office. *Civil Service Retirement: Financing and Costs.* Washington, D.C.: Government Printing Office, May 1981.

_____. *The Railroad Retirement System: Benefits and Financing*. Washington, D.C.: Government Printing Office, December 1981.

U.S. Congress. General Accounting Office. *An Actuarial and Economic Analysis of State and Local Government Pension Plans*. Washington, D.C.: Government Printing Office, 1980.

U.S. Congress. House. Committee on Post Office and Civil Service. *Background on the Civil Service Retirement System. A Report Prepared by the Congressional Research Service. Committee Print, April 20, 1983*. Washington, D.C.: Government Printing Office, 1983.

U.S. Congress. House. Committee on Ways and Means. Subcommittee on Social Security. *Termination of Social Security Coverage for Employees of State and Local Governments and Non Profit Groups, Committee Print, 1982*. Washington, D.C.: Government Printing Office, 1982.

U.S. Congress. Senate. Committee on Finance. Subcommittee on Savings, Pensions, and Investment Policy. *Pension Reform for State and Local Employee Retirement Systems. Hearing, March 29, 1982*. Washington, D.C.: Government Printing Office, 1982.

U.S. Department of Commerce. Bureau of the Census. *Finances of Selected Public Employee Retirement Systems*. Washington, D.C.: Government Printing Office, issued quarterly.

Chapter 6 - Individual Retirement Security

Articles

"Building a Base For a Savings Economy: A Major Boost Could Come From IRA's." *Business Week*, Sept. 7, 1981, pp. 86-87.

"Costs and Consequences of Tax Incentives: the Individual Retirement Account." *Harvard Law Review*. February 1981, pp. 864-886.

"The Widening Choices in IRA Investment." *Business Week*, Dec. 6, 1982, pp. 120-121.

Books

Egan, Jack. *Your Complete Guide to IRA's and Keoghs: the Simple, Safe, Tax Deferred Way to Future Financial Security*. New York: Harper & Row, 1982.

Individual Retirement Plans Under 1981 Tax Law: Individual Retirement Accounts; Individual Retirement Annuities; Government Retirement Bonds; Simplified Employee Pensions. Chicago: Commerce Clearing House Inc., 1981.

Jorgensen, James. *The Graying of America.* New York: The Dial Press, 1980.

Government Publications

U.S. Congress. House. Committee on Ways and Means. *Individual Retirement Accounts/Annuities (IRAs).* Staff report prepared by the U.S. Federal Trade Commission, March 1978. Washington, D.C.: Government Printing Office, 1978.

U.S. Congress. House. Select Committee on Aging. *The Future of Retirement Savings in America. Hearing, May 1, 1981.* Washington, D.C.: Government Printing Office, 1982.

_____. Subcommittee on Retirement Income and Employment. *A Guide to Planning Your Retirement Finances; A Guidebook. Committee Print, 1980.* Washington, D.C.: Government Printing Office, 1980.

INDEX

A

B

C

368.4   Congressional Quarterly Inc.,
C

        Social security and retirement

368.4   Congressional Quarterly
C   Inc.,

        Social security and
        retirement

                                    paper

DATE DUE	BORROWER'S NAME	ROOM NUMBER
FEB 1 1 1986	michelle Pardy Physics	
MAR 4 1986	R	
MAR 2 5 1986	MAR 1 7 1986	